SOME ALABAMA PIONEERS

Madge Pettit

HERITAGE BOOKS
2006

HERITAGE BOOKS
AN IMPRINT OF HERITAGE BOOKS, INC.

Books, CDs, and more—Worldwide

For our listing of thousands of titles see our website
at
www.HeritageBooks.com

Published 2006 by
HERITAGE BOOKS, INC.
Publishing Division
65 East Main Street
Westminster, Maryland 21157-5026

Copyright © 2001 Madge Pettit

Other books by the author:
The Families of Genery's Gap, Alabama
Memories of the Great Depression
Pioneers and Residents of West Central Alabama

Cover photo: Luther McClendon, a deaf teamster who worked in the timber woods in the Genery's Gap area soon after the turn of the twentieth century, with his log wagon and four-mule team. Even though deaf, he is said to have been a good worker and to have held his own in the very difficult work of the timber woods. He was married to Nancy Ida Ammons.

All rights reserved. No part of this book may be reproduced or transmitted in any form or by any means, electronic or mechanical, including photocopying, recording or by any information storage and retrieval system without written permission from the author, except for the inclusion of brief quotations in a review.

International Standard Book Number: 978-0-7884-1859-9

*To Bill and Holly—
of all life's blessings, the greatest by far.*

Contents

Introduction vii
Illustrations ix

James Madison Ammons 1
James T. Atchison 3
Rardon (Riordan) Bevill 12
James Carter 17
Hugh Clark 27
George W. Coburn 28
Thomas Cost, Jr. 29
James Dooley 32
Austin Gibson 38
John Harmon 40
Thomas Honeycutt 50
John Horton 63
Berryman Kimbrell 67
Madoc, Prince of Wales 77
Stark Porter 82
Thomas Seale, Jr. 106
John Smith 157
Uriah Smith 164
Sherrod Aaron Sturdivant 169
Ethelred Watson Thomas 183
John Thomas 188
Joseph Thompson 199
Enoch Tyler 210
Sidney Wilkerson 215
Fullname Index 217

INTRODUCTION

According to research, the first white man to set foot on the soil of what would one day be the state of Alabama was the Welsh Prince Madoc (later Modoc), who arrived there in the thirteen hundreds with a company of three hundred men. Penetrating to all parts of present-day Alabama, then to all parts of the southern United States, they married native women and established tribes of pale-skinned, Welsh-speaking Indians all across the South, and eventually all across the nation. With their roots in Alabama, they were called "White Indians," and their descendants live today in the remnants of the Tuscarora, Mandan, Modoc, and other tribes.

With the possible exception of a few Melungeons who may have drifted this far south, the next non-native inhabitants, who didn't arrive until some four hundred years later, were the adventurers, who had heard of the territory lying west of Georgia, and couldn't resist the lure of the new. These were always single men, who came with only the horse on which they rode, an ax for conquering the wilderness and building shelter, and a rifle for protection and the procurement of food. They lived among the native tribes and married indigenous women.

Today, it is hard to find a fifth or sixth generation Alabamian who does not claim some Indian blood. This is partly, but not entirely, because of the adventurers who married Indian women. It is also because the Indians and non-Indians mixed more easily here than in other parts of the country, and marriages between the races occurred more frequently.

After the adventurers, there appeared in the territory a few men who might today be called draft-dodgers. They wanted to avoid being involved in the Revolutionary War. I doubt that most of these were really slackers, but only strife-weary new Americans who only wanted to be left alone, having already had their fill of war. Some were, no doubt, Scotsmen who bore scars on their arms, from the blood oath they had been forced to sign in their own blood at Culloden Moor in 1746. Having forsworn war forever, they remained true to that oath. Others wanted no part of the war, for other reasons, however vague or unfounded.

Up until 1798, Alabama was part of the Mississippi Territory, but in that year, it became the Alabama Territory. A governor was appointed, and everyone knew that statehood was eminent. With this assurance, settlers began arriving with their families. By 1815 a steady stream of wagon trains was arriving from the Carolinas and Virginia, and the influx only increased with the attainment of statehood in 1819. The Creeks, who had tried to live peaceably with the whites, felt so overwhelmed by the influx, that they finally rebelled, and massacred a large number of settlers at Fort Mims, in South Alabama. They had already ceded all of the territory east of the Tallapoosa in 1832, but the massacre at Fort Mims precipitated their removal to a reservation in the west in 1836. Now, the state was wide open for settlement, and land could be had by applying at one of the land offices.

Most of the pioneer families included in this collection of genealogies had arrived by this time. They are what I think of as the real Alabama pioneers. Those who came later had a fairly easy time of it, compared to the original settlers, often settling on established farms and plantations as the original owners moved on westward. Many of them brought their slaves with them, which eased the burden of starting over in a new place.

As a group, the earliest Alabama pioneers were a hardy, hard-working, self-sufficient, God-fearing group. Many had previously known extreme hardship, and this was their chance for a new start. These earliest Alabamians, with their strengths and shortcomings were the roux which formed the basis for the present day "Heart of Dixie" state that we know.

Madge Pettit

June, 2000

John William Porter and part of his family, circa 1910.

Back row, left to right:
    Fannie Porter
    Jane Smith (his adopted sister)
    John William Porter
    Missouri Alice Kimbrel Porter (his second wife),
    holding Jack Porter
    Margie Eugenia Porter and Monroe Porter (by first wife)

Front row, left to right:
    Rufus Angus Porter
    Charlie Nelson Porter
    Minnie Moran Porter
    Mattie Lee Porter

Foreground: The grave of Rardon Bevill
Palmer Cemetery, Walker County, Alabama

His tombstone, like most of the others, was cut from local stone and engraved by a local artist. Rardon moved to Walker County with his wife Rutha Cost after the children from his first marriage migrated to Louisiana. Rutha is buried in another cemetery.

George Thomas (son of John Thomas, the Confederate veteran); Lennie and Ruby (daughters), Moriah (wife), Bertha (daughter-in-law), Bill (son). In front – Billy Thomas, son of John Thomas (brother to George) his wife and child. 1930's.

Margie Eugenia Porter Seales holding Madge Seales, who is investigating a sunflower, with Velma. 1920.

These three little barefooted kids are Madge Seales, Gene Seales, and Joe Seales in 1929. We never knew what shoes were in the summertime. This was taken at the old home place at Genery's Gap.

Department of the Interior.
Pension Office.

Washington, D.C. _May 31_, 1881

Sir

In your claim No 334,905 for Bounty Land Act of 1855. It appears that your service was performed in Georgia. That you are now a resident of California and that your attorney resides in the State of Maine. Please return this letter with an endorsement stating how you happened to employ an attorney who lives at so remote a distance from any place where you ever resided. State whether you ever had any acquaintance with him prior to the filing of your claim.

Very respectfully
J.A. Bentley
Commissioner

J.A. Sturdivant
Junction City
California

J. A. Sturdivant

This is a copy of a letter written by J.A. Bentley of the Military Pensions Office to Joseph A. Sturdivant in Junction City, California. Joseph Sturdivant had finally, in 1881, found out that he was eligible for a military pension, or a land grant, for his service in the Indian Wars, in which he fought on the side of the Cherokees against the Creeks, and had applied. As it happened, his lawyer was a man he had known in California, who had returned to his home in Maine. This letter, instead of dealing with the facts pertaining to his eligibility, zeroed in on the fact that his lawyer lived in Maine, while Joseph Sturdivant lived in California. Whether this had any bearing on the case or was pure nosiness in not known.

Jamestown City
June 15, 1881

Mr Bentley Dear Sir —
Yours of May 31 asking me
why I employed McCarty
at the time I made Application
Dr John Lord of the State
of Maine was living in Trinity
County Cal and in conversation
with him the case coming
came up relative to bring in
us Army I told him that
I had served in the creek
war — he asked me if I had
received a Land warrant I told
him no — I did not no that I was
intitled to One he said he
would rite to his friend
McCarthy and let him look it
up — I have no aquatance with
him those are the reasons
Yours Most Obedient J.A. Sturdivant

This is Joseph Sturdivant's answer, written two weeks later, in which he explains the situation. I was impressed by Joseph Sturdivant's handwriting, which is very good for a time when most people couldn't write at all. All of the Sturdivants were home schooled, and all were very well educated.

JAMES MADISON AMMONS

Born on July 16, 1853 in Houston County, Georgia, James Madison Ammons was one of eight children of Jesse Ammons (born 1803 in Robeson County, North Carolina, died 1860 in Houston County, Georgia) and his wife, Eliza Cannon (born 1815 in North Carolina), whom he married on August 5, 1835. Jesse's other children were: Maryann (1838), Allen (1839), Nancy (1842), Sarah (1844), Martha (1846), Stephen (1850), and Jake (1857).

Jesse Ammons was the son of Stephen Ammons, who was born in North Carolina in 1781 and died in Georgia, date unknown. Stephen had four other known children: Josiah, Hannah, Sarah, who was born in 1817 and married Berry Clarke on August 5, 1835, and Nancy, who married John F. Clarke on January 7, 1836.

James Madison Ammons, who died on May 14, 1925 in Bessemer, Alabama, had migrated to Alabama as a young man and married Sidney Emma Copeland, born 1858, died 1897, in Phoenix City, Alabama. They were the parents of eight children:

(I) Jesse Daniel (1878) married Nettie Lowery and had:

    (A) Jesse Daniel.

    (B) Henley.

    (C) Annie Marie.

    (D) James Edward.

    (E) Felix.

(II) Ellen, married Eli Copeland and had no children.

(III) Minnie Lou, married Bob Smith and had:

    (A) Henry Clayton.

    (B) Wilbur.

    (C) Odell, married Clyde Perry and had two children:

        (1) Wallace.

        (2) Ivy.

(IV) William Allen, married Minnie Lee Furcron and had nine children:

- (A) William Allen (Buster).
- (B) George Washington.
- (C) Clara Belle.
- (D) James Emmett.
- (E) Alice Agnes.
- (F) Bessie May.
- (G) Jack Madison.
- (H) Charles Edward (called Pike).
- (I) Mary Elizabeth, born 1917.

(V) Nancy Ida, married Luther McClendon, and had:
- (A) James Darcy (called Dart).
- (B) Thomas Luther (called Dick).
- (C) Ollie (called Pete).
- (D) Lillian, who was born in 1917.

(VI) James Thomas (called Dude), born 1888, died 1974, married Roxie Mae Henderson, born 1892, died 1985, (a cousin of this writer) and had:
- (A) James Wallace (1915).
- (B) Cecil Clayton (1916).
- (C) Troy Lee Madison (1917).
- (D) Harold Anderson (1924).
- (E) Harry Henderson (1924), twin to Harold Anderson.
- (F) Bobby Jean (1930).

(VII) John Roy, married Florence King.

(VIII) Henry Clayton, married Orell Caffe and had no children.

(Information contributed by Cecil Clayton Ammons and James Wallace Ammons, 1996).

JAMES T. ATCHISON

This Alabama pioneer came into the state about 1825, which would have been just six years after statehood, along with his wife and children, some of whom were already married and had families of their own. They settled at a place called Randolph, in Bibb County, and many of his descendants still live in the area, most in the town of Maplesville.

Born in Ireland in 1770, James T. Atchison was an only child and an orphan, according to family legend, who at about age sixteen ran away from his adoptive parents and stowed away on a boat bound for America. Landing in South Carolina, he spent the remainder of his youth in Edgefield District, where he married a Miss Henderson and became the father of ten children. He died in Alabama in 1847. His children were:

(I) Bennett Atchison, born in 1797 in Edgefield District, South Carolina, he moved to Alabama with his father's family, where he became a prominent citizen and church member. His wife's name was Eliza, born in South Carolina in 1802. Nothing is known of their children.

(II) Judia Atchison, who married Garrett Freeman.

(III) Elizabeth Atchison, who married Sinclair McCrary.

(IV) James H. Atchison, who was born in 1804 and married Sarah Atchison.

(V) Edmond Atchison.

(VI) Samuel J. Atchison.

(VII) Betty Atchison.

(VIII) Jackson Atchison.

(IX) Higdon Atchison.

(X) Yancy Dwyer Atchison: Born in South Carolina in 1809, Yancy Dwyer Atchison was about sixteen years of age when he came to Alabama. He was married twice, first to Susannah Gibson, by whom he had six children, and secondly to Eritta Jane Potts, by whom he had another eleven children.

Yancy Dwyer became a prominent landowner on Abner's Creek, near Maplesville, Alabama. During the Civil War he taught school and served on the Home Guard. He also worked as a blacksmith and did what he could to take care of the families of the soldiers who were away. At the end of the war, he freed sixty-eight slaves.

Yancy Dwyer is buried in an old neglected cemetery about three miles from the home of his son James Taylor Atchison, near Maplesville, Alabama. Not all the names of his children are known. Those that are known follow.

By Susannah Gibson:

(A) Newton Atchison was married twice, first to Ann Hosey, and secondly to Mary Vardman, and had several children. He was a successful farmer, and lived at Talladega Springs, Alabama.

(B) Lucy Atchison was married four times, to a Mr. Roper, a Mr. Crofford, a Mr. Coston, and a Mr. Ray. She lived in Bessemer, Alabama, and some of her descendants still live there.

(C) Jackson Franklin Atchison married Christine Weaver, and had several children. Christine was born December 25, 1835, and died in 1902. Jackson Franklin died in June of 1911.

(D) Mary Atchison married a Mr. Hand and had two sons, Belton and Crockett Hand, her husband was a sawmiller, and they lived near Bay Minette, Alabama.

By Eritta Jane Potts:

(E) Betty Atchison married Tyre Whatley. They raised an adopted daughter, Lucille Seal.

(F) Viney Atchison was married three times, to a Mr. Adams, a Mr. Densmore, and a Mr. Lawson, and had one daughter, whose name is unknown.

(G) Laura Atchison married Tom Morris.

(H) Charlotte Atchison married a Mr. Gentry and lived in the Talladega, Alabama area.

(I) Basel (Bass) Atchison, never married. He died about 1890, and is buried in the Walnut Grove Cemetery, Birmingham, Alabama. The grave is not marked.

(J) Edward Harrison Atchison, was married twice, first to a Miss Robertson, and secondly to Emma Rosella Letson.

(K) James Taylor Atchison married Sarah (Sally) Coburn, had a large family, and lived near Maplesville, Alabama. James and Sarah are buried at Mulberry Baptist Church. More on them later.

(L) William Yancy Atchison, was married three times, and raised a large family near Maplesville, Alabama. He is buried at Mulberry Baptist Church.

(M) Pickens Atchison, married Sally Weaver, a sister to Christine Weaver, who married his brother Jackson.

Now, back to James Taylor Atchison, child (K), above. He was born on Christmas Day, 1850, near Maplesville, Alabama, and lived his entire life within a few miles of the place. He was married on December 4, 1871, in Baker County, which is no longer in existence, to Sarah Coburn, born February 10, 1851 in Georgia. Sarah Coburn was the daughter of George W. Coburn, born 1817 in Georgia, died 1870 in Baker County, Alabama. Her mother was Amelia Danelly, born 1818 in the Carolinas.

James Taylor Atchison died on December 12, 1926, in Mulberry, Alabama, and Sarah died on June 4, 1938, also in Mulberry. Both are buried in the Mulberry Church Cemetery, and the graves are not marked. They were the parents of thirteen children.

(3) Robert Yancy Atchison, born September 6, 1872 near Maplesville, Alabama, died on August 31, 1956, at Maplesville, Alabama. He was married on November 9, 1893 at Bamford, Alabama (no longer in existence) to Beulah Porter, daughter of Mary Sturdivant and her second husband, John Abraham (Ibzan) Porter.

Ibzan Porter was a Confederate veteran, who had been a prisoner of war and who died in 1869 as a result of the treatment he had received in prison.

After that, Beulah was raised by William Harrison Sturdivant, Mary Sturdivant's brother, who owned a large farm and much land at Bamford, was a judge, a storekeeper, the postmaster, and had built a Baptist church at Bamford where he preached each Sunday. Both Mary Sturdivant and her brother William Sturdivant were half Cherokee, being the children of Sherrod Sturdivant and Elizabeth Dooley. More about Robert Yancy Atchison and Beulah Porter later.

(4) George B. Atchison, born January 1, 1874 in Alabama, married Minnie.

(5) Jessie Coburn Atchison, born March 26, 1877 in Alabama, he was married on December 12, 1895 to Nancy Sharpe. He died on August 7, 1952, and is buried in the Live Oak Cemetery in Selma, Alabama.

(6) John Henry Atchison, born November 29, in Alabama. He was married on October 21, 1906 in Fort Worth, Texas, to Lena Kate Elliott.

(7) Amelia Atchison, born December 1, 1880 in Alabama, she was married on December 31, 1902, to James L. Tyler.

(8) Mary Jane Atchison, born November 1, 1882 in Alabama. Never married.

(9) James Howard Atchison, born May 21, 1884 in Mulberry (Chilton County), Alabama, he was married on December 26, 1909 in Clanton, Alabama to Ruth Elizabeth Fritz. He died on May 10, 1961, and is buried in the Schultz Creek Cemetery.

(10) De Witt D. Atchison, born March 7, 1886 in Alabama. He married Roxie Elizabeth Moore.

(11) Catherine Atchison, born June 1, 1888 in Alabama, she was married on March 1, 1912 in Alabama to Walter Bailey.

(12) Sylvester Atchison, born April 1, 1890 in Alabama.

(13) Edgar C. Atchison, born June 3, 1892 in Alabama, he died on October 8, 1948, and is buried in the Mulberry Baptist Church Cemetery.

(14) Minnie Lee Atchison, born February 21, 1894 in Alabama, she married Thomas Pickens House.

(15) Homer Longshore Atchison, born March 23, 1896 in Alabama, he was married on March 6, 1916 in Chilton County, to Lela Cherry. He died on June 14, 1978 in Tuscaloosa, Alabama.

Now, back to Robert Yancy Atchison (1). He and his wife Beulah lived their lives on a farm near Maplesville, Alabama. As already stated, Robert Yancy died on October 31, 1956. Beulah died four years later, on March 23, 1960. They were the parents of eleven children, who were:

(a) James Clinton Atchison, born January 26, 1895 in Bamford, Alabama, and died on October 1, 1966 in Centreville, Alabama. He was married on July 9, 1912 to Julia Mary Ann Lovelady.

(b) Minnie Elizabeth Atchison, born December 11, 1897 at Bamford, Alabama, and died on November 3, 1967. She was married twice, first to Arthur Horton, and secondly to Tom Broadhead.

(c) Robert Hosmer Atchison, born February 2, 1900, he married Ethel Margaret Benton, and died on June 13, 1979.

(d) Joel Fisher Atchison, born September 15, 1902 in Bamford, Alabama, and died on February 8,1988, and is buried in the Elmwood Cemetery in Birmingham, Alabama. He was married on July 5, 1926 in Chilton County, Alabama, to Emma Victoria Hayes.

(e) Willie Gertrude Atchison, born August 3, 1905, and died on July 4, 1986, in Tucson, Arizona, and is buried beside her husband in Hobart, Indiana. She married Millard Garner in 1923, at Bamford, Alabama, the ceremony performed by her uncle, William Harrison Sturdivant. Willie had grown up at Bamford in the home of William Harrison Sturdivant and his wife Cynthia Ray Sturdivant.

(f) John Littleton Atchison, born September 5, 1906 in Mulberry, Alabama, died May 30, 1909, and is buried in the Mulberry Baptist Church Cemetery.

(g) Marvin Roosevelt Atchison, born March 27, 1909 in Mulberry, Alabama, died on August 8, 1987 in Maplesville, Alabama. He was married on November 10, 1930 in Centreville, Alabama, to Frances Lucille Stough. (see further).

(h) Harvey Longshore Atchison, born January 25, 1912 in Mulberry, Alabama. He was married on December 21, 1937 in the Chilton County Courthouse, to Effie Dee Simmons.

(i) Leroy Eason Atchison, born December 8, 1914, married Ollie V. Williams.

(j) Wheeler Eugene Atchison, born March 19, 1917, married on November 5, 1947 to Winnie Lee Williams. He married secondly Goldie Earnestine Mull.

(k) An unnamed baby boy, born on January 14, 1920, died five days later, on January 19, 1920, at Maplesville, Alabama.

Willie Gertrude Garner (child "e" above), married Millard Garner on January 3, 1923. Millard was born on February 13, 1902, died on February 22, 1979, and is buried beside Willie in the Evergreen Cemetery in Hobart, Indiana. They were the parents of twelve children, as follows:

(ea) Evelyn Lucille Garner, born on October 5, 1924, died on June 6, 1926. She is buried in the Sturdivant Cemetery at Bamford, Alabama, in a plot with her great-great uncle and aunt, William Harrison Sturdivant and his wife Cynthia Ray Sturdivant, and her great-great-grandmother, Elizabeth Dooley Sturdivant. This small family cemetery is now in deep woods, on land that is privately owned.

(eb) Millard Eugene Garner, Jr., born February 5, 1928 in Alabama, married Maudie Lee Hood on June 10, 1947.

(ec) Clyde Earl Garner, born March 19, 1931 in Alabama, married Ruby Jean Hood, sister to Maudie Lee Hood. He died on November 20, 1983 in Alabama, and is buried in Antioch Cemetery, near his sister, Jimmie Ruth Garner. Ruby Jean Hood Garner died in October 1988, in Valparaiso, Indiana, and is buried in the Angel Crest Cemetery in Valparaiso, Indiana.

(ed) Doris Faye Garner was born February 22, 1933 in Alabama, but lived most of her life in Indiana. She married first, Charles Fletcher. This marriage ended in divorce, and she married second, Roy Auguana, who died on October 19, 1998.

(ef) Pauline Virginia Garner, born September 20, 1935 in Alabama, she married first Arvel Pruitt on July 2, 1952, in Indiana, and they were divorced. Arvel Pruitt died on February 15, 1995, and is buried in

Kentucky. She married secondly Reif O. Shelby on April 15, 1966. Reif was born on February 17, 1927, in Mountain Grove, Missouri.

(eg) John Robert Garner, born January 22, 1938 in Alabama. He married Betty LaGrant and they were divorced. He died on April 29, 1978, In Indiana, and is buried next to his mother and father in the in Evergreen Cemetery in Hobart.

(eh) Myrtle Jo Garner, born September 13, 1939 in Alabama, married twice, first to Howard Edward Whitmer and secondly to John Price.

(ei) Laymon Wallace Garner, born January 20, 1942, died November 3, 1977, buried next to his parents in the Evergreen Cemetery in Hobart, Indiana.

(ej) Carolyn Sue Garner, born December 23, 1943.

(ek) Jimmie Ruth Garner, born September 14, 1945, died three months and eighteen days later, buried in Antioch Cemetery near her brother Clyde Garner.

(el) Hershel Wayne Garner, born March 30, 1947 in Alabama, married Phyllis Jean Shanks.

(em) Rosemary Garner, born August 3, 1953 in Gary, Indiana, married twice, first to Carl Whetsel, and secondly to Ramon Cruz II.

Marvin Roosevelt Atchison (child "eg" above) and his wife Frances Lucille Stough were the parents of twelve children as follows:

(eg1) Mary Frances Atchison, born February 16, 1932 in Maplesville, Alabama, married May 20, 1950 in Meridian, Mississippi, to Haywood Burt.

(eg2) Donald Olen Atchison, (a twin) born January 4, 1934, in Maplesville, Alabama, married on July 4, 1954 in Meridian, Mississippi, to Carol Virginia Martin.

(eg3) Ronald Eugene Atchison, (a twin to Donald Olen), born January 4, 1934 in Maplesville, Alabama, died on January 5, 1934 in Maplesville, Alabama.

(eg4) Shelby Jean Atchison, born January 15, 1937 in Maplesville, Alabama, married Billy Dwain Matchan on August 28, 1957.

(eg5) Robert Howell Atchison, born August 13, 1939 in Birmingham, Alabama, married on June 19, 1963 in Clanton, Alabama, to Betty Delois Jackson, born August 7, 1943 in Plantersville, Alabama. Robert Howell Atchison served in the U. S. Navy from November 13, 1957 to November 14, 1979. He and Betty Delois are the parents of three children:

> (eg5a) Robert Timothy Atchison, born September 21, 1964 in Pensacola, Florida, married on September 10, 1992 in Wawayanda, New York, to Marie Aleksew-Adair.
>
> (eg5b) Brenda Darlene Atchison, born April 7, 1966 in Pensacola, Florida, married on October 10, 1986 in Pea Ridge, Alabama, to Donald Joe Brantley.
>
> (eg5c) Donna Hope Atchison, born on November 5, 1973 in Meridian, Mississippi, married on July 17, 1992 in Rock Springs, Alabama to Steven Wayne Tate.

(eg6) Marvin Roosevelt Atchison, born on April 4, 1942 in Hillview, Jefferson County, Alabama, married on July 22, 1965 in Pinson, Alabama, to Alto Sue Mims. He was married secondly to Norma Jean Meeks.

(eg7) Doyle Lee Atchison, born September 7, 1944 in Hillview, Alabama, married on August 28, 1967 to Carolyn Sue Garner.

(eg8) Joel Andrew Atchison, born January 6, 1947 in Hillview, Alabama, married on December 9, 1967 in Maplesville, Alabama to Hilda Carol Hicks.

(eg9) Paul Anthony Atchison, born February 21, 1950, married Charlotte Wallace.

(eg10) Alice Faye Atchison, born February 20, 1952 in Clanton, Alabama, married on June 20, 1970 in Maplesville, Alabama, to Donald Brooks Burnett.

(eg11) Edward Earl Atchison, born September 22, 1953 in Maplesville, Alabama, married on April 26, 1975 in Maplesville, Alabama to Charlene Cecilia Deavers.

(eg12) Patricia Diane Atchison, born September 1, 1957 in Clanton, Alabama, married twice, to William Richard Cochran and Danny York.

Information on the Atchison Family is partly from personal knowledge of this writer, who is distantly related to this family through the Sturdivant and Dooley lines. The bulk of the information, however, was contributed by Polly Shelby, of Tucson, Arizona, and came from original research by Irene Walker Atchison. Irene Walker Atchison was my fifth grade teacher in a small elementary school in Alabama many years ago. Good work, Teacher, and thanks.

RARDON (RIORDAN) BEVILL

Rardon Bevill was a great-great-great-grandfather of your writer. The known history of this family goes back a thousand years to France, where the family name was Beauville. They lived in a village of the same name, and vestiges of the old manor house are said to still remain. In 1066 two of the sons of the family crossed the English Channel with William the Conqueror, and after the Battle of Hastings settled permanently in England, where the family remained for the next six hundred years. According to the *Domesday Book,* which was a detailed census of all the inhabitants of England in the years following the conquest, at that time the Bevills had vast holdings in the northwestern part of England, and the form of the name in use at that time was Boyvill. As the spoils of war, they had been given lands, homes, manors and titles. By the time they had been in England one hundred years, there were sixteen Bevill manors, and several of the Bevill men had been knighted. This was five hundred years and eighteen generations before our Bevill ancestors came to America.

The first Bevills came to America about 1670. One of them was the great-great-great-great-great-grandfather of Rardon Bevill, who was the first known Bevill to migrate to Alabama. His name was Essex Bevill, baptized in Chesterton, Huntingdonshire, England on March 15, 1639, he died in Henrico, Virginia in 1682, leaving a will. His wife was Amy Butler.

There is a legend in the family that two Bevill brothers came to America together shortly after the beheading of Mary Queen of Scots, their leaving England precipitated by that event. These two brothers, who were connected to the court of Queen Elizabeth I, objected to the beheading of Mary and were advised by a third brother, Lord Bruton Bevill, who had been a judge or an attendant at court at the time of the beheading, that considering Elizabeth's unpredictability when crossed, it would be better for their own safety as well as his, if they got out of the country, so they took his advice and got out.

In America, they settled in Virginia. Then the descendants of Essex Bevill drifted southward and westward into South Carolina, Georgia, Alabama, and on westward. After the death of Essex Bevill, his wife Amy married Henry Kent and thirdly, Thomas Bott, but had no children by them. Essex and Amy had five children:

(I) John, born about 1670, married Martha Colson. He died in 1735, leaving a will.

(II) Essex, Jr., who married Elizabeth _____. His will was written in 1729 and Elizabeth's in 1732.

(III) Mary.

(IV) Amy. In 1686, Amy wrote a deed of gift in Bristol Parish, Henrico Co.

(V) Elizabeth.

The line descends through the oldest son, John. He and Martha Colson had six children:

(A) John, Jr., who married Mary Eppes and died in 1767, leaving a will.

(B) Robert, who married Ann _____ and died in 1733, leaving a will.

(C) William, who died in 1771, leaving a will.

(D) Essex.

(E) Mary, who was married twice, to George Archer and then Joseph Royall.

(F) Martha.

The line descends through Robert Bevill. He and his wife had six children:

(1) James, born November 2, 1721, married Mary Archer.

(2) Robert, Jr., born October 10, 1723, married Sarah _____.

(3) William, born October 2, 1726, and baptized on October 30, married Sarah Colson.

(4) Edward, born 1728, married Parker Pride.

(5) Joseph, born December 11, 1730.

(6) Frances, born December 12, 1736, married John Ragsdale.

After the death of Robert Bevill in 1733, Ann Bevill married Thomas Bott. It is not known if this was the same Thomas Bott who had earlier married Amy Bevill, but this seems unlikely. Ann died in 1777, leaving a will.

The line descends through William Bevill. Up until this point, all the Bevills in Virginia had been tobacco planters. William became the first to break from this mold. About 1753, he migrated to South Carolina and became a rice and indigo planter. Born in Prince George County, Virginia, on October 20, 1726, he died in Union District, South Carolina, date unknown. He married Sarah Colson, widow of Abraham Colson, and had only one known child, Robert Bevill. Robert Bevill, born between 1740 and 1750 in Union District, South Carolina, died before 1820, in the same county. He married Elizabeth _____, born between 1740 and 1750 and died after 1820 in Union District, South Carolina. They had three children:

(a) Rardon (the Alabama pioneer), born February 26, 1793.

(b) William A.N., also went to Alabama, but little is known of him. He married Sarah Bentley. According to family historians, he had a son by Elizabeth Sharp before leaving South Carolina. The son went by the name of Napoleon D. Sharp and later Napoleon D. Bevill.

(c) Robert, who married Mary "Polly" Bentley. The Bentley girls were daughters of Joel Bentley of Union District, South Carolina, who migrated to Alabama with the Bevills.

Rardon Bevill (a), the Alabama pioneer with whom this piece is concerned, was born in Union District, South Carolina, and died in Walker County, Alabama on March 12, 1877. He is buried in the Palmer Cemetery, near Townley, Alabama, his grave marked by a very interesting marker chiseled from local stone. He was married three times and had a total of 15 children. The first marriage was to Mary Long and produced six children, all born in Union District, South Carolina:

(aa) William D., born December, 1815.

(ab) Sarah Ann, born January 20, 1817, died in Winfield, Louisiana sometime after the Civil War, married Stark Porter (they were the great-great-grandparents of this writer.)

(ac) Lucy (also called Susan), born June 11, 1819, married William E. Porter, brother to Stark.

(ad) Elizabeth, born May 15, 1821.

(ae) Rardon G., born November 18, 1822.

(af) Riley, born April 22, 1826, died January 7, 1879 in Winfield, Louisiana, married Mary Ellen Black. Names of Riley's children are unknown, but he had two known grandsons, R.D. Bevill and Joseph Bevill, who lived out their lives in Winfield,

Louisiana. He had only one daughter and she died at age two.

These six children from Rardon's first marriage all migrated to Louisiana with the Porter families after their mother died in Shelby County, Alabama on October 3, 1846 and their father remarried in 1847, was widowed, and married for the third time in 1849.

His second marriage was to Ann P. Mills, and they had one son:

> (ag) Adolphus Bevill, born on October 18, 1848, in Shelby County, Alabama.

His third marriage was to Ruthia Cost, who is thought to have been the daughter of Elijah Cost from his first marriage. Born August 12, 1828 in Shelby County, Alabama, she died December 13, 1911, and is buried in the Pleasant Grove Baptist Church Cemetery, five miles south of Carbon Hill, Alabama.

Five years after their marriage Rardon and Ruthia moved to Walker County, Alabama and settled at a place called Peach Cove, where they raised a very distinguished family. Rep. Tom Bevill, democratic representative of Alabama's fourth district for many years, is one of their descendants. They had a total of eight children:

> (ah) Chevis, born December 12, 1849 in Shelby County became a medical doctor. He died in Fort Smith, Arkansas.
>
> (ai) Zippar, born September 25, 1851, in Shelby County, Alabama.
>
> (aj) Francis K., born May 11, 1854, in Shelby County, Alabama, died in Bastrop County, Texas.
>
> (ak) Miriam, born March 16, 1856, in Walker County, Alabama.
>
> (al) Mary Ann and...
>
> (am) Martha Jane, twins, born November 16, 1857.
>
> (an) Paralee, born May 28, 1860.
>
> (ao) Simpson D., born May 29, 1868, became a medical doctor.

As a teenager, Rardon Bevill had served in the war of 1812, and in his old age he drew a veteran's pension. After his death in 1877, Ruthia applied for and received a widow's pension in Walker County, Alabama.

(Some of the foregoing is from personal knowledge of the writer, some from the Rardon Bevill Bible, owned by Vesta Fikes of Alabama, from Bevill-Burton Families *by Elizabeth S. Morris, p. 271-273, and from information sent by Florence Lewis of Whitewright, Texas. Some information on the early generations of Bevills is from Union County, South Carolina census records, and* Pioneering with Beville and Related Families in South Carolina, Georgia and Florida *by Asselia Lichliter).*

JAMES CARTER

The Carter name is an occupational name which originated in England many hundreds of years ago with the people who carted farm products and goods into town on market day. They came to be called "carters," and a single village might have many carters. Perhaps that is why the Carters are so numerous today; they have always been numerous.

This Alabama Carter line seems to be the same as the one mentioned in *Time Magazine* issue of August 27, 1977 on page 20, which, quoting Debrett of England, states that the line has been traced back to King's Langly, a village in Hertfordshire, eighteen miles north of London in the year 1361.

Many years after this date, a wealthy man by the name of William Glover, whose wife's name was Katharin, changed his name to Cranfield. He and his wife had two children, William and Elizabeth. William died young, so the daughter Elizabeth was to inherit the estate. She married William Carter, who by turn of circumstance became William Cranfield's heir. William Carter, who was born about 1515 and died about 1569, bought a manor from Anthony Denny called "Oakes Farm." The estate included significant parcels of land, as well as the manor house. (*Victoria History of the Counties of England, a History of Bedfordshire, Vol. III.*)

William and Elizabeth became the parents of five children:

(I) Paradise, who married Edward Williams.

(II) Winifred, who married a Hart.

(III) Mary, who married a Nicholls.

(IV) Millicent.

(V) William, who married Mary Ancell.

This line descends through William Carter, the fifth child. He died in 1605, leaving a will, which named ten of his children, all of whom were unmarried when the will was written in 1603. He is buried in the nave of Kempston Church.

His wife, Mary Ancell, who died in 1597, was the daughter of Thomas Ancell, Esq. of Barford, Bedfordshire, (1520-1591). Thomas Ancell's father was Edward Ancell, Gentleman, of Waltmanton and Townton, Somerset; and his mother was Wethleyan Powell, daughter of A.P. Powell of Wales. Edward Ancell was the son of John Ancell of Exeter, Devon. Mary Ancell's mother was Elizabeth Wheatley, daughter of Robert Wheatley (also known as Quitlawe of Joneby), Gentleman, of County Cumberland; and his wife, Catherine Fyssher, daughter of Richard Fyssher, Gentleman, of Pevenham, Bedfordshire. (*Victoria History of the Counties of England*, also *Genealogia Bedfordiensis*.)

The ten children named in the will were:

(A) Thomas.

(B) Ancell.

(C) Robert.

(D) Winifred.

(E) Amye.

(F) Elizabeth.

(G) Temperance.

(H) Anne.

(I) Ursula.

(J) Katherine.

The line descends through Ancell Carter, who was born in 1591 in Kempston, Bedfordshire, and became a London grocer. He married Jane Myles, daughter of John Myles of Gravely, Hertfordshire, and had seven children:

(1) Jane.

(2) George.

(3) John.

(4) Ansyle.

(5) William.

(6) James.

(7) Thomas.

These names were taken from *The Colonial Genealogist*, Vol. IV, No. 2, Fall, 1972, P. 73.

The line descends through Captain Thomas Carter, who became a captain of militia, county commissioner, and appraiser. He was a nephew of Colonel John Carter, who migrated to America and gained considerable fame and is said to have been the ancestor of President Carter.

Born about 1630 in London, Thomas died on November 14, 1700, in Lancaster County, Virginia, having come to America before his uncle Col. John Carter. He married Katherine Dale, born 1652, died May 10, 1703 in Lancaster County, Virginia, daughter of Major Edward Dale and his wife Diane Skipworth.

Thomas Carter first appeared in the Virginia records in 1653 when he paid tithes for himself and four servants. By 1663, he was paying for twenty persons. He purchased his first land in 1654 from his uncle, Col. John Carter, and paid for it with 12,852 pounds of tobacco and one hundred thirty Pounds Sterling.

He and Katherine were the parents of nine children:

>   (a) Edward Carter, born 1671, married Elizabeth Thornton.
>
>   (b) Thomas Carter, Jr., born 1673 in Lancaster County, Virginia, married Arabella Williams.
>
>   (c) John Carter, born 1674, married first Frances Ball, second Margaret Tedd.
>
>   (d) Henry Skipworth Carter, born 1674 in Lancaster County, Virginia, died in 1733.
>
>   (e) James Carter, born December 25, 1684, married Mary Brent.
>
>   (f) Elizabeth Carter, born 1680, married William George.
>
>   (g) Peter Carter, born 1688, married first his cousin, Catherine Rogers and second Margaret.
>
>   (h) Katharine Carter, born 1686, married first John Lawson and second a Mr. Tabb.
>
>   (i) Joseph Carter, born 1690, married Ann Pines.

Thomas Carter, Jr., child (b) above, became a captain of militia and a justice in Lancaster County, Virginia. Born in 1672 in Lancaster County, he died in 1728 in the same county. He married Arabella Williams, and they became the parents of ten children:

(ba) Thomas Carter, born ca. 1690.

(bb) James Carter, born 1693.

(bc) Joseph Carter, born 1696, settled in Spotsylvania County.

(bd) Jacob Carter, born 1698.

(be) Isaac Carter, born 1699.

(bf) Daniel Carter.

(bg) Peter Carter, born 1700. Peter married Judith Norris of Fauquier County, and had nine children:

    (bg1) Edward.

    (bg2) Henry.

    (bg3) Job.

    (bg4) Solomon.

    (bg5) Peter, Jr.

    (bg6) Thomas, who was an attorney and had two sons who moved to the Clinch River area.

    (bg7) Joseph, who was a tobacco inspector in Fauquier County, then moved to Spotsylvania. He married Catherine Stephens.

    (bg8) George, who lived his life in Fauquier County.

    (bg9) Norris who settled on the Clinch River.

(bh) Edward Carter.

(bi) Dale Carter, born 1709 (LDS archives).

(bj) Charles Carter. Charles had eight children:

    (bj1) Dale (1744-1773).

    (bj2) Judith (1747-1750).

    (bj3) Lucy.

    (bj4) Catherine.

    (bj5) Susannah.

(bj6) Elizabeth.

(bj7) John.

(bj8) Charles.

All of Charles' sons settled on the Clinch River in Washington County, Virginia. Dale settled there in 1773 and was scalped by Indians in 1776. John and Charles were deputy sheriffs in 1786, when Russell County was formed. A year later John's wife and six children were killed and the house burned down on top of them. John married again and moved to Russell County.

The Carters who moved into the Clinch River area, notably the descendants of Thomas, Norris, and Charles, were cousins to the musical Carter family (Alvin Pleasant Carter, his wife, the former Sara Elizabeth Daugherty, and his sister-in-law "Mama" Maybelle Carter) of country music fame, whose Carter ancestors had settled in the same area.

From here the line descends through child (bg), Peter Carter, son of Thomas Carter, Jr., and Arabella Williams, and Peter's son Joseph Carter (bg7). Joseph, born in 1696, died in 1751 in Spotsylvania County, Virginia. Proof of his descent from Captain Thomas Carter is found in the coat of arms on a deed made by Joseph in Spotsylvania County in 1734. This same coat of arms is on the will of Thomas Carter, who died in Lancaster County, about 1700.

Joseph Carter married Catherine Stephens, daughter of James Stephens of King and Queen County. Joseph Carter and Catherine Stephens had nine children, two of whom went to Tennessee, and one of these was the progenitor of the Alabama line. The nine were:

(bg7a) Sarah, born 1724.

(bg7b) Rachel, born 1730.

(bg7c) Elizabeth, born 1738.

(bg7d) Joseph Jr., born 1739, married Cynthia Carter.

(bg7e) John, who went to Tennessee.

(bg7f) Robert, born 1739, went to Tennessee, married Jean Crockett, sister of Davy Crockett.

(bg7g) George, born 1740.

(bg7h) Mary, born 1741.

(bg7i) Caty, born 1744.

(These names are from the will of Joseph Carter, Spotsylvania County, Virginia, February 9, 1750, Will Book B, p. 11.)

John Carter (bg7e), son of Joseph Carter and Catherine Stephens, was born in Spotsylvania County, Virginia, and died in 1811 in Greene County, Tennessee. He migrated to Greene County, Tennessee with his brother Robert (bg7f) after the death of their father. After his marriage to Jean Crockett, Robert lived in Cocke County, formerly part of Greene, then moved to Bledsoe County.

John Carter married Elizabeth Armistead. They were the parents of six children:

> (bg7ea) Abraham, born 1755, married Rebecca Edwards.
>
> (bg7eb) John, Jr.
>
> (bg7ec) Elizabeth.
>
> (bg7ed) Ezekiel, who married Martha Stanley in Greene County in 1800 and died there in 1853.
>
> (bg7ee) Elisha, who married Margaret, and died in Greene County in 1837.
>
> (bg7ef) James, who was born in 1765 in Greene County.

The line descends through John Carter, Jr. (bg7eb), born 1756 in Greene County, Tennessee. He married Phoebe Ballard, daughter of Isaac Ballard, in 1791, and they lived on Lick Creek in Greene County, near his brothers Abraham and Ezekiel. When he bought the land in 1788, it had been part of Davidson County, North Carolina. He died in Greene County about 1833.

He and Phoebe were the parents of seven children:

> (bg7eb1) Mashac Carter, born 1787 in Greene County, Tennessee, died 1858 in the same county, married Nancy.
>
> (bg7eb2) Elizabeth Carter, born January 21, 1791 in Greene County.
>
> (bg7eb3) James Carter, born July 10, 1795 in Greene County. James married Sarah Carter, migrated to Shelby

County, Alabama, about 1841, and remained there until his death.

(bg7eb4) John Carter (twin to James) was born on July 10, 1795 in Greene County. He married Polly Templeton on February 9, 1815, and apparently lived the remainder of his life in Greene County, Tennessee.

(bg7eb5) Abraham Carter, born about 1798 in Greene County, married Rebecca Edmonds.

(bg7eb6) William C. Carter, married Margaret. He died in 1839 in Greene County, Tennessee.

(bg7eb7) Ezekiel Carter, born in 1807, was married twice and had a total of fourteen children. His first wife was Mary Lynch, his second, Rhoda Munsey. He moved to Missouri with his second wife and lived out his life there.

James Carter, child #3 above (bg7eb3), was an Alabama pioneer, arriving in the state in 1841 from Greene County, Tennessee. He was granted land in Shelby County, Alabama on August 18, 1856. He had married his wife, Sarah Carter in 1837 in Greene County, Tennessee. Sarah had been born in 1810 in Tennessee.

They became the parents of five known children:

(bg7eb3a) Abraham Carter, born 1838 in Greene County, Tennessee.

(bg7eb3b) Mary Carter, born 1840 in Greene County, Tennessee.

(bg7eb3c) James Carter, Jr., C.S.A., born April 18, 1844 at Keystone, in Shelby County, Alabama, married Martha Carter. See further.

(bg7eb3d) Susan Carter, born 1845.

(bg7eb3e) Thomas Carter, married Mary Ann Cary in Shelby County, Alabama in 1865.

Nothing is known of any of James Carter's children, except James, Jr. It is thought that some of them may have gone west after the Civil War.

James Carter, Jr., C.S.A., was born On April 18 1844 in Shelby County, Alabama. James joined the Confederate Army in 1861 at Keystone, in Shelby County, Alabama, and served to the end of the war. He lived his entire life in Shelby County, except for the years he was away during the war.

He was married twice. On May 8, 1864, he married Laurana Glascock, who died soon after. In 1866, he married Martha Carter, who was the mother of all his children. He was the father of six sons, and no known daughters. The sons were:

> (bg7eb3ca) James Carter, born 1867, married Jenny Baker.
>
> (bg7eb3cb) Joseph D. Carter, born 1870, married Elizabeth Johnson, and had five children, William, Jack, Mattie, Molly, and Araminta.
>
> (bg7eb3cc) Robert E. Carter, born 1872, was married three times. His first wife was Lou McKinney, the second unknown, the third Mattie Porter, by whom he had three children:
>
>> (bg7eb3cc1) Ruth, who married Penn Milstead, and had several children:
>>
>>> (bg7eb3cc1a) Patricia Ruth, married a Mr. Eades, and had one child:
>>>
>>>> (bg7eb3cc1a1) Stephen.
>>>
>>> (bg7eb3cc1b) William Ronald, married but has no children.
>>>
>>> (bg7eb3cc1c) Larry Ray, married and has four children:
>>>
>>>> (bg7eb3cc1c1) Amanda.
>>>>
>>>> (bg7eb3cc1c2) Jade
>>>>
>>>> (bg7eb3cc1c3) Jarrod
>>>>
>>>> (bg7eb3cc1c4) Kyle
>>>
>>> (bg7eb3cc1d) James Donald, married and has one child:
>>>
>>>> (bg7eb3cc1d1) Timothy
>>
>> (bg7eb3cc2) James Robert, who married Nell McBurnett Webber and had two children:
>>
>>> (bg7eb3cc2a) Terry, married Christie Montoe and has two children:

(bg7eb3cc2a1) Megan.

(bg7eb3cc2a2) Katelyn.

(bg7eb3cc2b) Bobby Kay, married Horace B. "Nicky" Fancher, and has three children:

(bg7eb3cc2b1) Bryan.

(bg7eb3cc2b2) Melissa.

(bg7eb3cc2b3) Madison.

(bg7eb3cc3) Jimmy E. Carter, the third child of Robert E. Carter and Mattie Porter, never married.

(bg7eb3cd) Charles Carter, born 1874, married Lou Baker.

(bg7eb3ce) Reuben Green Carter, born 1876. According to Bobby Joe Seales, an Essman family researcher, Reuben Green was married first to Sintha Kate Essman, born 1876, daughter of Enoch Tyler and Comfort Lewis. They had no children. He married secondly Martha Viola Baker. More is known of Reuben Green Carter's descendants than some of thers of James Carter's sons.

(bg7eb3cf) Franklin Carter, born 1878. No further information.

Reuben Green Carter (bg7eb3ce) and Martha Viola Baker both died young, and are buried in the Elliotsville Cemetery in Shelby County, Alabama, near Keystone. They had four children who were then raised by their grandfather, Confederate veteran, James Carter, Jr. The four were:

(bg7eb3ce1) Reuben Lee Carter (called R. L.), married Estelle and had one son:

(bg7eb3ce1a) Bobby Lee.

(bg7eb3ce2) Estelle Carter married B.F. (Frank) Atchison, and raised four Atchison stepchildren, children of her cousin, Florence Carter, who was Frank Atchison's first wife.

(bg7eb3ce3) Walter Dean Carter. See further.

(bg7eb3ce4) Elvi Carter, married and has descendants.

Walter Dean Carter (bg7eb3ce3) was born in 1912 at Keystone, in Shelby County, Alabama. He and his siblings were left orphans at an early age, and were raised by their paternal grandfather, Confederate veteran James Carter at his home in Shelby County.

As a young man he moved to Jefferson County to find work. For many years he worked in a pipe shop in Bessemer, then went to work for the TCI Company at their plant at Ensley. On August 21, 1936 he married Velma Elizabeth Seales, daughter of Joseph Horace Seales and Margie Eugenia Porter. He died on January 20, 1979, at Bessemer, Alabama, and is buried in the Genery Cemetery at Genery's Gap, Alabama. For the names of his children and their descendants, see the material on the Seales family.

Information on the Carter family is from research in several LDS libraries, the National Archives, the Georgia Archives, the Jack Ladson Library, Vidalia Georgia, the Hayden Burns Library, Jacksonville, Florida, and talks with Carter relatives and neighbors.

HUGH CLARK

Lt. Col. Victor E. Clark, a retired air force officer of Dallas, Texas is the great-grandson of this Alabama pioneer. His father was Victor Earl Clark, Sr., who was born in Perry County, Alabama on November 24, 1888 and died on September 5, 1962, and is buried in Selma.

He was married on June 28, 1917 in Perry County, Alabama, to Ruth Mae Massey, born April 3, 1897 in Perry County, and died February 6, 1972 in Dallas County, Alabama, and is buried in the Live Oak Cemetery in Selma, Alabama, beside her husband.

Victor Earl Clark, Sr. was the son of James Crawford Clark, born June 13, 1853 in Perry County, Alabama, and died on March 23, 1910 in Selma, Alabama. He was married on November 4, 1884, in Perry County, Alabama to Dollie Adelia DeWitt, born July 12, 1869, died April 21, 1952 in Quantico, Virginia, and is buried in Selma, Alabama.

James Crawford Clark was the son of Hugh Clark, the Alabama pioneer born October 20, 1809, in Cumberland County, North Carolina, and died on October 29, 1897 in Perry County, Alabama. Migrating to Alabama as a young man, he was married on February 14, 1839, in Bibb County, Alabama, to Cinthia M. Perkerson, born March 15, 1818, in Jackson County, Georgia, died August 8, 1896, in Perry County, Alabama.

Hugh Clark was the great-grandson of Alexander Clark and his wife Flora McLean who came to America in the 1700's in a large colony of Scottish immigrants who came over as a group from the island of Jura. Jura is a cold and windswept island in the Inner Hebrides, off the western coast of Scotland. They settled as a group on the Cape Fear River in North Carolina.

From Hugh Clark, the Alabama line descends through his son Gilbert Clark and his wife Ann Alexander. Gilbert was born in 1723 on the Island of Jura, and died in 1798, in Cumberland County, North Carolina.

Their son David Clark was the father of Hugh Clark, the Alabama pioneer. David was born on September 10, 1756, in Cumberland County, North Carolina, and died on April 7, 1835, in the same county. The name of his wife is not known.

(*Information contributed by Lt. Col. Victor E. Clark, Jr., 1988.*)

GEORGE W. COBURN

This Alabama Pioneer brought his family into the state just before the Civil War. He was born in the year 1817 in Georgia, and died in 1870, in Baker County, Alabama. This county does not exist today, but was in central Alabama in the general area of where Chilton County is now. His wife was Amelia Danelly, born in the Carolinas. Both are buried in the Macedonia Church Cemetery in Chilton County, Alabama, in unmarked graves.

They were the parents of eleven children, all born in Georgia. They were:

(I) John L. Coburn, born, 1841.

(II) James M. Coburn, born, 1842.

(III) David F. Coburn, born, 1843.

(IV) William N. Coburn, born, 1845.

(V) Isaac M. Coburn, born, 1847.

(VI) George W. Coburn, Jr., born, 1849.

(VII) Sarah Elizabeth Coburn, born February 10, 1851, married on December 4, 1871 in Clanton, Alabama, to James Taylor Atchison. She died on April 6, 1938 at Mulberry, (Chilton County,) Alabama and is buried next to her husband in the Mulberry Cemetery; the grave is not marked.

(VIII) Charles J. Coburn, born on May 27, 1853, died January 28, 1935 in Mulberry, Chilton County, Alabama.

(IX) Ecsastis Coburn, born, 1855.

(X) Ambrose Coburn, born, 1857.

(XI) Jessie R. Coburn born, 1859.

Information on the Coburn family furnished by Polly Shelby of Tucson, Arizona.

THOMAS COST, Jr.

Thomas Cost, Jr., a native of Randolph County, North Carolina migrated to the Alabama Territory in 1817, two years before Alabama became a state, and settled in what is now Bibb County, but was at that time called Cahawba. Born in 1760, he was the son of Thomas Cost, Sr., born 1740. In June of 1827, Thomas, Jr. bought land in Shelby County and moved there, where he died in 1837, leaving a will. His children were:

(I) Thomas, born 1800, remained in Bibb County when his father moved. Later, when the county lines were permanently settled, he was in Chilton County, but not very far from his father, since they were in the area where Bibb, Shelby and Chilton join.

(II) John, who also remained in Bibb County, died there in 1847, leaving a will. He married Sarah Smith, who is thought to have been a daughter of John Smith, a Revolutionary soldier who had moved to Alabama from Halifax County, North Carolina after the war. He and his brother Uriah, who was a great-great-grandfather of this writer, were among the first residents of Bibb County when it was called Cahawba, and were the founders of Smith Hill, which was the original town where West Blocton is now.

John and Sarah had five children:

(A) William Cost, born 1823; on May 6, 1843 he married Nancy Alphin, who was born 1825 in Alabama. He died on April 28, 1862, in Richmond, Virginia, in the battle of Richmond. William had nine children:

(1) Bailey Cost, the son of William Cost (A) and Nancy Alphin, was also in the war and was a prisoner at Point Lookout.

(2) Robert Cost, who died in the Civil War.

(3) Elizabeth, who married J. R. Burnette.

(4) Nancy.

(5) Polly, who married Pink Robinson.

(6) Matt, who was a twin to Polly.

(7) Susie, who married J. Hinton.

(8) Samantha, who married J. Meroney.

(9) Jolly, died October 22, 1931, married Maria Martin September 22, 1878 and had:

   (a) Robert.

   (b) Norman.

   (c) Ephrian, who had one known son:

      (ca) Clarence.

   (d) Walter.

   (e) Clint.

   (f) Daisy.

   (g) Lizzie.

   (h) Fred.

(B) Yearby Cost.

(C) Adam Cost.

(D) Margaret Cost, who was deaf.

(E) Enoch Cost also died in the war, and is buried in Okolona, Mississippi. Before the war, three of his siblings, Yearby, Adam, and Margaret had been living in the house with him. By the time the war was over, Yearby and Adam had disappeared from the records, and Margaret, who was deaf, was living with her mother's people.

(III) Elijah Cost, the third son of Thomas Cost, Jr., the settler from North Carolina, married Caroline Ray, the daughter of a neighboring family, on September 24, 1844. In the 1850 census they had three children:

(A) Amos, 1841.

(B) Joseph, 1844.

(C) Thomas (1847).

Amos must have been from a previous marriage of one of the partners. At the time, Sarah Cost, Elijah's sister was also living with the family. After the 1850 census, this family disappeared from the records in Shelby County.

(IV) Peter, the fourth son of Thomas Cost, Jr., left no records in Shelby County. What is known is that he never married.

(V) Eli Cost, the fifth son, became a wealthy planter and slave owner in Shelby County. He married Barthena Lindsey, and had nine children. He died in 1855, leaving a will. His children:

  (A) James C., who married Miriam Byrum on July 5, 1841.

  (B) Allen, who married Emily D. J. Lee on October 1, 1857.

  (C) John, who married Martha Johnson on September 4, 1845.

  (D) Rebecca, who married James M. Johnson on January 25, 1847. Rebecca died at Pelham, in Shelby County, in 1868. James left the children in Alabama and went to Texas, where he died.

  (E) Thomas, who married F.M. McClendon on August 11, 1868.

  (F) Nancy.

  (G) Kinney.

  (H) Andrew.

  (I) Sarah Evaline.

(VI) Joshua Cost, born in 1802, the sixth son of Thomas Cost, Jr., apparently never married, and in 1850 was living in the household of John Cost, his brother.

(VII) Cathy.

(VIII) Nancy.

(IX) Sinda Cost married William Howard on October 2d 1839 and settled in Shelby County, Alabama.

(X) Elizabeth.

(XI) Sarah.

(XII) Mary.

(Some information courtesy Dave Cost of West Virginia, Cost family historian. Other information is from the Alabama State Archives, the Shelby County marriage books, and from the Shelby County Historical Society Quarterly.*)*

JAMES DOOLEY

James Dooley brought his family to Alabama about 1840, traveling with the Sherrod Sturdivant family. Elizabeth Dooley Sturdivant was his sister. They all settled in Shelby County near what was later called Bamford. James was the son of James Dooley, Sr. and his wife Mary of Butts County, Georgia. Mary is thought to have been a Ray.

Both the Dooleys and the Rays were Cherokee. All of James Sr.'s children were considered full blood Cherokee, which means they were at least three-quarters, since that is the percentage of pure blood one had to have to be considered full blood at that time.

James Dooley, Sr. had died in the middle-1830's, and Mary married William Ray from the same area of Georgia, and they moved to Coosa County, Alabama about the time of the Creek cession. The authority for this statement is the Alabama Legislative Journal for 1913, at which time William Harrison Sturdivant, son of Elizabeth Dooley Sturdivant, was a member of the Alabama Legislature, and in his biography stated that Mr. and Mrs. William Ray of Coosa County were his grandparents, although William obviously was a step-grandparent.

It is not known for certain how James Dooley, Sr. died, but according to the *Black Book of Georgia* by Robert Scott Davis, there was one James Dooley who was murdered in Columbia County, Georgia in 1834, by one John Ray, who was described as a large man with a red beard. No proof has been found by this writer, but it seems possible that this could have been James Dooley Sr., since he is known to have been an Indian agent and trader, and probably traveled all over Georgia and the Carolinas, and a dispute could have broken out between him and a rival trader.

The Dooleys had all been Indian agents and Indian traders and after several generations of marrying Cherokee women they were now considered full blood Cherokees themselves, having the required three-quarters Cherokee blood. They had originally been of Norman stock, and had come to England with William the Conqueror. The name at that time had the Norman spelling of Doully. In time, some of this name moved north to Scotland, and when the religious persecutions began, they fled to Ireland, where they were called Scotch-Irish. Some of them soon fled again, this time to America, arriving here in the middle 1700's, and settling mostly in Augusta County and Bedford County, Virginia. By this time, several forms of the name were being used, such as Dowley, Dula, Duley, Dooly, and of course Dooley.

Six young men named Dooley came over from Ireland at about the same time. It is not known how many of them were brothers or cousins, which was considered almost the same at that time, but it is assumed that some of them were. Three of these, Abraham, James and Henry, settled in Augusta County; Patrick and Henry settled in Bedford and Thomas alone settled in Orange County. All were very active in the Virginia militia, and Henry in particular was active in the civic and legal affairs of Augusta County.

Patrick, as a member of the militia, was "sent to Caroline" (South Carolina) to keep the Indians in check. He settled at Long Cane Settlement and continuously traveled among the Indian villages, settling disputes and generally acting as a go-between between the Indians and the authorities.

He and his wife Ann raised a very illustrious family. Their sons figure prominently in the history of Georgia, and their daughter Elizabeth married a Bibb from the same Bibb family that produced two governors.

James Dooley, who settled in Shelby County, Alabama, was a descendant of Thomas Dooley of Orange County, Virginia. Born in Ireland about 1710, Thomas came to America in 1752 and settled in Orange County, where he proved his importation from Ireland and was given fifty acres of land. He married Elizabeth ._____. He was an Indian trader, and evidently prospered, because in 1759 he and Elizabeth bought three hundred acres of land in Orange County and sold it in 1763. They had five children:

(I) Thomas, Jr. who was a Revolutionary soldier, was born in 1754 in Orange County, married Lucy Webb. He died after 1835 in Habersham County, Georgia.

(II) William, born 1756 in Orange County, married Elizabeth Downing, a Cherokee. Like most of this line, William was an Indian trader. (He was my fifth great-grandfather, and family tradition is that they were all Indian traders or Indian agents). He died after 1832 in Habersham County, Georgia.

(III) Margaret, married John Rains in Rockingham County, Virginia, in 1785.

(IV) Daniel, settled in the old Ninety-Sixth District of South Carolina. He was granted 200 acres in Ninety-Sixth on Beaver Creek, Waters of the Tugaloo River on January 21, 1785, and sold it to Frederick Lanier in 1799.

(V) Bennett, married a daughter of Seth Pogue and lived out his life in Wilkes County, N.C.

The line descends through child (II), William Dooley. Born about 1756 in Orange County, Virginia, he died about 1832, in Habersham County, Georgia. He married Elizabeth Downing, born about 1760 in South Carolina. According to *Old Cherokee Families and Their Genealogy* by Emmett Starr, Elizabeth was the seventh child of John Downing, who was a prominent Indian agent in South Carolina and an associate of Patrick Dooley. John Downing's wife was a full blood Cherokee of the Wolf Clan.

In 1776, William enlisted in the infantry under Capt. Hopkins in Rockingham County, Virginia. In 1790, he was in Edgefield District, South Carolina, town of Ninety-Six. According to the S.C. census of that year, he had one son and one daughter at that time. In 1793 he sold his land in Edgefield to Edward Couch. In 1832 he was in Elbert County, Georgia, where he petitioned for a Revolutionary pension, file # S31932. He and Elizabeth had four children:

- (A) James, born about 1775 in South Carolina, married Mary Ray, who was Cherokee. He died in Butts County, Georgia about 1835.
- (B) Nancy, born 1778, married Benjamin Neal.
- (C) Daniel, born about 1780.
- (D) Polly, married Barnabas Barron, a Cherokee.

The children of William were at least half Cherokee, probably more. At least two of them then married Cherokee, which means that their children were at least three-quarters, which one needed in order to be to be considered full blood. Polly, whose husband was Cherokee, was in Going Snake District in Arkansas in 1842, along with her husband, Barnabas Barron.

Joseph Sturdivant (a great-great uncle of this writer), who married Aerie Beck, a full blood Cherokee of the Grant Clan, had as an official taken a band of Cherokees from north Georgia to Going Snake District in 1836. These were friendly Cherokees who had fought alongside the whites, including Joseph Sturdivant and his brother Sherrod, in the Creek wars. The friendly Cherokees who had helped the whites were not included when the bulk of the Cherokee Nation was rounded up and sent to a reservation in 1838, but by then this group was already in Arkansas. Dragging Canoe, a prominent Cherokee warrior who was chief of the Chicamaugas and had fought with Andrew Jackson's army at Horseshoe Bend in 1814, went to Going Snake district with this group. These records can be found in the Cherokee collection at the University of Tennessee. In 1849, when gold was discovered in California, Joseph Sturdivant took the group on to the gold fields of northern California, and settled them on the Trinity River at a place that came to be called the Arkansas Bar.

The line descends through James Dooley. Born about 1775 in the old Ninety-Sixth District of South Carolina, he married Mary Ray about 1808 in South Carolina, and died before 1840 while residing in Butts County, Georgia. Mary Ray was born about 1780 in Abbeville District, South Carolina. James was an Indian trader and traveled among the Cherokee villages of Georgia and the Carolinas, according to family legend, living first in Edgefield District, South Carolina, then in Habersham County, Georgia, and finally in Butts County.

He and Mary were the parents of six children:

(1) William, born 1808, in Edgefield District, South Carolina, married Martha Holcombe in 1841. In 1835 he was granted 350 acres in Franklin County, Georgia, and in 1849, another 744 acres in Elbert County. He and Martha later moved to Texas.

(2) Elizabeth, born 1810 in Edgefield District, South Carolina, died September 24, 1900, in Shelby County, Alabama, and is buried in the Sturdivant Cemetery. She married Sherrod Sturdivant, son of John Sturdivant and Martha Hill (Patsy) Bass.

Sherrod had been a soldier who fought on the side of the Cherokees in their war with the Creeks and then had gone to north Georgia and lived among the Cherokees. Sherrod and Elizabeth had a total of thirteen children, but only six survived childhood:

(a) George W., born 1835 in Georgia. George died in the Civil War battle of First Manassas in 1862 at Falling Creek, Va. He married Sarah Estes Harmon, widow of John Harmon, who died about 1857. His widow Sara Estes Harmon is buried in the Shiloh Cemetery in Shelby County, Alabama.

(b) Mary, born 1843 at Stone Mountain, Georgia, died in 1893 in Tuscaloosa County, Alabama, is buried in Shelby County in the Shiloh Cemetery. She was married four times. Her first husband, Wesley Hinton was killed in the Civil War, leaving her with one child:

> (ba) Thomas Hinton.

In 1865, soon after the war was over, Mary married John Abraham (Ibzan) Porter, a Confederate soldier who had been a prisoner of war and was so weakened by disease that he didn't live long. These two were my great-grandparents. They had one child:

> (bb) John William Porter, who was my grandfather.

Mary next married _____ Mann, and had one child:

> (bc) Beulah.

Her fourth husband was Henry Bailey, by whom she had one son:

> (bd) Henry Bailey, Jr.

> (c) William Harrison, born June 15, 1845, at Stone Mountain, Georgia, died March 22, 1926, in Shelby County, Alabama. He married Cynthia Ray Whitten, a widow, and they had no children, but raised three of Mary's children and one of her grandchildren.

William Harrison was a planter, storekeeper, justice of the peace, postmaster, preacher, member of the Alabama legislature, and candidate for congress in 1913. He and Cynthia were buried near the Baptist church that he built near his plantation at Bamford in Shelby County, but now the church, and for that matter the rest of Bamford except for the name, is gone, and the small cemetery, called the Sturdivant Cemetery, is in deep woods.

> (d) Rebecca A., born 1847 in Georgia.

> (e) Elizabeth (called "Sis"), born 1851 in Georgia.

> (f) Sallie, born 1857 in Georgia.

The seven Sturdivant children who died young are buried in an old, long abandoned cemetery in deep woods in Stine's Bend on Cahaba River, near where Sherrod Sturdivant and his neighbor Michael Henderson lived after they migrated to Alabama in the 1840's. Some of the graves originally were marked, but were in deep woods for at least one hundred years, and now large, estate-type homes are being built in the area, so the fate of this old Sturdivant-Henderson-Harmon cemetery is not known.

(3) James F. Dooley, the third child of James Dooley and Mary Ray, was the Alabama pioneer. Born 1812 in Habersham County, Georgia, he was married on February 29, 1840, in Forsyth County, Georgia, to Martha R. Watkins. They moved to Alabama in the 1840's.

(4) Jesse: Married Sarah Ann Wilson and lived out his life in Habersham County, Georgia.

(5) Thomas, born 1826. Nothing else is known of him except that he had a son named William Harrison Dooley.

(6) R. J., married Permelia Hudson on December 22, 1838, in Forsyth County, Georgia.

(*Information from* Chalkley's Annals of Augusta County, Virginia; *Census records of Edgefield County, S.C.;* Habersham County, Georgia; Shelby County, Alabama; *Probate records in Shelby County, Alabama; tombstones in the Sturdivant Cemetery, Shelby County, Alabama; and interviews with now-deceased relatives.*)

AUSTIN GIBSON

According to Bob Curran, a very capable Alabama historian, Austin Gibson was a full blood Cherokee who had settled on the banks of the Cahaba River in Shelby County as a young man, and lived out his life there. In 1907, the last date any record of him has been found, he was one hundred and twenty years old, and was said to be the oldest man in Alabama and perhaps in the country.

According to Gibson's own account, he had fought with Andrew Jackson's army in the campaign against the Creeks in Alabama. From this it can be assumed that he was one of the friendly Cherokees who had come into Alabama with Jackson's army. Such Cherokees fought alongside the whites in the battle of Burnt Corn; the various skirmishes along the Alabama River; and the final great battle of Horseshoe Bend on the Tallapoosa, where they played a decisive part in the battle by stealing the canoes of the Creeks and thwarting their planned escape in the event of imminent defeat.

Austin Gibson was born in 1787, probably in Tennessee. By age twenty-five, he was in Alabama on the banks of the Cahaba River, where well into the twentieth century an ancient beech tree still stood, with "Austin Gibson 1812" carved into the trunk. A young man of good reputation who was an employee of Brown and Sanders, merchants of Calera, attested to this in 1907; he said he had seen the tree in 1906. Gibson said that a friend of his had done the carving, the reason for this most likely being that Gibson could not read or write.

Gibson owned forty acres of land on the Cahaba. This may have been a military grant.

In 1839, He was married in Shelby County to Sarah. Sarah probably was a Seals or Seales. In their extreme old age the couple were cared for by a Frances Seals or Seales, and Sarah said that Frances was her niece. Born in 1819, Sarah was twenty years old when she married Austin, and she said that he was much older than her father. When she died in 1907, they had been married for sixty-eight years. They had no children.

In his youth Austin Gibson had been a wily woodsman, many times escaping from the Creek Indians. At that time the Alabama woods were teeming with game such as black bears, panthers, civet cats, deer, fox, wolves, and numerous small game. Gibson was such a great hunter that he was compared to Nimrod, of Biblical account.

In 1906 Austin and Sarah were on display at the Alabama State Fair in Birmingham, their advanced age having made them an oddity. Austin was blind at the time, and had been for ten years. Such exploitation of vulnerable people would be unthinkable today, but in 1906, many things were featured in sideshows that would be offensive to modern sensibilities. Sarah died on April 27, 1907. The date of Austin's death has not been determined. A picture taken of him in his old age, shows him tall and slender, not stooped with age, with vestiges of the handsomeness that must have once been his.

(Some information courtesy of Bob Curran. Other information from an article by Rev. J. W. Cary, published in the Birmingham Age Herald *on April 28, 1907.)*

JOHN HARMON

This Alabama pioneer brought his family to Alabama from Georgia in 1820, soon after statehood. The Harmons were German in origin, all descending from one Melchior Hermann who emigrated from Germany in the year 1752, on the ship *Cunliss*, commanded by Captain Joseph Cletion, on the encouragement given to Protestants to emigrate.

Landing in South Carolina, he petitioned for land in 1752, and was granted two hundred and fifty acres on the fifth of December of that year. According to the *Cunliss* log, he had been accompanied by a wife, whose name was not given, and three children, and there is no record that he ever had any others. They were:

(I) John Leonhart Harmon, born in Germany in 1738, died in Newberry District, South Carolina in 1794. He married Mary Lankford, daughter of William Lankford of Newberry District. Today he has many descendants in Lexington and Newberry Counties in South Carolina.

(II) John Jacop (Jacob) Harmon, born in Germany in 1739, died in Lexington District, South Carolina about 1810. He married Hannah Turner of Newberry District. Most of his descendants left South Carolina for Georgia, Alabama, Mississippi, Tennessee, and on west to Texas and other States.

(III) Catherine Harmon, born in Germany in 1743, married Thomas Smith of Newberry District. Today she has many descendants among the Smith families of Lexington County, South Carolina.

The line descends through child (II), Jacob Harmon, and his son:

(A) John Harmon, who was born about 1775 in South Carolina. He migrated first to Jones County, Georgia, and from there to Shelby County, Alabama, arriving there sometime between 1825 and 1830. He died soon after migrating to Alabama.

John married Sarah _____. Born 1780 in South Carolina, she died on January 17, 1853 at Hero (a place no longer in existence), in Shelby County, Alabama.

John and Sarah were the parents of six children:

(1) Allen, who married Rebecca Lindsey.

(2) Martin, who married a woman whose name does not come down to us, and later Elizabeth.

(3) Sarah, who married Joseph Lindsey.

(4) Stephen, who married Mary Starnes, and after her death, Margaret Burke.

(5) John, married Sarah Estes. They had no children, and after his death Sarah married George Sturdivant, an officer of the Confederacy, and son of Sherrod Sturdivant and Elizabeth Dooley, who were neighbors.

(6) James, married Cynthia Brook.

Of Allen Harmon, child #1 above, the following is known: Born in Georgia about 1800, Allen was married about 1828 in Alabama to Rebecca Lindsey, who had been born in Alabama about 1800. On November 3, 1834, he was granted thirty-nine acres of land in Shelby County, identified in the records as the northeast quarter of the northeast quarter of section thirty-six, township twenty, range four west. This would be somewhere in the vicinity of the old settlement of Bamford, Alabama. Allen Harmon died in 1883, and Rebecca in 1900. They are buried side by side in the Shiloh Cemetery on County Road 13 in Shelby County, and their graves are marked. Allen and Rebecca were the parents of eight children as follows:

(a) Sarah, married Holly Henderson. The Hendersons were an old and distinguished family that had come to Alabama many years before statehood, from Tennessee, where they had been associated with the Boone family.

(b) Ann, married Anson Smithson.

(c) Manerva, married George Jordan on January 15, 1857. George was a descendant of Uriah Jourdan/Jordan, who had been in Alabama very early, coming there from North Carolina. The Jordans are a very old English family, and one Samuel Jordan had migrated to the Virginia Colony, probably from England in the early 1600's. George and Manerva had six children:

(ca) Charlie (married Martha Howard).

(cb) Ben (married Rose Peel).

(cc) Jim.

(cd) Sarah (married Frank Carter).

(ce) Georgean.

(cf) Ludie.

(d) Joseph, never married. He was a soldier in the Confederate Army, became ill while in the army, and was sent home, where he lingered for a while and then died.

(e) Martin, never married. He also was a soldier of the Confederacy, came down with the measles while in the army, developed pneumonia, and died.

(f) John H., married Mary Cost. See further.

(g) Lydia, married John Nicholas.

(h) Parthenia, married Richard Honeycutt.

Further information is only available on John H. Harmon, child (f). John was the only one of Allen and Rebecca's sons to live long enough to have a family. He was born in Shelby County, Alabama, on September 26, 1843 and died June 10, 1930. In 1862, he married Mary A. Cost, born March 27, 1845, died November 8, 1935. They are buried side by side in the Genery's Cemetery on the crest of Shades Mountain on the line between Jefferson and Shelby counties in Alabama, and the graves are marked.

John served in the Confederate Army, and was wounded in the foot and had a finger shot off. These wounds didn't seem to affect his life span, however, as he was the longest surviving Confederate veteran in the state of Alabama.

John and Mary lived in a log house at the end of Shades Mountain. The logs were hand-hewn, and at last account the house was still standing, after more than a hundred years. John became a justice of the peace, and was greatly respected in the community. He was respectfully known as "Squire Harmon" throughout most of his lifetime. John and Mary Harmon were the parents of eight children, as follows:

(fa) William A., married Rosa M. Harkness.

(fb) James L., married Martha Benton.

(fc) Sarah, never married.

(fd) John H., married Allie Tyler.

(fe) Rufus N., never married.

(ff) Joseph E., married Mary Benton.

(fg) Iona, never married.

(fh) Dora, never married.

Let us now step back a few generations to the second son of John and Sarah Harmon, Martin Harmon: Born in Georgia about 1810, he married about 1834, and his wife's name is unknown. She died between 1846 and 1849, leaving six children:

(1) Mary.

(2) Stephen, who married first Tilda Vining, and second Sara Ward.

(3) David, who married Martha Houston.

(4) William J., who was killed in the Civil War in Virginia on July 2, 1863.

(5) Elijah.

(6) John L., who married Cynthia Norwood.

Martin Harmon married for the second time on January 31, 1849, in Coosa County, Alabama, to Elizabeth Blankenship. They lived in Coosa County for a time, then returned to Shelby County. On May 10, 1834, Martin was granted thirty-nine acres of land in Shelby County. He died between 1862 and 1870. Elizabeth appeared on the 1870 census as head of the household, but by 1880 she has disappeared from the records. Martin Harmon is buried in an unmarked grave in Shelby County. Elizabeth's place of burial is unknown.

Martin and Elizabeth were the parents of four children, making a total of ten children for Martin Harmon. They were:

(7) Lydia.

(8) Mary.

(9) Peter, who married Tempie Norwood.

(10) Nancy.

Stephen Harmon, the oldest son of Martin Harmon, was born about 1835, in Shelby County, Alabama. He had one son by Tilda Vining:

(a) "Little Steve."

Then on November 30, 1872, he married Sarah Ward and they had two children:

> (b) Melisha, who married Newie Howard, then Thomas Anderson, then Zebedee Buckelew.
>
> (c) Chris, who married Lela Booth.

Little else is known of Stephen. On the 1870 census he was living with his uncle, Allen Harmon. He does not appear on the 1880 census, and Sarah and her two children are shown living in the house with her mother. Sarah does not appear on the 1880 census. Stephen is buried in an unmarked grave in Shelby County, Alabama.

"Little Steve" Harmon (a) married Ellen Bunn and had:

> (aa) Ira, who married Jona Oglesby.
>
> (ab) Elizabeth, who married Lannern Clark.
>
> (ac) J. William LaFayette, who married May George.
>
> (ad) Steve Luther, who married Audrey Howard.
>
> (ae) Eula, who married Joe Higginbotham.

Chris Harmon (c) married Lela Booth and had:

> (ca) James L., married Joyce Pitts.
>
> (cb) Ada, married Phillip Brewer.
>
> (cc) Emma, married Lee Carter.
>
> (cd) Daisy, married Clarence Boyd.
>
> (ce) Clarence, never married.
>
> (cf) Tillman, died young.

David H. Harmon was the second son of Martin Harmon. According to his tombstone, he was born in 1827, but census records and his military records indicate he was born about 1842. On November 12, 1863, he married Martha Houston, who was born in 1845, and her death date is unknown.

On March 24, 1862, David joined the Confederate Army as a private, in Co. E (or D, the record is dim), 44th Alabama Regiment. Wounded in the leg at Seven Pines, he was given a disability discharge in August that same year. He died of pneumonia on February 11, 1921, and is buried in a marked grave in Old Blue Creek Cemetery in Jefferson County, Alabama. Martha is buried in an unmarked grave in the Shiloh Cemetery in Shelby County. David and Martha were the parents of seven children:

- (a) Charles, who married Betty Patterson and had:
  - (aa) Annie.
  - (ab) Lela.
  - (ac) Lila.
  - (ad) Othie.
  - (ae) Elser.
  - (af) Agnes.
- (b) Johnnie, who died at about age thirty and was never married.
- (c) Annie.
- (d) Martin, who married first Ida Holsenbeck and had:
  - (da) Kate.
  - (db) William.

Later he married Callie Thompson and had:

- (dc) Elbert.
- (dd) Louie.

- (e) Val D., who married Nancy Parsons, and had:
  - (ea) Robert.
  - (eb) Ethel.
  - (ec) Jack.
  - (ed) Alice.
  - (ee) Virgil.
  - (ef) Ruth.
  - (eg) Edna.
  - (eh) Alva.

(ei) Earl.

(ej) J.M.

(f) James F., who married first Hattie Thompson and had:

(fa) Frank.

(fb) Marty.

then married Pearl Cates and had:

(fc) Stella.

(fd) Elizabeth.

(fe) Marie.

(ff) Warren.

(g) Mary, who married Major Holcomb and then William Brookshire.

William James Harmon, the third son of Martin Harmon, was born about 1842. He married Nancy P. Boram on August 23, 1860. No record of any children has been found. He was killed in action on July 2, 1863, in Virginia. Nancy subsequently married M. H. Heth.

Elijah Harmon, the fourth son of Martin Harmon was born in 1844 and died young.

John L. Harmon, the fifth son, was born in 1845 in Shelby County, Alabama, and died on February 15, 1897, is buried in Old Blue Creek Cemetery in Jefferson County, and the grave is marked. On May 4, 1870, he married Cynthia J. Norwood, who was born about 1847 in Alabama. The date of her death and place of burial is unknown. In the 1870 census, they were living in the house with John L.'s first cousin, "Squire" Harmon.

An interesting fact in connection with John L. is that he had a son named John (#1) who married Ollie Howton and they had a son named John (#2), who married Annie Pierce. John #1 was shot and killed by a man named Lockhart in 1905. John #2 was shot and killed by a man named Norwood in 1931. They are both buried in Old Blue Creek Cemetery, and the graves are marked.

John L. Harmon and Cynthia J. Norwood were the parents of six children:

(a) James Frank, who married Laura Tibbs, and had two sons,

(aa) John Thomas Andrew.

(ab) Wheeler D.

(b) Elizabeth, called "Dutch," who married Philip Robins.

(c) Luna, called "Lou," who married Melvin Patterson.

(d) John, who married Ollie Howton and had three sons:

(da) John, married Annie Pierce.

(db) James, married Letha Carroll.

(dc) Willie.

(e) Lillian, who married Tom Kennedy.

(f) Rosie, who died young.

Peter Harmon, the sixth and youngest son of Martin Harmon, was born about 1858. On November 8, 1876, he married Tempie Norwood, and his cousin, "Squire" Harmon, performed the ceremony. Tempie was born about 1861. She may have been a sister to Cynthia Norwood, who married Peter's older brother, John Harmon, but this has not been verified.

They had three children:

(a) John.

(b) Wiley.

(c) Oscar.

In about 1883, when Peter was only about 25 years of age and Tempie was about 22, they and their oldest child all died within a short period of time, possibly in an epidemic of some kind. Their place of burial is unknown.

Their son Wiley D. married Cynthia J. Norwood and had six children:

(ba) Walter, who never married.

(bb) John M., who never married.

(bc) Nannie, who married James Kelly.

(bd) Lillian, who married Charles Hammond.

(be) Oscar, who never married.

(bf) Henry S., who married Mynia Love.

Peter and Tempie's son Oscar married Bertie Fish and had one child:

> (ca) Frank, who married Alice Slovensky and had no children.

Stephen G. Harmon was the third son of John and Sarah Harmon. Born about 1818 in Georgia, He married for the first time in 1841 in Shelby County, Alabama. His wife was Mary Starnes, and they had two children:

> (a) Lydia.
>
> (b) Martin.

Nothing is known of Lydia. Martin, born about 1842, married Malinda McCraw on February 8, 1865. Mary Starnes died about 1842 or 1843, and in 1844 Stephen Harmon married Margaret Burke, from Jefferson County.

Stephen and Margaret left Shelby County, Alabama and settled in Pontotoc County, Mississippi about 1844 or 1845, and remained there for the rest of their lives. Most of their descendants live in Mississippi today. Stephen is buried in Edington Cemetery, near the town of Pontotoc, Mississippi. The place of Margaret's burial is not known.

Stephen had an additional nine children by his second wife:

> (c) Sarah E.
>
> (d) John S.
>
> (e) Rebecca.
>
> (f) William R., married Ida Nolan.
>
> (g) Joseph A., married Callie Eddington.
>
> (h) Gilbert M., married Georgia Ann Jones in Mississippi, and later Margaret E. McDougal in Alabama.
>
> (i) S.W., married Miss Morgan Moore.
>
> (j) M.D., married Tom White in Alabama.
>
> (k) Thomas, married M.A. Marshall.

John Harmon was the fourth son of John and Sarah Harmon. He was born about 1820 in Georgia. John married Sarah Estes on August 10, 1856. He died about a year later. Sarah then married George Sturdivant, son of Sherrod Sturdivant and Elizabeth Dooley. John is buried in an unmarked grave in Shelby County, Alabama. He left no descendants.

James Harmon was the fifth and youngest son of John and Sarah Harmon. Born in Georgia about 1825, he married Cynthia Brock on February 9, 1842. They had three children:

    (a) William A.

    (b) Sarah L.

    (c) John M. William.

John M. William Harmon was killed in action on June 1, 1865, near Suffolk, Virginia. He was never married. Nothing is known of the other two siblings. James Harmon died between 1850 and 1853. Probate records in Shelby County show that Samuel Hamaker, Allen Wide, William Brock and John Brock became guardians of the children.

(Information on the Harmon pioneers was furnished by David H. Harmon of Adger, Alabama, who is a son of Virgil Harmon, son of Val Harmon, son of David Harmon, son of Martin Harmon, son of John and Sarah Harmon, the pioneer couple who brought their family to Alabama from Georgia in the 1820's.)

THOMAS HONEYCUTT

Thomas Honeycutt (also spelled Hunnicutt), was born about 1760, probably in North Carolina. The first record of him as an adult was in Baldwin County, Georgia, when a certain William Anderson went to claim land he had won in the 1805 Georgia Land Lottery, and found Thomas Honeycutt and his family "squatting" on the land. Evidently, the situation was settled amicably, and William Anderson and Thomas Honeycutt's daughter, Mary Honeycutt, born 1786, were married on March 6, 1806, this according to their granddaughter, Ann Mariah Honeycutt Redding, born May 19, 1825, and told to this writer by Ed Honeycutt of Durant, Oklahoma. Mrs. Redding stated further that Thomas Honeycutt and all his family except his daughter Mary Honeycutt Anderson migrated to Alabama.

Thomas was on the 1802 tax digest for Hancock County, Georgia, and registered for the 1805 land lottery from that county. He was on the 1807 tax digest for Baldwin County, Third District, where he paid poll tax. He purchased land in Jasper County (which had been formed from part of Baldwin) in 1808, and sold it in 1817. This is probably when he left for Alabama.

The earliest record of Thomas Honeycutt in Alabama was on November 19, 1818, when his daughter Lucinda married Sidney Bates, and Thomas gave his consent. Agrippa Atkinson performed the marriage ceremony. Then on December 11, 1818, in Montgomery County, Thomas Honeycutt's daughter Patience and Phillip Coker applied for a marriage license and Thomas gave his consent. Nine years later, his daughter Martha married Elisha Henley on January 11, 1827, in Bibb County, consent of Thomas. (*Marriage Book A&B*, p.143).

In *A History of Mulberry Church 1820-1870*, by Ulysses H. Abram, there is a record of Thomas Honeycutt and his wife Josephine, this being the first indication of his wife's name. Mulberry Church is in Bibb County. Among the marriages recorded in the book is that of their daughter Sally Honeycutt who married Henry Henly on October 15, 1820, and a son, James Honeycutt, who married Bethney Cobb on December 22, 1823.

Thomas and Josephine seem to have had a rather large family, but at the time of the 1830 census, there were only two sons and one daughter remaining in the household. Thomas does not appear in any subsequent census records, which has led some researchers to speculate that he may have participated in the Creek Roundup of 1836 and was killed. This could hardly be, since Thomas would have been about 76 years old at the time of this encampment.

There was a Thomas R. Honeycutt who participated in the Creek roundup of 1836 mustered in on June 19, 1836 at Cowager (?), for three months. He mustered out at Montgomery, Alabama, on July 21, 1836, his company having camped eighteen miles south of Fort Mitchell, which was located on the Federal Road below present day Phoenix City in Russell County, Alabama. This road ran from Milledgeville, Georgia, the state capital at that time, to Vicksburg, in the Mississippi Territory. This Thomas Honeycutt has been determined to have been his grandson, Thomas R. Honeycutt, born in 1818, son of William Honeycutt, who would have been eighteen years old in 1836.

A complete list of Thomas and Josephine Honeycutts's children is as follows:

(I) William Honeycutt, born 1790, in Bibb County, Georgia. On November 2, 1812, he married Martha Elizabeth (Patsy) Smith on October 18, 1814 in Georgia (*Marriage Book A*, p. 70). After migrating to Alabama, they lived in the Mulberry Community in Bibb County for some years, then moved to Autauga County.

The court records there reveal some tantalizing clues as to William Honeycutt's fate. Mr. Edward Honeycutt of Durant, Oklahoma, having also heard stories passed down in the family, went to a great deal of trouble to ferret out this mystery.

In Autauga County, Alabama, the minutes for the Commissioners Court for August 1848, an entry indicates that James Lawhr, coroner, was paid twenty-four dollars for holding inquest over the dead bodies of Mr. and Mrs. Honeycutt. The same body met again in February of 1849, and the minutes indicate that one Wiley Heath was paid four dollars for going to Centreville, which was in Bibb County, for prisoner Bagley. In these same minutes were comments on the inspection of and the paying of Mr. I. G. Graham for the building of an iron cage within the jail.

In the records of the Alabama Penitentiary System for 1850-51, is listed one Jacob Bagley, prisoner #151, age 33, 5'5" tall, born in North Carolina, convicted at Montgomery. The story passed down through the generations of the Honeycutt family, and verified by research is that someone killed William Honeycutt and his wife with an ax from the yard, in an attempt to steal a trunk full of gold the murderer thought Honeycutt had. The thief-murderer was their son-in-law, Jacob Bagley.

The inventory of William's estate indicates that he was indeed a wealthy man, but at this point, no one knows if there really was a trunk full of gold. He was the father of thirteen children:

- (A) Elmira Bagley, born 1814.
- (B) Elizabeth, born 1814.
- (C) Louisa, born 1816.
- (D) Thomas R., born 1818.
- (E) William T., born 1820.
- (F) Sarah B., born 1822.
- (G) James J., born 1825.
- (H) Martha Jane, born 1827.
- (I) Zachariah, born 1827.
- (J) Pall O., born 1835.
- (K) Edward Henry, born 1835.
- (L) Doctor, born 1837.
- (M) George W. F., born 1839.

(II) Mary Honeycutt, born 1786, married William Anderson. She remained in Georgia with her husband and family when the rest of the Thomas Honeycutt family migrated to Alabama. William Anderson was born in Norfolk County, Virginia on January 8, 1763. He was a Revolutionary soldier. After the war, he migrated to Georgia, where he met and married Mary, and subsequently had six children. William Anderson died on May 6, 1844. Mary Honeycutt Anderson died on March 3, 1861. The above is from a D.A.R. application written by their daughter, Ann Mariah Redding in 1902.

(III) Lucinda Honeycutt, born 1802, married Sidney Bates.

(IV) Sally Honeycutt.

(V) James Honeycutt was born in 1803, in the Mulberry community of Bibb County, Alabama. On December 22, 1823, he married Bethany Cobb, daughter of Alexander Cobb, a well-to-do farmer, and the only one in the area who owned slaves. They appear on the 1830 and 1840 census records for Bibb County. In 1850, they were in Shelby County with eight children. Their names and ages were listed on the census record thusly:

- James Honeycutt, age 47, born in Georgia.
- Bathsheba, age 45, born in South Carolina.
- Lucinda, age 17.
- Tennessee, age 15.
- George M. age 14.
- Jasper Marion, age 12.
- Angeline, age 10.
- James M., age 8.
- Riley M. (Monroe), age 5.
- Amanda, age 1.

According to Mr. Edward Honeycutt of Durant, Oklahoma, there was another son, who for some reason is not listed on the census record. He was:

- Levi Anderson Honeycutt, born in 1827 near Montevallo in Shelby County.

As a young man Levi went to Lauderdale County, Mississippi, where there are various jury lists showing that he served on the jury many times. On February 16, 1848, he married in Bibb County, Alabama, a Miss Harriet B. Collier, daughter of Vic Collier. He had met her in Lauderdale County, Mississippi. By 1850 he was back in Lauderdale County, but by 1860, he was again in Bibb County, Alabama. He was a minister of the gospel, and this may account for his moving around so much.

Levi died on November 5, 1860, and his father James was appointed administrator of his estate. Among other items listed in the settlement were a pair of oxen, an ox wagon, 11 head of cattle, 14 sheep, 15 goats, 17 hogs, and 80 acres of land. Some of the people attending the estate sale were Benjamin Glasscock, H.B. Honeycutt, C.B. Cobb, Z.H. (Zachariah Honeycutt?), G.W. Honeycutt, G.W. Prestridge, G.W. Randall, T.G. Robertson, G.W. Golhard, and Leroy Busby.

James Honeycutt was killed by a band of marauders on February 6, 1865. This was during the Civil War era and such murders were very common in this part of the south. The perpetrators were usually northern renegades and southern scalawags, and robbery was usually the motive, as was the case here. They thought that James had gold hidden on the premises, and tore up the place searching for the gold or anything else they could steal. They stole most of the livestock, including Bartheny's pet horse.

Bartheny later heard that her horse had been sold to someone down near Selma, and went to get him back. By then, the horse had been mistreated and had turned mean, but Bartheny went into the corral against the advice of the owners, whistled for the horse, who came running. She had the horse to kneel, whereupon the owners told her to take her horse and go, which she did.

In the 1870 census for Baker (now Chilton) County, James' widow and the children remaining at home, plus two who were grandchildren, appear thusly:

- Besteny (Barthena), age 66.
- Riley M. (Monroe), age 25.
- Mandy, age 21.
- Martin J. B., age 28.
- William, age 2.
- George, age 1.
- H. Honeycutt, age 29.

The "Mandy" above is Amanda Honeycutt Martin, wife of Isaac Bird Martin, listed here as J. Martin. The two children are theirs.

In the 1880 census for Chilton County this family is listed in this manner:

- Isaac B. Martin, age 35.
- Amanda, age 30.
- William, age 11.
- Clarance, age 7.
- Mary, age 3.
- Ballina, age 74.

"Ballina" is Barthena, and the census taker has misspelled her name again. She was at that point living in Amanda's household. Amanda died on February 27, 1884. Isaac was born on February 9, 1843, and died on November 12, 1912. Both are buried in the Providence Cemetery.

(VI) Patience Honeycutt, married Phillip Coker.

(VII) Temperance Honeycutt, born 1804.

(VIII) Martha Honeycutt, born in 1808, married Elisha Henley.

(IX) Anderson Honeycutt was born on August 25, 1813, died on January 28, 1891 and is buried in a small family cemetery in the woods of Chilton County, Alabama. His wife Mary was born on June 8, 1817, and died in August of 1895. She is buried beside Anderson.

Anderson had been born in the Mulberry Community of Bibb County, and on June 3, 1829 filed for a tract of land there, namely W/2 of SW/4 Section 1, TWP21N, R13E warrant 4379. Half of a quarter-section would have been eighty acres, and not claiming to be a surveyor, I think that Range 13E would have been on the southern perimeter of the county. Anderson would have been only sixteen years old at the time, so his father may have filed for him.

Eighteen years later, on November 15, 1847, he was in Shelby County and filed on forty acres there, namely NE/4 of SW/4 Sec18 TWP15E R23N. This parcel was in the northeastern part of the county, near some of his brothers and sisters who had settled there. However, Anderson had resided, or at least owned property, in Shelby County before this.

In Deed Book G, pages 406-407, it is recorded that Anderson Honeycutt sold on February 17, 1838, 120 acres in E/2 of SW/4 and SW/4 of SW/4 of Sec 15, TWp 23N, R15E. According to his obituary published in the Chilton Review, Anderson Honeycutt, identified as the father of Mr. J. J. (Jefferson Jasper) Honeycutt of Jumbo neighborhood, "died at the residence of his son-in-law near Strasburg (now Thorsby) on the night of 28 inst. (January 28, 1891). He had reached the age of seventy-six years."

Anderson and his wife Mary had twelve children:

(A) Leah Malinda, born 1834.

(B) Jefferson Jasper, born 1836 (more on him later).

(C) Jane Sabrine, born 1840.

(D) Arena, born 1841.

(E) Eliza, born 1844.

(F) Catherine, born 1845.

(G) Nancy, born 1849.

(H) Susan, born 1851.

(I) Lewis, born 1854.

(J) Elmira D., born 1855.

(K) Mary, born 1859.

(L) Martha, born 1862.

(X) Unknown male, born 1820-1830. This may have been either John Honeycutt or Elisha Honeycutt. Both are thought to have been sons of Thomas and Josephine, but for some reason were not listed on the census record.

The information on this unknown was supplied from the research of Ed Honeycutt of Oklahoma, with help from William Hines of Arkansas and his grandmother, Lelia Ernestine (Goodwin) Carter, (born in 1874, granddaughter of Isadora Honeycutt, born in 1852.)

In the 1840 census, John Honeycutt and Elisha Honeycutt were in Cherokee County, Alabama. An elderly woman of 80-90 years old was in the household with John and his family. Since Thomas Honeycutt was not on the 1840 census for Bibb County, it can be assumed that he died before 1840, and that his wife Josephine was listed as living in the household of her son. Others in the household were John's wife, four sons, and one daughter. Elisha had in his household his wife, two sons and one daughter. Elisha had married Fanny Whatley in Hancock County, Georgia on October 31, 1814, according to *Marriage Book A,* page 86. This date must be incorrect, as the 1840 census shows Fanny to be 20-30 years old, so she would have been a small child in 1814. According to information provided by William Hines to Ed Honeycutt, Elisha Honeycutt died in Winston County, Mississippi in 1847, and Fanny died in Ashley County, Arkansas in 1850.

(XI) Unknown female, born 1815- 1820, (1830 census.)

(XII) Alexander Honeycutt. Alexander has been put at the end of the list of Thomas and Josephine's children because his relationship as a son has not been verified. However, all the available evidence indicates that he was. Sometime after 1830 the Honeycutts left the Mulberry Community of Bibb County and moved into the area of Jumbo, then Shelby County, now Chilton.

In the land plat book at the Alabama State Archives, a record can be found where six of Thomas' children applied for grants within the same section (Sec 18, 23 N, 15 E). Alexander's name appears among them. He applied on October 19, 1836, and was granted patent #20964. Also, the Shelby County court records show that Anderson Honeycutt and Alexander Honeycutt transacted business on the same days; they witnessed each other's legal documents, land sales and mortgages. The two even obtained mortgages from the same person in Bibb County. Each had a son named Jefferson Jasper. Alexander had another son named Thomas Anderson, while he and a third brother each had sons named Doctor.

Alexander was born in Georgia in 1808. His wife Louisa, whom he married in 1827, was born in 1809 in South Carolina. Alexander died in 1869 in Arkansas. He and Louisa sold their land in Alabama in 1838, and moved to Ashley County, Arkansas, where he appears on the 1850 census. They evidently stopped in Mississippi for a time, since two of their children were born in Chickasaw County.

To get to Chickasaw County, they probably traveled the federal road into Mississippi and connected with the Natchez Trace, which was another federal road, and followed it to Chickasaw County. The Natchez Trace at that time was plagued by robbers and murderers and proved very dangerous for travelers. In any event, Alexander and Louisa with their family made their way along it to Chickasaw County, and thence into Arkansas.

They had a total of twelve children:

(A) Jane P., born 1828 in Shelby County, Alabama.

(B) Alpha Ann, born 1830 in Shelby County, Alabama.

(C) James Matthew, born 1834 in Shelby County, Alabama.

(D) William, born in 1836 in Shelby County, Alabama.

(E) George Newton, born in 1838 in Shelby County, Alabama.

(F) Thomas Anderson, born in 1840 in Alabama, probably en route to Mississippi.

(G) Jefferson Jasper, born in 1841 in Mississippi.

(H) Francis Asbery, born in 1842 in Mississippi.

(I) Doctor Blewford, born in 1844 in Mississippi.

(J) Charles W., born in 1847 in Chickasaw County, Mississippi.

(K) Sarah, born in 1853 in Ashley County, Arkansas.

(L) Lucinda, born in 1853 in Ashley County, Arkansas.

Now we return to Jefferson Jasper Honeycutt, son of Anderson Honeycutt, son of the Alabama pioneer Thomas Honeycutt. His is the line on which we have the most information, since it is the line of Mr. Edward Honeycutt, who has done many years of research on the Honeycutt family. Jefferson Jasper Honeycutt was born in 1836, in the Mulberry community of Bibb County. In the 1850 census of Shelby County, Alabama, he was listed in his father's household and was 16 years of age.

The next record of him was his marriage to Emily A. Marcus, on December 19, 1855, in Shelby County, Alabama. His Civil War record, which is housed in the National Archives, show that he was mustered in on March 22, 1862 at Mims' Cross Roads (present day Union Grove) by Captain James Cobb, and served with the 31st Alabama Volunteer Infantry Regiment. The following May, at Camp Goldwattie at Talladega, the unit became Cobb's Co. G of the 31st, or "Hundley's" Infantry Regiment.

At the time of his enlistment, Jefferson Jasper Honeycutt was twenty-six years old, had been married to Emily Marcus for six years, and had one son—Edward, or Eddard—who was three years old.

Soon after being activated, the 31st was pressed into service. They were at Knoxville in June, after having pushed the Federals out of the Cumberland Gap. In July, they became part of the 1st Division, commanded by Gen. Steveson. As part of the 1st Division, the 31st saw action at Tazewell, Tennessee in July and August, then spearheaded into Kentucky. In October of 1862, they were in the battle of Corinth, Mississippi. In this battle the Federals were attempting to gain control of the major north/south, east/west railway intersection. In December, the division was transferred to Vicksburg, Mississippi. There were a number of battles in April and May of 1863, leading up to the siege of Vicksburg.

The siege of Vicksburg lasted until the 4th of July, 1863, at which time the southerners surrendered. After the surrender, there were 29,491 southern soldiers paroled, and given 30-day furloughs. In September, the regiment was assigned to Pettus' brigade, but still in Steveson's 1st Division.

They were then shipped to Tennessee, where Gen. Bragg was laying siege to Chattanooga. In September and October, things went well, but on November 24th Gen. Grant had taken charge of the Federal forces, and had begun to break out. The 31st was pushed off Lookout Mountain to Missionary Ridge, east of Chattanooga. Then Pettus' brigade, which included the 31st, was assigned to the north end of Missionary Ridge, to defend a railway tunnel. On Wednesday morning, November 25, 1863, Gen. Sherman moved against Tunnel Hill and the north end of Missionary Ridge. At the same time, five miles south, Gen. Hooker moved against the southern end of the Confederate line, and Gen. Thomas moved against the center. The center, then the south end, gave way, and Pettus' Brigade had to fall back when the center failed. At this point, Jefferson Jasper Honeycutt was captured, and subsequently spent the remainder or the war in the northern prison at Rock Island, Illinois.

After the war, Jefferson Jasper Honeycutt settled in Baker (now Chilton) County Alabama, in the Chestnut Creek area. He appeared on the census there in 1870 and 1880.

In 1880 the family was listed as follows in Beat 1, household 46:

- Jefferson Jasper was listed as age 43.
- Emily, age 41.
- Daniel, age 17.
- William (Billy), age 15.
- Leah Paralee, age 12.
- Ward, Age 9.

The oldest son, Edward, had married and established his own family. He and wife Mary were listed as living in househhold 176, also in Beat 1.

Before the Civil War, Jefferson Jasper Honeycutt had, on October 18, 1859, applied for 260 acres in Section 24, Township 23, Range 14 east (page 23 of the Cahaba Book), patent # 37652. Then, on August 4, 1860, he filed on 80 acres in Section 18, 23N, 15E. The former land description is where the Davis/Honeycutt Cemetery is located.

After returning from the war, Jefferson Jasper became a county commissioner, and a farmer. Then in 1891 he was living in Strasburg (now

Thorsby,) and engaged in business with Mr. J. Brice (*The Chilton View*, February 5, 1891.) He died on September 22, 1891, and is buried in the Providence Cemetery near Thorsby, beside his wife and youngest child, Ward Honeycutt.

Jefferson Jasper and Emily were the parents of five children:

(A) Edward Walter, born March 26, 1859.

(B) Daniel Crawford, born November 5, 1863.

(C) William L. (Billy), born February 7, 1865.

(D) Leah Paralee, born about 1868.

(E) Ward, born June 7, 1871.

The line of Mr. Edward Honeycutt descends through the oldest son, Edward Walter Honeycutt. Edward, whose birth date is recorded in his family Bible as March 26, 1859, married Mary Missouri Thames on December 19, 1878, at the home of her father, James Thames, according to their marriage certificate. The ceremony was performed by W.B. Crowson. Their first child Jesse Garfield Honeycutt, was born on September 12, 1882.

On December 11th of that same year, Edward bought 120 acres of land from J.A. and Mary Ann McNeal, for which he paid one hundred and fifty dollars. Land description is N/2 of SE/4 and S/2 of S/2 of N/4, Sec 8 Twp 23, R14E. The farm was located on the Calera road about a quarter mile north of what used to be called Mims' Crossroads, now known as Union Grove. This community is about five miles east of Jemison, Alabama. The Jemison exit off I-65 takes in a portion of the farm.

Edward was a fairly well-to-do farmer, a Methodist minister, and the bookkeeper for the local Rocky Mount Union #22. He built a church about three quarters of a mile from his home, and a cemetery was begun next to the church. The church no longer stands, but the cemetery is still extant, now called "Old" Rocky Mount Cemetery. There is another church in the same area called Rocky Mount, which probably post-dates Edward's church of the same name.

An undated letter written by Edward's wife, Mary, to their son Jesse, who was living at Piper in Bibb County, tells Jesse he must come because "Pa is poorly, and complains of hurting in his breast and jaw. The doctor came and said it is his teeth." Mary was lonely, with "only the two little boys" with her. These two are thought to have been Virgil and Glois Martin, her grandsons. Then there is a P.S. written by Edward on May 30, 1920, which says: "I think I will make it if I don't have another setback." He died two days later, on June 1, 1920, according to his death certificate.

The farm was bought by Benjamin Glasscock, husband of Tennessee Honeycutt, daughter of James Honeycutt.

Edward Walter Honeycutt and his wife Mary Missouri Thames were the parents of three children:

>(a) Jesse Garfield, born September 12, 1882 in Chilton County, Alabama; and died August 12, 1941.
>
>(b) Emily (Emma) Elizabeth, born July 6, 1885, died February 28, 1951.
>
>(c) Eva Dora, born September 17, 1891, died February. 1973.

The line descends through the son, Jesse Garfield Honeycutt. On September 25, 1902, he married Mary Ozanna Creel who was born on February 8, 1875. Her father was Joshua Creel, who was born on October 9, 1822, died February 20, 1900, and is buried in Providence Baptist Cemetery. To reach this cemetery, go north from Jemison on US 31 to State 155, then left about 2.8 miles to the church and cemetery on the west side of the intersection. Mary Ozanna Creel's mother was Mary Frances Horton, born in February of 1840.

Sometime between 1913 and 1916, Jesse Garfield Honeycutt gave up farming, moved to Bibb County, and went to work in the coal mines at Piper. Eventually becoming out of work there, he opened a butcher shop. Shortly before 1930, he moved again, this time to Lee's Junction, about two miles west of Bessemer, Alabama. It is now called Five Points, and is considered part of Hueytown. He worked at the Mulga coal mines, but lost his job when the depression of the 1930's hit. His son Herschel managed to hold on to his one-day-a-week job at Woodward Furnace, and managed to make the house payments for the family. Then, to help their situation, the family moved to the community of Mudd Creek and farmed for one season, but then returned to Lee's Junction. Their home there sat on three lots, so Jesse farmed the two vacant lots, and rented additional land nearby to grow corn, vegetables and peanuts.

Jesse died on August 19, 1941. He was working at the Woodward Coal Mines, changing out timbers, and the roof fell in on him. His wife Mary died of a stroke in June of 1965. Both are buried in Valhalla Cemetery,

Bessemer, Alabama, Lot 155, Section 7. They were the parents of five children:

>(aa) Arvel Jefferson Honeycutt, born June 22, 1903
>
>(ab) Herschel McKinley
>
>(ac) Hazel Cecil Honeycutt, born November 23, 1910.
>
>(ad) Vera Agrath Honeycutt, born August 10, 1913.
>
>(ae) Vivian Nellie Honeycutt, born October 21, 1916

The line descends through Arvel Jefferson Honeycutt, the oldest child, who was the father of Mr. Edward Honeycutt, of Durant, Oklahoma, a well-known researcher. After leaving his father's house while they were living at Piper in Bibb County, Alabama, he went to work for Woodward Iron Co. Soon after that he met his future wife, Iris Duffey, and they were married on January 1, 1925. They subsequently became the parents of six children, one of them being:

>(aa1) Edward W. Honeycutt, born July 16, 1930.
>
>Edward W. Honeycutt spent his career in the Air Force as a flight engineer. While stationed in Durant, Oklahoma, he met Eyvonne O'Donley, and they were married on June 1, 1951. They became the parents of two children:
>
>>(aa1a) Glen Edward was born at Perrin AFB in Texas in 1952.
>>
>>(aa1b) Amy Denise was born at Great Lakes Naval Station in Chicago.

Information on the Honeycutt generations was furnished by Mr. Edward Honeycutt of Durant, Oklahoma, who says he was given invaluable help by Mr. John David Glasscock of Chilton County, Alabama, whom he considers the unofficial Chilton County historian.

JOHN HORTON

The first Horton in the British Isles is said to have been a Roman soldier serving under the Emperor Hadrian, in the years of the Roman occupation of Britain. The first Horton of record in America was a Mistress Mary Horton who left England in 1609 on the "Sea Adventure," bound for Virginia. The ship ran aground in one of the coastal waterways and crew and passengers were stranded on the island until 1610, when they were rescued and transported to Virginia. She witnessed the wedding of Pocahontas about 1614-1615, and her grandson is identified by relationship in the etching depicting the wedding scene. (This is from a letter from Perry Horton of North Carolina, March 10, 1985)

John Horton, the Alabama pioneer, came to Alabama from North Carolina about 1815, settling first in Montgomery County, later moving to Bibb about 1825. He was joined there by his nephew, Nimrod Wells Horton, son of Nimrod Horton, born 1759 in North Carolina, died 1830 in South Carolina, who married Susannah Wells in Lincoln County, North Carolina in 1803.

Nimrod's father is thought to have been James Horton, born about 1760, died about 1773 in North Carolina, a Revolutionary War veteran who was killed by the British or by Tories while home on furlough. Nimrod Horton was the father of twelve children, of which six were sons and six daughters. Of these, only one, Nimrod Wells Horton has been identified.

John Horton, the subject of this piece, lived out his life in Bibb County, Alabama, after moving there from Montgomery County. He had been born in Halifax County, North Carolina about 1755, the son of William Horton, and died after the 1830 census in Bibb County, Alabama.

He was a Revolutionary soldier, having enlisted in the North Carolina Continental Line in Halifax County on October 1, 1778. He became a corporal, then a sergeant in Col. W.L. Davidson's company. In 1782, his name appeared on a petition to Governor Alexander Martin on behalf of William Dale, convicted of horse stealing. William Horton was captain of the petition. (*State Records of North Carolina,* collected and edited by Walter Clark, Vol. 19, p.934, Vol 16, p.1072, and Vol. 14, p.294.)

William Horton, who was John Horton's father, was born about 1710 and died after 1784 in Halifax County, North Carolina. He was the son of Hugh Horton, born about 1660 in Henrico County, Virginia, and died in 1735 in Bertie County, North Carolina. Hugh is thought, but not proven, to have been the son of Isaac Horton, born about 1610 in England, who died about 1680 in Henrico County, Virginia.

John Horton, the Alabama pioneer, probably had a large family, but the names of only two are known, the two being:

(I) John Horton, who settled in the area of Elyton (now Birmingham), Alabama and raised a large family.

(II) James M. Horton. James M. moved to Coosa County, Alabama after it was opened for settlement in 1832, and lived out his life there, in the Hatchet Creek Area. Born in North Carolina in 1800, he died in Coosa County, Alabama in 1856, leaving a will. The will indicates that he was quite wealthy, owning a plantation and slaves.

He married Violetta Patterson, born 1812 in South Carolina, and thought to have been the daughter of Adam Patterson, who was living near them in Coosa County in 1840.

In the 1850 census, there had been a notation that James M. Horton was blind.

After James M. Horton's death in 1856, Violetta married Judge Ebenezer Pond, who owned a neighboring plantation. In the 1870 census, Ebenezer's two children who had been in the household in 1860, were on their own, as was Margaret Emeline, who was James' and Violetta's daughter. Violetta's mother, age 71, was in the household, however, as was John W. Horton and his wife Martha. Also in the household, was Prince Horton, age 60, a black farm worker, born in North Carolina. Speculation is that this was a former slave who had been with James M. Horton since childhood, and chose to remain with them after the emancipation.

James M. Horton and Violetta Patterson were my great-great-grandparents. They were the parents of two children, Margaret Emeline, and John W.:

(A) Margaret Emeline Horton, who was my great-grandmother, was born in Coosa County, Alabama on October 20, 1846, and died on March 16, 1905, in Tuscaloosa County, and is buried in the Union Cumberland Presbyterian Church Cemetery at Vance, Alabama, which is in Tuscaloosa County.

In 1865 she married John M. Thomas from a neighboring plantation in Coosa County. The ceremony took place at the home of John Horton in Elyton, Alabama. John M. Thomas had been badly wounded in the Civil War and spent time in a northern prison camp. Because of his wounds, he had been afforded transportation back to Jefferson County, Alabama after the war, whereas the southerners who were able to walk had to walk back to their homes, and many died along the way.

After his return from the war, Margaret Emeline and John Thomas settled in Tuscaloosa County near Thomas relatives and lived out their lives there. They had an extremely difficult time because of John's wounds, and because of the hardships and deprivations that all southerners suffered for many, many years after the war's end.

They became the parents of nine children:

(1) Mary Jane Thomas, born 1866, died 1930, married Joshua Vining.

(2) Margaret Fatima Thomas, born 1867, died 1899, married John William Porter and had three children:

(a) Margie Eugenia.

(b) John Monroe.

(c) Samuel David, never married.

Margie Eugenia Porter married Joseph Horace Seales, and has many descendants. (See the John William Porter and Joseph Horace Seales families for more on Margie Eugenia's descendants.) John Monroe was married twice, to Ruby Howard and Lessie Jordon, and also has many descendants.

(3) John Thomas, born 1869, married Ethel.

(4) Robert Thomas, born 1871, married Viola Crider.

(5) Martha Thomas, born 1874, died 1885 as a child.

(6) George Thomas, born 1876, married Moriah Wilson. They had two daughters and one son:

(a) Lennie.

(b) Ruby.

(c) William.

(7) Missouri Thomas, born 1878, married Starling Whaley, and had five children:

(a) Paul.

(b) Clarence.

(c) Otto.

(d) Leona.

(e) Irene.

After the death of Starling Whaley, Missouri married a Mr. McFerrin.

    (8) Emma Thomas, born 1880, married Roman Vining.

    (9) Coleman Thomas, born 1882, died 1906, married Josephine Wright, one daughter, Colie.

Little is known of the later generations of most of this Thomas/Horton family by this writer. Margaret Fatima Thomas Porter died young, Margie Eugenia Porter (my mother) was raised in Jefferson County, Alabama, in the home of her foster grandfather, and, sadly, in the struggle of day-to-day living and raising families, contact was lost.

    (B) John W. Horton, the second child of James W. Horton and Violetta Patterson, was born in Coosa County, Alabama in 1852, and was married in October 1869 to Martha, born 1840. In 1870, the couple was living in the home of Ebenezer Pond, John's stepfather. Nothing further is known of them.

Information on the Horton family is from research by Madge Pettit in the archives and census records of Virginia, North and South Carolina and Alabama, with special emphasis on the Alabama counties of Shelby, Bibb, Coosa, and Tuscaloosa. Much help was also received from Perry Horton of Oak Hill, Ohio.

BERRYMAN KIMBREL

Born in Tennessee in 1803, Berryman Kimbrel came to Alabama about 1835. He died in Shelby County, Alabama in 1887, and is buried in the Higginbotham Cemetery. In 1838 he married Feriby Vining, born 1808 in Georgia, daughter of John Vining, born 1784 in Georgia. This seems to have been Berryman's second marriage, although this has not been verified. However, Ransom Kimbrel, born 1824 in Tennessee, is known to have been his son, so it is thought that he married young, about age 20 or 21, in Tennessee, and that his wife may have been an Indian but no record has been found of the marriage. On February 28, 1839, Berryman received a land patent in Bibb County, Alabama, and that is where he raised his family. More about Berryman later.

The Kimbrels descend from the ancient English house of Kembolde. This name gradually evolved into Kemball, Kimble, Kimbull, and in America, Kimbrel and Kimbrell. The first Kemball immigrant of record migrated to America about 1635, and settled in Massachusetts. The Kimball (using this form of the name) immigrant from whom the Kimbrels of Alabama descend, however, came to America about forty years later and settled in the Virginia Colony. He was Joseph Kimball, born about 1650 in England, and died in 1713 in Surrey County, Virginia. His estate was closed on June 17, 1713, in Surrey County. He was the father of three sons, all of whom settled for a time in Brunswick County, Virginia. They were:

(I) William, born about 1675 in Surrey County, Virginia. By 1728, he was in Brunswick County, Virginia, where he sold land to Ralph Jackson. In 1752 he owned land with his brother Joseph on Fishing Creek, Just across the state line in Granville County, North Carolina.

(II) Joseph: Born about 1810 in Surrey County, North Carolina, he married Winnie Gilliam. In 1732 he was in Brunswick County, where he sold land to Adam Sims. In 1760 he bought 650 acres in St. John's Parish, in Granville, County, North Carolina. Bartholomew Kimball (probably his son) was one of the sworn chain carriers. In those days acreage was measured in chains and links rather than in yards and feet. A chain carrier was just what the name implies: one who was responsible for carrying one end of the 32-foot-long measuring chain. About this same time Joseph bought 530 acres on Reedy Fork of Anderson's Swamp, joining Bartholomew Kimball. He owned a mill on the North Fork of the

Swamp. In 1754 he had bought 626 acres on Indian Creek in Granville County. Joseph had a son Peter Kimball and Peter had a son Buckner Kimball, born 1746, who died in 1830 in Granville County. Buckner married Pattie Harris, daughter of West Harris. Their daughter Sarah Kimball was the second wife of Penuel Woods. They also had a son named Harris Kimball (1778-1825). Buckner Kimball was a captain in the Revolutionary War. In 1805 Buckner Kimball and Peter Kimball were in the land lottery in Greene County, Georgia. On February 14 1769, Joseph Kimball sold his furniture, cattle, and a negro woman named Mell to Miles Williams.

(III) Charles: Born about 1682 in Surrey County, Virginia. He seems to have been a somewhat remarkable man, a surveyor's helper, planter, carpenter, Indian trader, foreman of the first jury ever assembled in Granville County, North Carolina, and a wealthy landowner and influential member of the community, first in Brunswick County, Virginia and later in Granville County, North Carolina. By 1717 he was living in Brunswick County, Virginia, and trading with the Tuscaroras. There he got into trouble of sorts and was called before the county council and questioned for trading independently with the Tuscaroras, and not being a member of the Indian Company monopoly. This was against the law. This law had come into being because some of the traders were suspected of stirring up trouble between the Indian tribes, and the Tuscaroras and Senecas in particular. What Charles Kimball traded to the Indians was most likely hemp. The name Tuscarora means "hemp gatherer," and the tribe was given the name Tuscaroras because of their extensive use of this plant. In the 1700's many of the planters in Virginia and the Carolinas grew hemp as a cash crop. Hemp is the same thing as "apocynum cannabinum," or as it is known today, "cannabis," and one variety is known as marijuana. In the 1700's the growing and marketing of hemp was not illegal, nor did it carry any stigma or elicit any social or political backlash.

It is not known whom Charles Kimball married. A thorough search of the records has failed to reveal this information. His wife may have been a Tuscarora woman. The Indian traders almost always married Indian women. Traveling into the remote Indian villages was extremely dangerous, especially at that particular time in history, since the Tuscaroras had not long since fought two bitter wars with the whites, one in 1711, another in 1712 to 1714. A trader's chances were greatly enhanced if he was allied with the Indians in some way, preferably marriage. There were five sub-tribes of Tuscaroras—the Tulelos, Waccamaws, Waterees, Waxhaws, and Weapemeocs. They lived in fifteen towns scattered along the Roanoke, Tar, Pamlico and Neuse rivers in eastern North Carolina. A single trip to visit all the Indian villages, traveling on horseback from Brunswick County, Virginia over the Indian trails probably took at least a month. The traders were accompanied by pack-horse men, who took care of the horses and the cargo, which was usually furs on the return trip. The pack-horse men were usually a rough, burly lot; expert woodsmen, crack shots with a muzzleloader, and deadly hand-to-hand fighters—real "knife artists."

In addition to his Indian trade and other pursuits already mentioned, Charles Kimball owned vast amounts of land in Surrey County, Virginia, where he grew up, then in Brunswick County, Virginia, and Granville County, North Carolina. He also is in many of the land records as a surveyor's helper, which means that he probably was a bonded chain carrier which was a position of some honor. Kimball's Creek is mentioned in some of the Granville County records. On October 21, 1728 Charles was granted 200 acres in Cumberland County, North Carolina.

On July 27, 1761 he witnessed a deed in Granville County for Richard West. He is thought to have died soon after this, as he disappeared from the records. No will has been found. He had five known children, but there probably were others. The five were:

(A) Benjamin: Born about 1700 in Brunswick County, Virginia. He used the Kimbell form of the family name. As a young man he moved to Granville County, North Carolina, and when Warren County was formed from what had formerly been Granville, he was in Warren County, near the town of Warrenton. On September 28, 1728 he was granted a patent for 520 acres of new land in Brunswick County on the Maherin River. About this time he was married to Lucy Shearin, daughter of Joseph Shearin. It is through these two that the Alabama line descends, so more about them later.

(B) William: Born about 1705 in Brunswick County, Virginia. In 1728 he owned land in that county on the Maherin River, next to his brother Benjamin. Nothing further is known of him.

(C) Lewis: Born about 1710, married Alsey Jackson. He died young.

(D) Peter: Born about 1715 in Brunswick County, Virginia, married Alsey Jackson Kimball, widow of Lewis Kimball, and settled in Warren County, North Carolina.

(E) Buckner: Born about 1720. Little is known of him, but he is documented as a brother to Benjamin and Peter in *Genealogies of Virginia Families,* Vol. 2, p.106.

Now back to Benjamin Kimbell, the eldest son: By 1748 he was in Granville County, North Carolina, and owned land on the Hub Quarter Creek. On October 26, 1753, he bought 320 acres on the north side of Fishing Creek. He and his brother Peter also owned land on Kimball's Creek. About 1765 Benjamin bought land in Bute County, North Carolina, and was on the tax lists there in the 1760's and 1770's. However, on the 1785 census, he was back in Warren County, where he remained until his death. His wife evidently preceded him in death, since she is not named in his will which was probated in November, 1794, in Warren County. He and his wife are thought to have been buried in a family burial plot on his plantation. The children are named in his will, along with the specifics of how the real estate and slaves are to be divided among them. They are as follows:

(1) David: Two negroes, Amanda and Hannah and their increases, and one half of a sixty-acre plot.

David served in the Revolutionary War. In 1807 he migrated to Clark County, Georgia, but later moved to Muscogee County, Georgia, where he had been granted land. He died in Muscogee County, leaving a will. He was the father of eight sons:

(a) Benjamin.

(b) John.

(c) Christopher.

(d) Gideon.

(e) Thomas.

(f) Ransom.

(g) Robert.

(h) David.

(2) James: Four Negroes, Betty, Fanny, Andrew and Hilah, and their increases, and one half of sixty acres adjoining his

property. (James was called Francis on the deed when he and his siblings sold the remainder of their father's land after his death.)

(3) Benjamin: Four Negroes, Mengo, Rose, Esther, and Hannah, and their increases. (Benjamin settled in Warren County, North Carolina and lived out his life there.)

(4) William: One Negro man, one girl, Lucy during his natural life, two cows, two calves, other young cattle, and one half the land he now lives on. (William lived out his life in Warren County, North Carolina.)

(5) Leonard: Two Negroes, Riddle and Peg, two cows and calves. (No further records were found in North Carolina. Leonard is thought to have died young.)

(6) Ransom: Three negroes, Lilah, Indah, and Peter and their increases. (Ransom's wife died in 1806 in Warren County, North Carolina, and Ransom migrated to South Carolina.)

(7) Charles: One Negro girl Susanna, one Negro man, Ned, one boy Marc, "provided my son shall have lawful heirs, this my will that they should inherit the estate." (Charles migrated to Tennessee, and his descendants were among the Alabama pioneers. See further.)

(8) Rebekah: Twenty pounds. (Rebekah married Capt. William Armistead, a Revolutionary soldier of Randolph County, North Carolina, who was born in Virginia. She died fairly young and Armistead remarried and migrated to Alabama.)

(9) Armistead: Twenty pounds. (No further information.)

(10) A daughter, name unknown, who died before the will was written, leaving a daughter named Polly Jones. She had married Ridley Jones, son of Francis Jones. Polly was given a cow and calf, one feather bed and furniture (a bedstead) to be delivered at legal age or marriage.

Charles Kimbrell (he used this form of the name) was the progenitor of the Alabama line of Kimbrels. He was born in Warren County, North Carolina, but migrated at an early age to Anderson County, Tennessee. He appeared on the tax list there in 1806, along with a Peterson Kimbrell, who is thought to have been a first cousin. Peterson eventually settled in Roane County, Tennessee and had several children (Sally, who married Matthias

Parr in 1819, Betsy, who married Thomas Williams in 1821, Jenny, who married William Wilson in 1821, Benjamin, who married Catherine Luttrell in 1827, Crowder, who married Nancy _____, date unknown, and Rachel, who married James Manning in 1835.)

In the next generation this family scattered into Illinois and Missouri. Peterson Kimbrell eventually went to Sparta County, Illinois, where he died. Charles Kimbrell lived out his life in Anderson and Knox Counties, Tennessee. He is thought (but not documented) to have been an Indian trader like his grandfather Charles Kimball, and his wife may have been a Cherokee or Creek, or perhaps even Crow, as there were a few of this tribe along the border between Tennessee and the Alabama Territory, which would later become the state of Alabama. In the next generation in Alabama it was well known that the Kimbrels were part Indian. My family has known the Kimbrel family for approximately 150 years, and one of the Kimbrel ladies became my mother's stepmother, so I have some personal knowledge of this family. Charles Kimbrell died about 1840 in Knox County, Tennessee. He was the father of four known children.

- (A) Berryman: Born 1803 in Tennessee, he migrated to Alabama. See further.

- (B) Thomas: Born 1813 in Tennessee, he migrated to Alabama. He died in Jefferson County, Alabama on December 4, 1904, and is buried in the George Cemetery. His wife was Elvy Loveless. They had two known children: Charles M. (1856-1936), who is buried at Green Pond, and Jacob (1838-1901) who is buried at Bucksville. Thomas received a land patent in Tuscaloosa County on April 11, 1850.

- (C) Jesse, on whom no further information is available.

- (D) John, about whom all that is known is that he received a land patent in Shelby County, Alabama on January 23, 1855.

Berryman Kimbrel obviously was only one of several sons of Charles Kimbrel who became pioneers in the new state of Alabama, but he is the only one of whom very much is known, hence he became the subject of this entry. As already noted, he was born in 1803 in Tennessee, died in 1887 in Shelby County, Alabama, is buried in the Higginbotham Cemetery, and was married in 1838 to Feriby Vining, born 1808 in Georgia, the daughter of John Vining, born 1784 in Georgia.

Berryman's marriage to Feriby evidently was his second marriage, since Ransom Kimbrel, born 1820 in Tennessee is verified as his son by the

Mormon Church records. He evidently married young in Tennessee, but no record has been found, so his wife is thought to have been an Indian. He migrated to Alabama about 1835, and on February 28, 1839 received land in Bibb County, where he settled. He and Feriby had six more children. All of Berryman's children were:

(1) Ransom: more is known about him than the others. See further.

(2) Nancy: Born 1842.

(3) Charles: Born 1843, married Mary Pleasant Evaline Henderson, daughter of Pleasant Henderson and Elizabeth Seamons. According to Henderson researchers they migrated to Texas, but they must have returned, since in 1920 they appeared on the census in Bibb County, Alabama. Charles at the time was 63 years old, Mary, 65, and three children at home, Pleasant, age 24, Belle, age 20, and Gracie, age 16.

(4) John: Born 1844, married Permelia Williams.

(5) Martha J.: Born 1846.

(6) William: Born 1848.

(7) James B.: Born 1852, married Amanda Bunn on October 11, 1890 in Shelby County, Alabama.

Ransom Kimbrel was born July 13, 1824 in Tennessee. His tombstone gives his birth year as 1822, but according to all the other available records, this is incorrect. He died on October 19, 1908 in Shelby County, Alabama, and is buried in the Genery's Cemetery, which is on the crest of Shades Mountain on the Jefferson-Shelby County line.

He came to Alabama as a teenager with his father Berryman Kimbrel and other relatives. In the 1850 census he was living in the household of his uncle, John Kimbrel. He married Rachel Heflin, who was born January 30, 1839, died January 22, 1912, and is buried in the Genery's Cemetery beside Ransom. She was the daughter of William C. Heflin and Rachel Johnson of Bibb County, Alabama.

At the beginning of the Civil War, Ransom joined the Confederate cause and served until the end of the war. While he was away, Rachel stayed on the farm, deep in the Shelby County woods, took care of the children, who were small at the time, and kept the farm going.

To understand the extraordinary strength and courage she displayed in doing this, one has to understand something of the times in which it occurred. Renegade northern soldiers and southern scalawags roamed the countryside in gangs, robbing and killing. Then Wilson's Raiders came through, stealing anything they could and usually burning what they couldn't use. They camped on Cahaba River, not far from the Kimbrel homestead. There was no way of knowing what the northern soldiers might do, since they were under orders to live off the land, and that could be open to broad interpretation. Ransom survived the war, returned to Shelby County, and raised a large family. When the boys grew up, several of them worked on the Southern Railroad, which had been put through in 1875. In their old age, Ransom and Rachel lived in section houses (small frame houses built near the stations here and there along the tracks as residences for the "section hands" who worked that section of the track) here and there up and down the track, wherever the boys were working.

Ransom and Rachel Kimbrel were the parents of eleven children:

>(a) George: Born 1858, married Mary Tatum. In 1924 they had three children in Shelby County schools, Helen, age 10, Nellie, age 8, and G.C., age 6. This according to the school census. These may have been grandchildren.

>(b) William: Born 1861. In 1920, he was living in Bibb County, age 60 and wife Lucinda, age 58.

>(c) Melvin.

>(d) Nelson: Married Neata Della Hollingsworth, no children. They lived out their lives in the Genery's Gap community, and are buried in the Genery's Cemetery. In 1925, Nelson shot and killed his brother-in-law, Kimsey West, husband of Neata's sister, Maggie Hollingsworth. This is a matter of public record.

>(e) Thomas: Died at age 32.

>(f) Jacob: "Jack," Married Arlevia Hollingsworth, sister to Neata and Maggie. They had only one child a son, Clayton Kimbrel. Jack was shot and killed at an early age at the train station at Elvira, according to the story passed down in the family. Some of the young men from the Genery's Gap community would often meet the train at Elvira and engage some of the passengers in a game of chance. This time something went wrong, and Jack ended up dead.

(g) Joe: Married first Sadie Tatum and had two children, a son, Jesse, and a daughter, Genie. In 1920 they were living in Jefferson County, Alabama. Joe married second, Rose Peel Jordan, no children.

(h) Missouri Alice: Born February 3, 1867, in Shelby County, Alabama, she married John William Porter and had nine children: Fannie, Mattie, Charles, Minnie, Rufus, Jack, Jesse, Lucion, and Gladys.

This was a second marriage for John William Porter. His first marriage was to Margaret Fatima Thomas, daughter of John M. Thomas, a Confederate veteran of Tuscaloosa County, Alabama, and his wife Margaret Emeline Horton.

John William Porter had three children from his first marriage to Margaret Fatima Thomas:

(1h) Margie Eugenia.

(2h) John Monroe.

(3h) Samuel David.

John William Porter and Margaret Fatima Porter were the maternal grandparents of this writer, and Missouri Alice Kimbrel Porter was my step-grandmother.

(i) Susan Lee Anne: Born 1870, she was married in 1886 to William Andrew Jackson Tyler. They had 21 children:

(ia) Belle, who married a Goodwin.

(ib) Maude, who married a Sullivan.

(ic) Minnie, who married a Gunter.

(id) Willie, who married a Blow.

(ie) Rosie, who married a Bailey.

(if) Mary, who married a McClendon.

(ig) Nora, who married a Hodge.

(ih) Flora, who married a Herring.

(ii) Lottie, who married a Higginbotham.

(ij) Nettie, who married a Cruse.

(ik) Ruby, who married a Brown.

(il) Bob, who never married.

(im) Oscar, who married a Benton.

(in) George, who married a Ledbetter.

(io) John, who never married.

(ip) Grover, who married Mae _____.

(iq) Homer "Tiny," who married Jeannette_____.

(ir) Fannie, who died at age four.

(is), (it), and (iu) three who died unnamed as infants.

(j) Caroline: Married Henry Henderson and had three children:

(ja) Horace.

(jb) Willard.

(jc) Daisy.

Henry and Caroline are buried in the Mount Carmel Cemetery, West Blocton, Alabama. According to descendants, Caroline was the last of five marriages of Henry Henderson, but proof has been found of only one other, that being to Martha Jordan at an early age in Shelby County. They had two daughters, Florence and Nora.

(k) Sally, married Pete Howard and had five children, one being Ruby Howard who married John Monroe Porter, son of John William Porter and Margaret Fatima Thomas.

Information on the Kimbrel family is from personal knowledge, oral family histories, and research at the courthouses of Shelby and Bibb Counties, at several Morman history centers, and the National Archives.

MADOC, PRINCE OF WALES

Anyone who is a student of the Indian civilizations of the southeast has heard of Prince Madoc and the legendary "white Indians" of Alabama. His story is a fanciful tale, part legend, part provable fact, and altogether interesting to anyone who likes to delve into Indian lore. It goes like this: About a thousand years ago a Welsh prince named Madoc was for some reason thrown out of his country, and set out in a boat to find a place where he might take refuge.

Madoc was one of seventeen sons of Owen Gwyneth, Prince of Wales, and the reason he was thrown out of his country is thought to have been because he was different in some way. He may have had a disfiguring birthmark, red hair, dark skin, or crossed eyes. Whatever the reason, he and a small entourage set out from the coast of Wales in a boat. On the Atlantic they were caught up in a storm and carried in a southwesterly direction to the shores of the New World, and eventually into the present Gulf of Mexico. They finally came ashore at the present location of Mobile, Alabama.

In the wilderness that would one day become the State of Alabama, Madoc and his company of about 300 men took Indian wives. Their descendants formed the many tribes which later were known as "White Indians." Prince Madoc's name eventually, through usage, devolved into "Modoc." His name can be traced in the histories of many Native American tribes which are found today in southern states reaching from Alabama to North Carolina, but also in certain western groups in California and Oregon.

When I was a child growing up in Alabama there was an area in Shelby County on Cahaba River that was called "Modoc." No town was there, not even a village, just dense woods and the river, and here and there a backwoods farmer. I remember asking many times why it was called Modoc, and no one seemed to know – an unusual situation in an area and time where most of the place names had an identifiable source.

Then, there was another mystery: On the tract of land adjoining our homestead, which was just over the line in Jefferson County, lived a family who had been there since pioneer days. This location would have been six or seven miles from Modoc. The family had settled there about 1890, according to my mother, whose own family had settled there in 1840, just four years after the land was ceded by the Creeks. Her grandfather had taken part in the roundup and removal of the Indians, so my mother knew the entire history of the area from its first European settlement—everything, that is except the origin of the name "Modoc."

My mother told me that the wife of the neighbor family told her that when they first came to the property and were clearing the land that they felled one tree in which they found a small clay doll near the top. My mother said that a crow (crows are terrible thieves) had stolen it somewhere and brought it there. This didn't make sense to me, since the nearest homestead where a doll might presumably have been found was miles away, and also a doll made of clay would be quite heavy, and even a very large crow couldn't carry it very far.

My mother told me many stories about "the Old Place"—about how the mother of the family who settled there was always uneasy and afraid. She told of hearing things at night. Sometimes it would be the sound of a large dog walking across the bare floor, when all the doors were closed and there was no dog in the house. Sometimes it would be the sound of a woman moaning. Sometimes at night they would hear a tapping noise, like someone driving tacks. When the wife became frightened, her husband would tell her not to worry, that it was just old man Golden pegging shoes, whereupon he would turn over and go back to sleep. Old man Golden was an older man with no family who had lived on the land briefly some time before this family moved there, and in those days people still made their own shoes.

Then, as the children grew older and roamed in the woods near the home and up and down Rice Creek, which ran through the property, they reported seeing things which really frightened them. As my mother put it, the boys of this family weren't ordinarily afraid of anything, "not even the Devil himself."

I interviewed the oldest living member of this family in 1996, she being the only one of the children of the family still living at that time, and she confirmed all of this. She was ninety-two years old, but very lucid. She remembered seeing the little doll, and described it as being hand-molded out of clay and "about the length of my hand," which I took to mean that it was about seven inches long. She said you wouldn't believe all the scary things they saw and heard while growing up over there. She said that even a short time before, she and a relative had been at the old place picking blackberries and had been nearly frightened out of their wits by the sounds of a woman moaning. She died a few months later, so I never had the opportunity to talk with her again.

I remember one other very strange thing concerning the Old Home Place. After the family grew up and the old folks died, the place became deserted and we kids were able to roam it at will. Even so, I don't remember ever being at the Old Place but once. On that one occasion I was a teenager, and had gone with my mother to look for the milk cows. I remember it as a sad, haunted place. At the time there were huge, freshly-dug holes in the ground in several places. I asked my mother what it meant, and her reply was that people had been digging for gold. I couldn't understand that. The family who had lived there were just farmers and had raised a large family, and old man Golden, if he had had any gold, would surely have taken it with him when he moved on westward. So, I figured out that it must have been Indian gold they were seeking, and this idea plus the story of the little doll found in the treetop started me to thinking that this must have been the site of an Indian village.

From earliest times and up until the Indians were rounded up and relocated to Oklahoma in 1836, there had been a brisk trade between the tribes of the present day Gulf Coast states and the present mid-Atlantic states over the Great Trading Path, which ran from present North Carolina in an arc that swooshed through central Alabama and on to southwestern Mississippi. The Cherokees had been mining gold in North Georgia for many, many years, and some of it reached Alabama through trade, along with trade items such as quartz and obsidian for arrow and spear points, and peach seeds. Peaches, which originated in Egypt, were brought to America very early by the English adventurers and soon were spread across the continent by way of the trading paths as the Indians bartered using the prized peach seeds.

After I grew up and began researching my history and Alabama history in general, and eventually the history of the many Indian tribes who had inhabited the area before the white man, I discovered Prince Madoc and his tribes of white Indians. As already stated, the legend is that about a thousand years ago this Welsh prince was for some reason banished from Wales and set out in a boat to find refuge wherever he might. The boat was caught up in an Atlantic sea storm, carried far off course, and eventually tossed into the Gulf of Mexico and onto land at the spot where Mobile, Alabama is today. From there, Madoc, who came to be called Modoc, eventually moved northward with his party, intermarried with the local Indian women, and established several tribes of so-called "white Indians " in the area. Their religion was centered on a fertility rite, and involved masked figures performing fertility dances. In the center of each Modoc village was a large living tree, and in the top of the tree was affixed a small doll which symbolized fertility. This is where their religious ceremonies were performed.

I believe the old homestead of my memory was built on the exact spot where there formerly had existed a Modoc village on the banks of Rice Creek. As for the gold someone thought was buried there, I don't believe there was any Indian gold.

Many times, when the Indians were removed by force they left behind their treasures, buried ten feet deep in the ground in an Indian treasure hole, no doubt hoping to return later and retrieve them. I have heard stories of Indian treasure maps, passed down from parents to children to grandchildren of the location of these treasures, and I have heard of gold figurines and exquisite stone effigies said to have been taken from such troves. I personally once saw an unbelievably beautiful stone effigy in the form of a snake, which I was told had been taken from a treasure hole in northern Mississippi; however I don't think this sort of treasure is buried at this location.

The Modoc Indians who I think lived there left of their own free will, probably pushed out or harassed out by the Creeks. In any case they weren't being rounded up and sent on a forced march to a reservation in Oklahoma, as later happened with the Creeks and Cherokees. Chances are that when they left, they probably took whatever they owned.

The large holes my mother and I saw most likely were dug by some treasure hunter with an early metal detector (a "needle") who made a hobby of visiting old home sites looking for gold buried by some pioneer. As for the noises the original family heard, and things they saw, it may have been Indians returning to the site for one reason or another, perhaps to visit the burial site of an ancestor.

I think there were at least two other Modoc villages, perhaps more, on Cahaba River, in the aforementioned area known as Modoc. Then, there is a place on the south side of Shades Mountain, a circular rock formation, where according to legend, Indian chiefs once held their tribal councils. Because of the location, I suspect that these chiefs, if the legend is true, were Modocs. There they probably sat and talked about their harassment by the Creeks, where their hunting parties could safely hunt and their women fish, smoked their pipes and cast their cares and grievances into the council fire, Indian style, where they rose with the smoke to the Great Father.

The Indians always traveled the high ground, and one of their trails traced the length of Shades Mountain. Today, a paved road follows the same route. Another trail ran the hog's back of Bluff Ridge, and according to my ancestors, one of their hunting camps was on Bluff Ridge right where the original pioneer family later had their cotton fields and a small cotton house, on the ridge overlooking their home place. They grew cotton on the top and down the north side of Bluff Ridge. The top of the ridge is an airport now.

When the Modocs left the area, they traveled north to the Tennessee River, according to legend, then north on the Tennessee to the Ohio, thence to the Mississippi, and up the Mississippi to the estuary of the Missouri River, where they joined other descendants of Prince Madoc, who had several towns on the banks of the Missouri. They were there known as Mandans, and they are extinct today, reportedly killed off by smallpox.

In the meantime, Prince Madoc had continued to father Indian tribes all across the continent. The Tuscaroras of coastal North Carolina are said to be his descendants. This includes the Waxhaws, Weapemeocs, Waccamaws, and Waterees. There are also places bearing his name, and presumably indicating his presence at one time, in Georgia, and South Carolina, and on across the country in Illinois, Indiana, Kansas, and continuing westward to northern California and Oregon, where the Modocs are widespread and numerous, and include the Salems of Oregon. No one knows what finally became of Prince Madoc, but he is one early immigrant to Alabama who left his name and his genes behind in many places.

This piece is gleaned from a lifetime interest and research into the Indian civilizations of the southeast; visits to the sites of Indian settlements dating back as much as fifteen thousand years; from a lifetime of studying Indian artifacts; and interviews with people, now departed, who lived close in time to the Indians who once freely roamed the great forests of the south.

STARK PORTER

Stark Porter came to Alabama from Union County, South Carolina about 1845, and settled in Shelby County. He traveled with his brothers Hancock Porter and William Edward Porter, and members of the Jolly and Bevill families. The Porters are a very old family, in both English and American history.

In England they trace back to William De La Grande, a Norman knight who came across the English Channel with William the Conqueror in 1066. In reward for his services in the Norman Conquest, he was given vast holdings of land in Warwickshire, and his son Ralph later was given the position of Grand Porteur in the court of Henry I. This title meant that he was the Keeper of the Doors at the Court, a position of great importance. He served in this position for some twenty years, beginning in 1120 and ending in 1140. This is where the name "Porter" began, as the French word "Porteur" (gate-keeper) gradually became anglicized to "Porter." The Porter coat of arms features a replica of a gate, with three bells and a gatekeeper's helmet. The Porter motto is "Vigilantia et Vertuti," which means "Watchfulness and Bravery."

In America, the family line of the Alabama pioneer Stark Porter, who was my great-great-grandfather, traces back to October 24, 1635, when Edward Porter landed at the Chickacoan Indian District on the Virginia Coast. He had sailed from Bristol, England on the ship *Constance*, with Capt. Clement Chapman. He was 35 years old at the time, having been born in England in 1600. His wife's name was Mary. In Virginia, he settled in Westmoreland County, and he and Mary became the parents of five children, all born in Westmoreland County. They were: Robert, Jacob, Edward, Thomas, and Francis. Little is known of any of these except Thomas.

Thomas Porter was born about 1660 in Westmoreland County, Virginia, and died in Lancaster County, Virginia, date unknown. He was married about 1690 in Westmoreland County, Virginia, to Elizabeth Wood, and they became the parents of five children, all born in Lancaster County, Virginia. They were: Ann, Elizabeth, twins William and Peter (born May 28, 1693), and John. John Porter was the ancestor of the Alabama pioneer Stark Porter.

John Porter was born on June 23, 1695, in Lancaster County, Virginia, and died in 1756 in the same county. He married Sarah Sanders, daughter of a sea captain and ship owner named Edward Sanders and his wife Elizabeth. Edward Sanders lived at Cherry Neck Point, Northumberland County, Virginia, but traded throughout the Carribean. He was the son of Dr. Edward Sanders, a physician and surgeon. His mother was Mary Hudnall, widow of John Hudnall. The Sanders family had been in Virginia since the early 1630's, and Edward had been sent back to England for his medical education. John Porter and Sarah had three known children, Edward Sanders, John, and Samuel. The line descends through Edward Sanders.

Edward Sanders Porter was born in Lancaster County, Virginia in 1720, and died in Union County, South Carolina in 1791. He was a wealthy planter in Lancaster County, Virginia, and later in Union County, South Carolina. His will does not name his wife, but speculation is that she may have been a Hancock. Neither does his will name all of his children, only Hancock, Landlot, Calvin, and Epaphroditus, and no daughters. (Will Book I, Sec. A, p. 8, Union County, S.C. 1791). The following is thought to be a complete list of his sons, plus one daughter:

(I) Landlot Porter, Revolutionary soldier. Landlot was born in Lancaster County, Virginia about 1747, and died in Hinds County, Mississippi on February 6, 1831. He married Winneyfred Palmer, who was born in Virginia, and died between 1820 and 1830 in Mississippi. Both were buried on the banks of the Homochitto River, which has changed its course many times over the years, and the graves are lost. In the Revolution, Landlot had been in Col. Brandon's Regiment in Union County, South Carolina. On September 26, 1808, he claimed a tract of 160 acres on the Homochitto River in Southwest Mississippi. A year earlier, on July 7, 1807 his four sons, William, Joseph, John, and Shadrach had each claimed 160 acres on the Homochitto. (American State Papers, Class VIII, Wash. D.C., 1834, Public Lands, Vol. II, p.244) Landlot was the father of six children, all born in Union County, South Carolina. They were:

(A) William Porter, born 1779, he died on September 9, 1834 in Hinds County, Mississippi, and was buried on the banks of the Homochitto River. His wife's name was Sarah, and she may have been a Retty. She died in Franklin County, Mississippi, and was buried beside William. They were the parents of eight children:

(1) Lucinda, born in South Carolina, married James Owens on July 23, 1824.

(2) Elizabeth, born about 1803 in South Carolina, died March 19, 1860. She was married three times, first to Gabriel Cowan, on January 3, 1819, secondly to William Crofford on October 21, 1830, and thirdly to Gadi Owen.

(3) Jeremiah "Jerry," born December 9, 1802 in South Carolina, died on December 29, 1851 in Holmes County, Mississippi. He married Susan Elizabeth Anderson. After Jeremiah's death, she married Alfred ____. Jeremiah and Susan were the parents of five children:

(a) John H., born about 1830 in North Carolina.

(b) Prentiss, born about 1838 in Mississippi.

(c) Pernesia, born about 1841 in Mississippi, married John Fullilove.

(d) Elvira, born about 1845 in Mississippi, married Washington Beall.

(e) Martha Louise, born about 1848 in Mississippi, married Frederick King.

(4) Landlot, born in 1805 in South Carolina, died after 1880 in Jasper County, Mississippi. He married Elizabeth ____, and they had six children, all born in Mississippi:

(a) James Palmer (1832).

(b) Susan (1834).

(c) Martin (1838).

(d) Martha Ann (1840).

(e) Russell (1845).

(f) Saphronia Paulina (1849).

(5) William Jr., born 1809 in Franklin County, Mississippi, died on October 18, 1860 in Hinds County, Mississippi, married Martha Fortner, widow of Arthur Fortner on December 21, 1836. She had no children of her own, but two stepchildren, Sarah Fortner, who married Josiah Stovall on June 6, 1838, and Susan E. Fortner, who married William H. Rose on May 8, 1841. Arthur Fortner and three other Fortner children are buried with the Porters in Hinds County, Mississippi.

(6) Draper Roman, born May 11, 1812 in Franklin County, Mississippi, died January 15, 1875, in Hinds County, Mississippi, city of Raymond, married Elizabeth Louise Helen Forbes on January 10, 1837. She was born on October 5, 1819 in England, the daughter of William and Elizabeth Forbes, and died on April 27, 1912 in Tyler, Smith County, Texas. They were the parents of nine children:

(a) William Forbes, born October 5, 1838 in Holmes County, Mississippi, died October 20, 1838.

(b) Benjamin Franklin, born May 14, 1840, died in the Civil War Battle of Sharpsburg on September 17, 1862.

(c) James Walden, born January 14, 1843, died October 28, 1909, married Saphronia Horton on August 4, 1867.

(d) George Washington, born October 19, 1845 in Holmes County, Mississippi, died on March 20, 1934, married Mary Elizabeth Newsome Owen on August 17, 1866.

(e) John Wesley, M.D., born October 19, 1848 in Holmes County, Mississippi, died April 4, 1911, married Lizzie Sugg on December 7, 1871. In his adulthood, he changed his name to Robert Chandler Porter.

(f) Addison Thomas, born August 9, 1851, no further information.

(g) Sarah Elizabeth, born May 8, 1854, died September 5, 1903, married twice, first to a Johnson, and secondly to Phillip B. Scott.

(h) Pinkney Prentiss, born January 1, 1857, married Idella Ross on March 23, 1876.

(i) Jefferson Davis, born on November 26, 1861, died April 28, 1923, married Cora_____.

(7) Juliann Retty, born in 1815 In Franklin County, Mississippi, died in 1861, married Blanton Crisler on October 4, 1832, and had seven children:

(a) James.

(b) William.

(c) Julius W.

(d) Catherine.

(e) Joseph.

(f) George.

(g) Lucinda.

(8) Palmore, born March 1820 in Franklin County, Mississippi, died on October 24, 1833 in Hinds County, Mississippi.

(II) Hancock Porter, Revolutionary soldier, was born in 1748 in Union County, South Carolina, and was still alive there at age 92 in 1840. He was a wealthy planter in Union County. The name of his wife is not known. He had five children:

(A) Shadrack Porter, born about 1790 in Union County, South Carolina, died in the War of 1812.

(B) William Porter, born in 1784 in Union County, South Carolina, died about 1870 in Shelby County, Alabama, and was probably buried on the home place, as he is not listed in the Shelby County Cemetery Census, published by the Shelby County Historical Society. He was married twice, first unknown, second was Rhoda Porter, whom he married about 1841 in Union County, South Carolina. He was the father of four known children, all born in South Carolina:

(1) Dedima, born 1831, married A. P. Bradford.

(2) Jane, born 1842.

(3) Nancy, born 1843.

(4) William, born in 1847.

(C) Nancy Porter.

(D) Dedima Porter, born 1795 In Union County, South Carolina, married George Crawford. They settled in Shelby County, Alabama.

(E) Hancock Porter, Jr., born about 1780 in Union County, South Carolina. No further information.

(III) Edward Porter, Revolutionary soldier, was born in 1750 in Lancaster County, Virginia, and died between 1820 and 1830 in Union County, South Carolina. On January 7, 1789, one Edward Porter was married in Westmoreland County, Virginia to Mary

McClanahan. This may have been his son Edward, who was born in 1770, so would have been nineteen years old at the time. So far as can be determined, this is the only child he had.

Edward may have spent most of his youth in an English prison. There is a record that in 1782, one Edward Porter of South Carolina was in Mill Prison, Plymouth, England. There was a total of 590 prisoners there, most from South Carolina, and some had been there for many years. (*South Carolina Historical and Genealogical Magazine*, Vol. 10, #2, P.121, April 1909).

In 1820 Edward and his wife, both over 60, appeared on the census for Union County, South Carolina. A younger Edward Porter, he and his wife both age 50-60, were living next door, with three sons and three daughters. In 1830, the older Edward was no longer there. In 1850, the younger Edward was on the census in Georgia.

(IV) William Porter, Revolutionary soldier, was born about 1752 in Lancaster County, Virginia, and died on April 26, 1818 in Union County, South Carolina. He was a private in Col. Thompson's Regiment of South Carolina Rangers. In 1775 his age was given as 23, born in Virginia, height 5'9". This regiment was formed in 1775 to protect the backwoods inhabitants from the Indians. (*South Carolina Provincial Troops*, by A. S. Salley, p. 164).

William was married twice, first to Mary Sandy, daughter of Uriah and Ann Sandy, and secondly to Winney____. Winney is named in William's will, but nothing further is known of her. He had three children by his first wife, and two by the second. They were:

(A) Jedithan, who had daughters named Jane and Cynthy. He died at age 23, so these two most likely are all the children he had. His wife's name is unknown, and it appears she may have preceded him in death, as she is not mentioned in the only two documents found pertaining to this family, a deed (m-10-1813) in which Jedithan "with love and affection gives his two daughters Jennett and Synthy all his personal estate," and another deed (m-12-1813) in which William Porter Sr. gives to his granddaughters Jane and Cynthy Porter and to his son Jedithan, a negro named Jack.

(B) Landlot, born 1792, migrated to Autauga County, Alabama.

(C) Uriah, born 1795 in Union County, South Carolina, married Phoebe____, born 1805 in Georgia. After the death of his father in 1818, Uriah migrated to Georgia, then moved into Alabama in the 1830's and settled in Russell County. He had seven children, according to the 1850 census for Russell County, Alabama. They were:

    (1)   William, born 1828 in Georgia.

    (2)   Elizabeth, born 1830 in Georgia.

    (3)   John, born 1832 in Georgia.

    (4)   Jane, born 1835 in Georgia.

    (5)   Pleasant, born 1838 in Alabama.

    (6)   Mildred, born 1842 in Alabama.

    (7)   Phoebe, born 1845 in Alabama.

(D) Chloe.

(E) Jemima.

(V) Jedithan Porter, who was my fourth great-grandfather was the fifth child of Edward Sanders Porter. Born in Lancaster County, Virginia about 1755, he died on October 29, 1804 in Union County, South Carolina. He married Rhoda Palmer, born about 1754 in Virginia, the daughter of Ellis Palmer of Edgefield District, South Carolina. After the death of Jedithan Porter, Rhoda married Capt. Joshua Palmer in 1830, at age 76. It was the second marriage for both. Rhoda died in 1841. In her will she left everything to the five then surviving children of John Palmer Porter. (Will Book 3, p. 293, Union County, S.C., 1841).

Jedithan Porter had been a planter and an extensive land owner in South Carolina, his holdings extending from Union County almost to Columbia. He was the father of thirteen children, named in his will, all by Rhoda Palmer, and all born in Union County, South Carolina. The original will is still on file in the Union County Courthouse, and is readily available to researchers (Box 1, Pkg 37, 1792, Union County, South Carolina). His thirteen children were:

    (A) Avis Porter, born about 1782. Nothing further is known of him.

    (B) Comer Porter, birth date unknown, he died in 1866 in Union County, S.C.

(C) Nancy Porter, born about 1784, died about 1866 in Union County, married a Comer.

(D) Edward Porter, born about 1786.

(E) Elisha Porter, born in 1787, died in Chickasaw County, Mississippi, date unknown, married Holly Cooper.

(F) Cier Porter. This was my third great-grandfather. His real name was Hezekiah, but he was called "Kiah," or "Kier," and it was written up as "Cier" in the will. He was born in 1785 and died at about age 40, leaving four known children, and there may have been others. The name of his wife is not known. His known children were:

  (1) Hancock Porter, born 1811 in Union County, South Carolina, died in Louisiana, married Letitia Jolly. He migrated from South Carolina to Shelby County, Alabama in 1838. About 1855 he then migrated to Winnsboro, Louisiana. He and Letitia Jolly were the parents of seven children, all born in Shelby County, Alabama. They were:

  (a) Nancy A. (1838).

  (b) Josephus (1841).

  (c) Clovis A. (1843).

  (d) Mary C. (1845).

  (e) Zachary Taylor (1846).

  (f) Sara J. (1848).

  (g) Jedithan.

These names, all but Jedithan were taken from the 1850 census for Shelby County, Alabama. Jedithan probably was born between the time of the 1850 census and the family's migration in 1855: Mr. Walter Simpson of Houston, Texas, in a letter dated March 22, 1985 stated that Hancock Porter had a son named Jedithan who had sons Henry and John, and that he descends from John.

  (2) Stark Porter, born 1818 in Union County, South Carolina, died in 1859 in Winnsboro, Louisiana, married Sara Ann Beville. (See further.)

(3) William Edward Porter, born about 1815 in Union County, South Carolina, died in Louisiana in 1880, married Susan Beville. They had five children, all born in South Carolina, except the last two. They were:

(a) Elizabeth (1840).

(b) James T. (1842).

(c) Ann (1846).

(d) John Backster (1847).

(e) Paralee (1849).

(4) Jedithan P. Porter, born on April 13, 1813 in Union County, South Carolina, he died on September 2, 1874 in the same county, and is buried in the McKissick Cemetery, which is located in the extreme northern part of Union County, near the Pacolet River and not far from the Cherokee County line. He married Margaret McKissick, who was born on October 3, 1819 and died on February 17, 1861 in Union County, and is buried in the McKissick Cemetery beside Jedithan P. They were the parents of five children:

(a) Rhoda Palmer Porter, born about 1850 in Union County, South Carolina, died in Chickasaw County, Mississippi, married Eli M. Gordon. She was sued in the Chancery Court of Houston, Mississippi by the children of Elisha P. Porter, who was her uncle, and who had deeded 100 acres of land to her. She won the suit, and the record of this proceeding proves her to have been a daughter of Jedithan P. Porter, and a niece of Elisha P. Porter.

(b) G.N.E. Porter, born May 5, 1856 In Union County, South Carolina, died February 20, 1878 in the same county. He was a captain in the Confederate Army. He is buried in the Porter Cemetery in Union County, South Carolina, which is located in the northern part of the county, between the Pacolet River and the Broad River.

(c) Hezekiah Sylvanus Porter, born May 5, 1843, in Union County, South Carolina, died on April 26, 1878 in the same county, and is buried in the Porter Cemetery. He married Mary Susan Gallman, born May 7, 1841, died July

1, 1903, buried in the Porter Cemetery beside Hezekiah Sylvanus.

In 1860, Hezekiah Sylvanus Porter was in Chickasaw County, Mississippi with his sister, Rhoda Palmer Porter Gordon and her husband Eli M. Gordon. He joined the Confederate Army from Houston, Mississippi, was wounded, came out of the army for a while, went home to South Carolina to visit, rejoined the army, finished his service, returned to South Carolina, raised a family, and died there.

He and Mary Susan Gallman were the parents of five children, all of whom lived their entire lives in Union County, and none of whom were ever married. They were:

    (ca) Margaret (November 5, 1867-February 3, 1958).

    (cb) Sallie (July 2, 1870-December 13, 1940).

    (cc) Joseph N. (February 2, 1873-January 15, 1941).

    (cd) David (October 24, 1875-August 2, 1953).

    (ce) Melvina (July 20, 1881-).

    Child # 1, Margaret is buried in the Mount Joy Baptist Church Cemetery in Union County. Her gravestone identifies her as the daughter of Hezekiah S. Porter and Mary Susan Gallman. Joseph, David, and Sallie are buried in the Porter Cemetery in Union County.

    (d) Stark W. Porter, born about 1840, died 1895. He was a Confederate soldier. Nothing further is known of him.

    (e) Joseph Porter: He was a lieutenant in the Confederate Army and was killed at Gettysburg.

This concludes the line of Hezekiah Porter, the sixth child of Jedithan Porter, son of Edward Sanders Porter, but we will return to it later and pick up and enlarge upon the line of Stark Porter, son of Hezekiah, since, even though he migrated to Louisiana and died there, his descendants are the ones of this Porter line who have remained in Alabama to this day.

We now continue with the line of Jedithan Porter.

    (G) John Palmer Porter, was the seventh child of Jedithan Porter and Rhoda Palmer. Born in Union County, South Carolina about 1793, he died in Pontotoc County, Mississippi in 1883. He married Dorothy Teague, who died before 1850 in Pontotoc

County, Mississippi. Their children (those surviving in 1841) inherited the entire estate of their grandmother, Rhoda Palmer Porter. (Will Book 3, p. 293, Union County, S.C., 1841). The names of all their children were:

(1) John Palmer Porter, Jr., born 1825 in Union County, South Carolina. He lived in Redlands, Mississippi, then Okolona, Mississippi, then moved to Hillsboro, Texas, where he died. He married Massina West, born 1823, and had two known children:

(f) Ophelia, born 1847, in Pontotoc County, Mississippi.

(g) Camillus, (male) born 1849, in Pontotoc County, Mississippi.

Ophelia and Camillus were the only children of this family listed on the 1850 census for Pontotoc County (p.116, #81), though others may have been born later.

(2) Frances Porter, born 1828 in Union County, South Carolina. She married Ferdinand Gregory in South Carolina, and they migrated to Pontotoc County, Mississippi. Ferdinand Gregory died before reaching Mississippi, and Frances remarried. Nothing further is known.

(3) Hosea Holcomb Porter, born 1829 in Union County, South Carolina. He was a dentist and made his home in Troy, Mississippi. He was married twice. According to relatives, both wives left him and went to Texas.

(4) Lemuel Teague Porter, born 1831 in Union County, South Carolina, died In Alabama.

(5) Marthe Porter, born 1833, died before 1841.

(6) Emeline Porter, born 1836 in Union County, South Carolina, married in Mississippi to an Abernathy, died in Jonestown, Mississippi.

(H) Landlot "Lotty" Porter, the eighth child of Jedithan Porter and Rhoda Palmer, was born in 1796 in Union County, South Carolina, and died before 1876 in Chickasaw County, Mississippi. He married Antoinette Susannah Comer, born 1797 in South Carolina.

Antoinette Susannah Comer was a sister to Jason Comer of Union County, South Carolina. She had a sister who married a Mardis, one who married a Baldwin, and one who married a Gregory.

She and Landlot became the parents of twelve children:

(1) John N. Porter, born 1818 in Union County, South Carolina, married Mildred, born 1824 in South Carolina. At the time of the 1850 census, he was in Chickasaw County, Mississippi living three doors from Landlot, and had four children:

(a) Joseph Anthony, born 1838 in Georgia.

(b) James N., born 1841 in Mississippi.

(c) Milly S., born 1843 in Mississippi.

(d) Francis A.E., born 1847 in Mississippi.

(2) Andrew Jackson Porter, born about 1822, probably in Union County, South Carolina. He died in Houston, Mississippi in 1864 from wounds received in the Civil War, and is buried in an unmarked grave in the Prospect Methodist Church Cemetery, south of Houston, Mississippi. He was married twice, first to Mary Ann Wiley, born October 21, 1825, died July 24, 1856 in Houston Mississippi and is buried in the Prospect Methodist Church Cemetery. They had five children:

(a) M.J. Porter, born 1845 in Itawamba County, Mississippi.

(b) John M. Porter, born 1846 in Itawamba County, Mississippi.

(c) Andrew Jackson Porter, Jr., born December 1, 1850, died August 9, 1909 in Chickasaw County, Mississippi, buried in Macedonia Cemetery, east of Houston, Mississippi. He married Frances "Frankey" / "Fannie" Gilliam on December 14, 1874. She was born on June 1, 1857 and died on January 6, 1937 in Houston Mississippi, buried in the Macedonia Cemetery.

(d) Lemuel Lott Porter, born 1851 in Mississippi. He is verified as a son of Landlot by notes of Homer Porter (Porter Collection, Book 7, #1, Dallas Public Library). He may have been the Civil War soldier from Chickasaw

County, Mississippi who died in a Civil War hospital in Atlanta, Georgia and was put into the hospital records as "S. Lott Porter."

(e) Mary Ann Porter, born 1854 in Mississippi, married Francis McCullough in Houston, Mississippi on May 19, 1873.

Andrew Jackson Porter married secondly Sarah _____. After Andrew Jackson's death, she moved back to Lamar County, Alabama about 1880, and probably died there.

She and Andrew Jackson Porter had four children:

(f) James Robert Porter, born 1859 in Alabama. In 1882, he was living in Lamar County, Alabama.

(g) Andrew Jackson G. Porter, born June 3, 1861, died on January 14, 1926 in Woodruff County, Arkansas. Andrew is buried in the Fakes Cemetery in McCrory, Arkansas. Andrew Jackson G. was a Baptist minister, and was serving a charge in Arkansas. He married Sarah Autrey and they had twelve children, all born in Chickasaw County, Mississippi. They were:

(g1) Theda Porter, born January, 1881 in Chickasaw County, Mississippi died 1925 in McCrory, Woodruff County, Arkansas. She married first S.J. Jolly, and second Roy Porter.

(g2) Florah Porter, born January, 1882, married first G.C. Porter, and second James Pendergrist.

(g3) Mamie Porter, born May, 1885, married Jake Bishop.

(g4) James H. Porter, born January 1886, married Grayce.

(g5) Cluff Porter, born December 1887.

(g6) Nannie Porter, born November 1889, married Luther Jones.

(g7) Oscar Porter, born August 1891.

(g8) Jackson Porter, born December, 1896.

(g9) Newbert Porter, born May, 1899.

(g10) Grace Porter, born February 1895.

(g11) Paul Porter, born 1902.

(g12) Odellus Porter, died in Chickasaw County, Mississippi, and is buried in the Prospect Methodist Church Cemetery in Houston, Mississippi.

(3) Julia A. Porter, born 1833 in Union County, South Carolina, married Julian F. Gilliam in Chickasaw County, Mississippi.

(4) Waitus Porter, born 1836 in Union County, South Carolina, died in the Civil War Battle of Franklin, Tennessee. He was married and had a daughter, Virginia Elizabeth, who went to Texas.

(5) Gillis Porter, born 1838 in Union County, South Carolina. He was married in Arkansas, moved to Greenville, Texas, and later to Oklahoma. He ran a wagon train from New Orleans to Indian Territory in Oklahoma.

(6) Adeline Porter, born 1841 in Union County, South Carolina, died October 22, 1879 in Chickasaw County, Mississippi, married Andrew J. Ashby.

(7) Christopher Columbus "Lum" Porter, born February 7, 1841 in Union County, South Carolina, died May 29, 1914 in Chickasaw County, Mississippi, married Oregon Baird on April 30, 1881 in Mississippi.

(8) Jane Porter, born 1845 in Union County, South Carolina, married L.A. Bingham.

(9) Holly Porter, born 1848 in Mississippi.

(10) Laura Ann Porter, born March 4, 1851 in Mississippi, died May 22, 1918 in Greenville, Texas. She was married twice, first to George Joseph Gideon, and secondly to Isaac Sterling Hancock.

(11) Frances Porter, born about 1854 in Houston, Texas, died in Greenville, Texas, married Daniel Murphy Gideon.

(I) Omia Porter, the ninth child of Jedithan Porter and Rhoda Palmer, was born about 1794 in Union County, South Carolina. She is named in Jedithan's will, but nothing further is known.

(J) Jedithan Porter, Jr, the tenth child was born about 1797 in Union County, South Carolina and died in 1856 in Franklin County, Georgia. He married Jane Jolly, a widow with two children, Mahala and Lucinda Lucy, who are named in Jedithan's will. In 1850 John and Annice Jolly were in the house with Jedithan and Jane Porter in Franklin County, Georgia.

(K) Hancock Porter, the eleventh child of Jedithan Porter and Rhoda Palmer was born about 1795 in Union County, South Carolina and died on May 27, 1852 in the same county. His wife's name was Elizabeth. His will was written on October 15, 1842 and witnessed by his brother John Palmer Porter and his nephew, John Palmer Porter, Jr. (Book C, p.45, Union County, S.C.) Hancock and Elizabeth were the parents of three children:

(1) Joshua P. Porter.

(2) Simpson Porter, born 1833 in Union County, South Carolina.

(3) Marion Sanford Porter, born 1838 in Union County, South Carolina, died in 1876 in the same place, married Sara Araminta Fant. His will can be found in Box 69, pkg. 3, 1879 in Union County, South Carolina.

(L) Russell V. Porter, the twelfth child, was born July 16, 1800 in Union County, South Carolina, and died on May 4, 1883 in Pontotoc County, Mississippi. He married Mary Jolly. He migrated to Shelby County, Alabama about 1838, but after the death of the elder Jollys there and the migration of Stark Porter and Hancock Porter, his nephews, to Winnsboro, Louisiana, he joined other Porter relatives in Mississippi.

(M) The name of the thirteenth child of Jedithan Porter and Rhoda Palmer is not known. He/she is referred to in Jedithan's will as being not yet born. (Book A, p.191, Union County, S.C.)

(VI) Epaphroditus Porter, the sixth child of Edward Sanders Porter, was born about 1757 in Union County, South Carolina, and died there sometime after 1830. The name of his wife is not known. He served on the petit jury for Union county in January and June of 1799. On the 1820 census for Union County, both Epaphroditus and his wife are shown to be over age sixty with three other males and five other females in the household with them. They were still there in 1830, and at that time, Epaphroditus Jr. appeared on the same page, living in a separate household.

(A) Epaphroditus Porter, Jr.: Epaphroditus, Jr. is the only child of Epaphroditus Porter, Sr. whose name has been extracted from the records. He was born in 1773 in Union County, South Carolina, and died in November, 1860, in Walton County, Georgia. Married twice, the name of his first wife is unknown. His second wife, whom he married on September 27, 1841 in Franklin County, Georgia, was Sarah Chandler, who had been born in Georgia in 1802, and was the widow of James Chandler, who had died in 1837.

In 1850 Epaphroditus and Sarah were living in Walton County, Georgia, family #601, dwelling #601, his age given as 77. According to the mortality schedule for the state of Georgia for 1860, he died at age 96, of old age. He was the father of three known children, all apparently by his first wife, judging by the birth dates. They were:

(1) Jedithan, born 1800 in Union County, South Carolina, whose wife's name was Sarah. He died in July, 1829, in Fayette County, Georgia. His wife Sarah died in 1878 at nearly one hundred years of age. She was appointed administrator of Jedithan's estate in Pike County, Georgia, on July 11, 1829 with son Isom as security.

She and Jedithan's orphans drew in the 1832 land lottery, Sarah drawing in Floyd County, land which she sold in 1853, in Henry County. The orphans drew land in Gilmer County which was also sold in Henry County in 1853.

Jedithan and Sarah were the parents of seven children:

    (a) Tillman.

    (b) Tresuvar.

    (c) Rebecca, who married Charles W. Elliott.

    (d) Sarah, who married a Weldon.

    (e) Susan, who married a Barrett.

    (f) Emaline, who married Seaborn Lewis on June 27, 1853 in Henry County, Georgia. No record has been found of this family.

(g) Martin, who married Lucinda Rogers on June 27, 1833 in Henry County, Georgia, according to the Leon Hollingsworth card files. He is the only one of Jedithan and Sarah's children who is known to have remained in Georgia. He died in Colt County, Gerogia, date unknown.

(2) Epaphroditus III, the second known child of Epaphroditus II and Sarah, was born in 1811 in Union County, South Carolina, and migrated to Shelby County, Alabama, about 1840. He operated a ferry at Harpersville, on the Coosa River, and was a justice of the peace there for many years.

His wife, also named Sarah, was born in 1813 in South Carolina. Epaphroditus disappeared from the Shelby County records after 1860, and is thought to have moved westward with the Porter and Beville families. He and Sarah had only one known child, Martha, born 1848 in Shelby County, Alabama.

(3) Less is known of the third known child, whose name was Landlot. He lived in Autauga County, Alabama.

(VII) Calvin Porter, the seventh child of Edward Sanders Porter, was born about 1759 in Union County, South Carolina, and died after 1791 but before 1820 in the same place. The ony record of Calvin found to date is in his father's will in which he receives above his pro-rata share "one bay mare named Doe." He does not appear on the 1820 census, so he probably died before then.

(VIII) Uriah Porter, a Revolutionary Soldier, and the eighth child of Edward Sanders Porter, was born about 1760 in Union County, South Carolina, and died during the years of the Revolutionary War, although it is not known that he died in actual battle. In the months of August and September in the year 1779, Uriah Porter, a private, is recorded as being in Captain John Herrington's Company of South Carolina Troops. He is thought to have died unmarried between 1779 and 1791. A younger Uriah Porter, thought to have been his nephew and a son of William Porter, was living in Russell County, Alabama, in 1850.

(IX) Jonathan Porter, the ninth child of Edward Sanders Porter, was born about 1761 in Union County, South Carolina, and died between 1780 and 1820 in the same place. His wife's name was Sarah. In 1790 Jonathan appeared on the census for Union County, South Carolina with his wife, four sons under age 16, and three daughters.

In 1820, Sarah appears as a widow with three daughters. Nathaniel Porter and Matthew Porter owned land in Union County, and are thought to have been Jonathan's sons, but this is not proven. Also, a J.S. Porter (Jonathan S.?) born December 30, 1830, died December 23, 1887, is buried in the Gregory Cemetery in Union County. This may have been Jonathan's grandson, but again, this is not proven.

(X) David Porter, a Revolutionary Soldier, and the tenth child of Edward Sanders Porter, was born about 1762 in Union County, South Carolina, and died after 1830 in the same place. David appeared on the 1790, 1820, and 1830 censuses for Union County, and records from the Revolutionary War show that he served in that conflict from 1783 to 1786. Nothing further is known of him. A Gideon Porter who served on the petit jury for Union County on December 28, 1790 could have been his son, but this is only speculation.

(XI) Nancy Porter, the eleventh child of Edward Sanders Porter, left few records behind. She is known to have married a Jesse Holcomb, and may have been the mother of Rev. Hosea Holcomb, a Baptist preacher who migrated to Alabama and preached throughout the state in the middle of the nineteenth century, and in 1840 published a history of the Baptist church in Alabama up until that time. He is buried in Sadler Cemetery near Bessemer, Alabama. His relationship to Nancy Porter Holcomb, however, has not been proven by this researcher.

Thus the history of this Porter line is completed; we now return to Stark Porter, the pioneer who came to Alabama in the 1840's then migrated westward and in the circle of time his grandson returned to Alabama, where his descendants remain to this day.

Stark Porter, son of Hezekiah Porter, was born in 1818 in Union County, South Carolina. His mother is thought (but not documented) to have been a Stark—John Stark was the Sheriff of Union County, and is thought to have married a Porter daughter. After a few years had passed, John Stark's daughter became the wife of Hezekiah Porter and the mother of Stark Porter, according to speculation.

On January 20, 1837, Stark Porter was married in Union county to Sara Ann Beville, daughter of Rardon Beville and his first wife, Mary Long. He brought his family to Shelby County about 1845 and remained there until about 1855. Three of their children were born there, and another was born in Mississippi while they were migrating to Winnsboro, Louisiana.

According to Mr. Walter Simpson of Houston, Texas, Stark Porter ran a store which was located behind the court house in Winnsboro. After his death there in 1859, Sara Ann Beville Porter moved the family to Winnfield, Louisiana to be near relatives.

Stark Porter and Sara Ann Beville were the parents of seven children as follows:

> (a) Hezekiah Porter, the oldest child of Stark Porter and Ann Beville was born in 1838 in Union County, South Carolina. As a young man he migrated to Alabama and then on to Louisiana with the family, and later settled in Texas.

> (b) Rardon Porter, the second child of Stark Porter and Sara Ann Beville was born in 1841 in Union County, South Carolina. He joined the Confederate Army in Winn Parish Louisiana with his brother Ibzan at the beginning of the Civil War and served until the conflict was ended. On returning to Louisiana after the war, he found only devastation, so according to family legend, having no other means of travel, he walked all the way to Leon County, Texas, started a new life, and lived out his years there.

> (c) John Abraham Porter (called Ibzan) the third child of Stark Porter and Sara Ann Beville, was born in 1843 in Union County, South Carolina. He joined the Confederate cause in Louisiana at the beginning of the Civl War, was captured at the siege of Vicksburg, and spent the rest of the war years in a northern military prison at Rockford, Illinois. At the end of the war he had to walk all the way back to the south, dodging northern sympathizers, begging food and almost starving along the way.

According to Confederate records, Ibzan Porter was not a large man, standing only five foot seven, and having blond hair and blue eyes. I can imagine him, not much more than a boy, traveling the dusty back roads of the north and through dense woods, always keeping the morning sun to his left and the evening sun to his right, to make sure he was still traveling south. He would have had to grapple fish from the streams with his bare hands, and kill an occasional hare with a hurled stone, having no gun or other means of killing.

Instead of returning to Louisiana, where nothing was left of his home or family, Ibzan went to Lowndes County, Mississippi, where he had close relatives. There he married Mary Sturdivant, daughter of Sherrod Sturdivant and Elizabeth Dooley, his Cherokee Indian wife. The Sturdivant family had recently moved there from Shelby County, Alabama. Ibzan Porter and Mary Sturdivant had only one child, a son whom they named John William Porter. As a result of the bad treatment he had received in the northern prison camp, Ibzan Porter lived only four years after his release, dying in 1869 in Lowndes County, Mississippi, when his son was three years old.

His son, John William Porter, was my grandfather. I remember him as an old man, talking about his father. His only memory was that as he lay dying he called my grandfather to his bed and told him to meet him in heaven. All the Porters seem to have been very, very religious, so this is in character.

>(ca) John William Porter was brought from Lowndes County, Mississippi, to Shelby County, Alabama, to near the place where his grandfather Stark Porter and other relatives had lived in the 1840's and 1850's. His grandfather Sherrod Sturdivant had died in Lowndes County, Mississippi about the same time as his own father, Ibzan Porter, and his uncle William Harrison Sturdivant became leader of the family and brought them all back to Alabama.

His mother soon married again and John William became a ward of William Harrison Sturdivant, who became a very important man in Shelby County. John William Porter stayed with his uncle until age six at which time he was allowed to be adopted by John Thompson of Genery's Gap, who was a friend of William Harrison Sturdivant. He had a good life with the Thompsons, became an experienced woodsman, trained in Indian lore. He had an excellent teacher in John Thompson, who had fought in the Indian Wars, as had his father before him.

As a young man John William Porter would take jobs in the town of Elyton (now Birmingham), in the winter when the farm work was finished. When the town of Bessemer was being established, he helped to lay out the streets. One pay day night he was on his way back to Genery's Gap when he was attacked by robbers. Back then, workers didn't work just eight hours a day, but from daylight until dark, so by the time my grandfather got on his way home, it was black dark. The road where he was attacked is no longer there, but I still know the exact spot where it happened. Several men jumped out at him, grabbing at him and the horse's harness. As it happened, he was riding a blooded thoroughbred horse, which John Thompson had acquired in a trade with a northern soldier during the Civil War. Smart as he was, the horse sensed danger long before it happened, took one giant leap and was gone down the road, thereby no doubt saving my grandfather's life.

In 1893, my grandfather received word that his mother, who was living in Tuscaloosa County at the time, was ill and not expected to live, so he traveled to Tuscaloosa County to visit her. A young woman named Margaret Fatima Thomas, daughter of John M. Thomas, a partially disabled Confederate veteran, and his wife, Margaret Emeline Horton Thomas, was caring for his mother. The Thomases were devout Presbyterians and leaders in the nearby Union Presbyterian Church. The young couple quickly fell in love.

John William Porter's mother died and he brought her back to Shelby County to be buried in the Shiloh Cemetery.

Soon after this John William Porter and Margaret Fatima Thomas were married and settled near her parents in Tuscaloosa County. They lived in a small cottage, got water from a nearby spring, farmed the surrounding acreage and tried to avoid falling into a huge sink hole which took up a large portion of their yard. The hens would sometime build their nests deep in the sink hole, and my mother said that my grandmother wouldn't let her go down and get the eggs, telling her that she might fall through to the other side of the world. The job of gathering the eggs fell to my grandfather.

All three of their children were born on that Tuscaloosa County property. They were as follows:

> (ca1) Margie Eugenia Porter was born in Tuscaloosa County, Alabama, on July 16, 1894; died April 4, 1982 at Bessemer, Alabama. She is buried in Genery's Cemetery. More follows on Margie below.
>
> (ca2) John Monroe Porter was born about 1896, died about 1965, and is buried in Genery's Cemetery. He was married twice, first to Ruby Howard, daughter of Pete and Sally Howard of Shelby County, and had one son:
>
>> (ca2a) William Porter.

John Monroe Porter was married secondly to Lessie Jordan by whom he had six children. Their names are not known.

(ca3) Samuel David Porter was born in 1899 and died about 1970. Samuel David was never married. He is buried in Genery's Cemetery.

The mother of these children died of typhoid fever when Margie was only five years old. Samuel, the youngest child, was only three months old. I remember Margie talking about how her mother's death broke her five-year-old heart. She said she went outside and sat on the ground in the corner between the chimney and the side of the house and cried her eyes out.

The family stayed with the Thomases for a time, but their grandparents were old, so the father soon took them back to Genery's Gap, where he had grown up in the home of John Thompson. My mother talked about how broken-hearted she had been upon leaving her Thomas grandparents, who had been very good to her and her brothers, but the Thompsons were so good, kind, and caring, that she soon adjusted and was happy. Her aunt Missouri Whaley, her mother's sister, had taken Samuel, who had had "brain fever," (polio) as an infant and was a hunchback. She kept him until he grew up.

Margie Porter and her brother Monroe attended school at Morgan, about a mile and a half away from the Thompson homestead, where Miss Madge McDonald (later Roy, after she married widower Andy Roy) taught school in a one-room schoolhouse. Miss Madge taught several generations of the local children and was universally loved. My mother and her brother, and later their half brothers and sisters all dearly loved her. The school only taught through the eighth grade, and there was no high school anywhere in the area, so my mother and all the ones she grew up with never went higher than the eighth grade.

The Porter family had only been living in the house with John Thompson about ten months when John William Porter was remarried, this time to Missouri Alice Kimbrel, daughter of Ransom Kimbrel and Rachel Heflin. My mother was six years old at the time, and from then on, her life was rather bleak. Her stepmother wouldn't allow her and her brother to call her, "Mama." She had to be addressed as "Miss Alice." John William and Alice Missouri began having children very fast, and by the time my mother had finished school, they had six. A good portion of the work fell on my mother's shoulders, and she no longer had Miss Madge for solace, since she no longer went to school. Her relationship with her stepmother deteriorated over the years, until finally, after she was married, they no longer had any contact.

John William Porter had a total of nine children by his second wife, Missouri Alice Kimbrel:

 (ca4) Fanny, married Mayhew McClure.

 (ca5) Mattie, married Robert E. Carter.

 (ca6) Charles, married Alline Phillips.

 (ca7) Rufus, never married.

 (ca8) Minnie, married Junior Lambert.

 (ca9) Andrew Jackson married Flora _____.

 (ca10) Jesse married _____.

 (ca11) Lucian married _____. No children.

 (ca12) Gladys, married Leonard Moore and _____.

 All are deceased.

On August 21, 1912, Margie Eugenia Porter married Joseph Horace Seales, who had recently moved to Jefferson County from Bibb County, Alabama. The ceremony was performed at Bamford by her great uncle, William Harrison Sturdivant. The wedding party rode to Bamford in a horse-drawn buggy. Margie's brother Monroe and her stepmother accompanied them.

The newlyweds spent the first year of their marriage living on the old Elijah Cost place in Shelby County, but then moved back to Jefferson County and bought ten acres and a small house adjoining John Thompson's property. Joseph Horace Seales had formerly lived in the house as a bachelor while working in the timber woods of the area. About 1919 they built another, bigger and better house a hundred yards down the hill, and there lived out their lives.

Now we return to the children of Stark Porter and Sara Ann Beville:

 (d) Stark Porter, Jr., the fourth child of Stark Porter and Sara Ann Beville, was born in Shelby County, Alabama in 1845, soon after the family arrived there from South

Carolina. The family migrated to Louisiana when he was about ten years old, and nothing further is known of him.

(e) Mary Porter, the fifth child, was born in Shelby County, Alabama, in 1846, and migrated westward with the family at about age nine. Nothing further is known of her.

(f) John B. Porter, the sixth child, was born in Shelby County, Alabama, in 1849. He was about six years old when the family migrated to Louisiana, and nothing further is known of him.

(g) The seventh child of Stark Porter and Sara Ann Beville was born in Mississippi while the family was migrating to Louisiana. They had relatives there, and stopped with them long enough for the child to be delivered. Nothing further is known.

Information on the Porter family is from many sources. Special thanks must go to Mr. and Mrs. Walter Simpson of Houston, Texas. After many, many years of searching, I had been unable to take this family any further back than my grandfather, until they identified my great-grandfather as John Abraham (Ibzan) Porter, and furnished enough information about the Porters in Louisiana and Texas that I could take it from there.

Special thanks also go to Mr. Robert Porter of Tupelo, Mississippi, who was of immeasurable help to me. Information also came in letters from Elizabeth Burnett of Nederland, Texas, and Pinney H. Nobles of Roseland, Louisiana. Help also came from the court house employees in Union County, South Carolina, who helped me locate several Porter wills and gravestones in the New Hope Cemetery, the McKissick Cemetery, the Episcopalian Cemetery, the Mount Joy Cemetery, and the Porter Cemetery in Union County.

Other information came from census records in Chicasaw County, Mississippi; Shelby County, Alabama; Union County, South Carolina; and Jefferson County, Alabama.

THOMAS SEALE, Jr.

This Alabama pioneer came into the state about 1835, but before that had already pioneered in five other southern states. Whenever and wherever the Indians were pushed back and the land opened for settlement, the Seale family was soon there. This particular Seale was my great-great-grandfather.

The Seale family is a very old one, going far back in English history. In America, they date back to 1656, when two brothers, William and Thomas Seale (Seile) came to America. They were the sons of one Henry Seile, (he still used the Norman form of the name), a London bookstore owner, who was bookseller to the king, Charles I. They were also associated with the royal family through ties of friendship and marriage.

Charles I, who was of the Stuart line, was beheaded in 1649, and this was followed by many years of upheaval during which anyone who was related to the Stuarts or closely associated with them in any way was murdered and their homes and family destroyed. It was during this time that Henry Seile disappeared from the records, but whether he was murdered is not known. Seven years later two of his sons, William and Thomas, came to America. William's wife was a Bury (Berry,) and they are thought to have come to America with some members of the Bury family. All were brought into the Virginia Colony by one John Wood, who was granted one thousand acres of land for bringing twenty new settlers into the colony. Little is known of Thomas Seale, except that he lived his life in Frederick County, Virginia, and died there in the early 1700's. The Administrator's bond can be found in *Administrations Book 1750-Frederick-A*. The Alabama line descends from William.

William Seale was born about 1624 in England, married about 1650 in England, and died about 1695 in the Virginia Colony. He was a tobacco planter. He and his wife were the parents of two known children:

(I) William Seale Jr., born about 1658, who married Elizabeth Markham.

(II) Anthony Seale, born about 1659 and died about 1726, in Prince William County, Virginia. The Alabama line descends through Anthony, who was a tobacco planter in Prince William County. The name of his wife is not known. He had three known children:

(A) Anthony Seale II, born 1695 in Virginia, died on October 15, 1781 in Prince William County, Virginia married Ann Bristow. (See further).

(B) David Seale, born 1698 in Virginia, married first Jael Clendenning and secondly Sarah Stringfellow. Names of his children are not known.

(C) Charles Seale, born 1700 in Virginia, married Elizabeth _____.

Anthony Seale II is the pivotal link in the Seale family line in America. Probably ninety-five percent of those bearing the Seale name in America descend from this man. He was a tobacco planter and a surveyor of roads in Prince William County, Virginia.

Anthony Seale II was married on December 24, 1720 to Ann Bristow, born about 1700, died about 1787, daughter of John Bristow and Michal Nichols. John Bristow was a Virginia planter and the father of eleven children:

- James.
- Johannah.
- William.
- Michal.
- Thomas.
- Elizabeth.
- Sarah.
- Nicholas.
- Anne.
- Jedediah.
- Mary.

All but two of these children were by Michal Nichols; Jedediah and Mary were by his second wife, Mary Carter. John Bristow died in Middlesex County, Virginia in 1716.

Anthony Seale II and Ann Bristow were the parents of seven children, as recorded in the Seale family Bible, now in the possession of the Stribling family. They were:

(1) William Seale, born December 3, 1722 in King George County, Virginia, died 1797 in Moore County, North Carolina. He was married twice, first to Sophie Pope Muse, and secondly to Winnifred _____.

(2) Mary Elizabeth Seale, born February 25, 1724 in King George County, Virginia, died 1784 in Prince William County, Virginia. She was married twice, first to a Mr. Buckner and secondly to Lt. William Brown. Her descendants are said to have settled in the northern states.

(3) Thomas Seale, born August 17, 1727 in King George County, Virginia, died about 1806 in Baldwin County, Georgia, married Elizabeth _____. He was a patriot in the American Revolution, and his descendants are eligible for membership in the DAR. (See further).

(4) Charles Seale, born February 10, 1729 in King George County, Virginia, married Lydia Muse, died about 1799 in Fairfield County, South Carolina.

Charles and Lydia had a large family including eight sons and several daughters. Of the sons, this is what is known:

(a) James settled in Butler County, Alabama.

(b) Thomas settled in Greene County, Alabama, and has often been confused with his cousin, Thomas Seale, Jr. in the records.

(c) Joshua settled in Marion County, Mississippi, where he was joined by Thomas Seale Jr. and Thomas' brother David Seale.

(d) Enoch settled in Shelby County, Alabama, where he has many descendants.

(e) Elijah settled in Shelby County, Alabama.

(5) Anthony Seale, born April 10, 1732 in King George County, Virginia, died about 1794 in Wilkes County, Georgia, married Ann Jarvis.

(6) John Seale, born June 30, 1736, in Prince William County, Virginia, died 1788 in the same county, married Sarah ____.

(7) Dorothy Seale, born June 17, 1739 in Prince William County, Virginia, died 1796 in Wilkes County, Georgia, married Francis Stribling.

Thomas Seale (child #3 above), was the father of Thomas Seale, Jr., the Alabama pioneer. Born on August 17, 1727 in King George County, Virginia, he moved with the family to Prince William County, Virginia when he was about eight years old. He was married about 1755 to Elizabeth _____, born about 1737 in Henrico County, Virginia. On July 13, 1756, he enlisted in the French and Indian War. At that time his age was given as thirty-two. This would put his birth year at 1724, not 1727, as is recorded in the Seale family Bible. Some family historians have contended that his birth date and that of his sister Mary Elizabeth Seale were transposed in the Seale family Bible, and this record makes that a virtual certainty.

Thomas was described in his military record as being six feet one inch in height. The height of most of the other men in the company (Captain Henry Harrison's Company) ranged from five feet one inch to about five feet ten inches, so Thomas was considerably taller than most of his companions. Being familiar with the personal characteristics that run in this family, I further imagine him as being blonde, with blue eyes, and a self-possessed bearing.

The record of Thomas' enlistment was found in Prince George's County, Maryland, just across the Potomac River from Prince William County, Virginia. There the Seale plantation was located where Chainbridge, Virginia is today. Thomas' occupation was recorded in his army enlistment as "smith" (blacksmith), but this was only one of the several occupations he followed during his lifetime.

After his military service, Thomas and Elizabeth moved from Prince William County, Virginia to Cumberland County, North Carolina. There they owned a plantation on Overton Road which was on Deep River in the northern part of the county, and was considered to be some of the best land anywhere in the county. This was in the part of Cumberland County that later became Moore County.

Besides being a planter in his new home, Thomas was also a collector of taxes and a merchant; he may have owned a store. When loyalist Alexander Morrison was divested of his holdings and deported to Scotland, he submitted a list of the people to whom he owed money. On this list was the name of Thomas Seale, to whom he was in debt to the extent of three pounds, five shillings for osnaburg (a type of cloth), rum, and sugar. The fact that Thomas Seale was a merchant may explain why traditionally, less has been known about him than other members of this family. The probability is that most of his assets, whatever the amount, were kept in hard money (rather than land and slaves) and consequently few records were left. Hard money (coins made of precious metal) in those days often meant Spanish reales or "eight-bit pieces" and the usual method of safekeeping was to bury it in the ground.

The records seem to indicate that Thomas remained in Cumberland County for about twenty years. During the Revolutionary War he is recorded as having performed patriotic duty. Being about fifty-two years of age at this time, he probably would have been considered too old for active duty, so his patriotic duty had to be in the form of troop support. Some of the troops suffered extreme privations, and those citizens who could do so furnished food, horses, blankets or cattle. Thomas, being a storekeeper, may have been in a better position to help than most.

In 1782, he gift-deeded his plantation to his daughter Ann James (Deed Book G, p.108). For the next fourteen years, Thomas seems to have been in South Carolina part of the time and Georgia part of the time. In 1785, he appeared in Wilkes County, Georgia, which had been opened for settlement in 1783. There he received a grant of six hundred acres, but sold it within six weeks to Andrew King for one hundred fifty pounds sterling (Grant Book III, p.59, Deed Book A, p.78, and Deed Book AA, p.30). In 1796, he was in Hancock County, Georgia. There are land records for him there, and his name appears on the tax lists. He is also mentioned in the court records on several occasions when he performed jury duty or served as a witness.

Elizabeth was a member of the Island Creek Baptist Church, along with a Sophia Seale, who may have been Thomas and Elizabeth's daughter. She later is found with them in Hancock County, and in 1807, after Thomas and Elizabeth's deaths, she received a land grant, spinster status, in Wilkinson County, when it was formed. Thomas and Elizabeth later found themselves living in Baldwin County when it was cut out of Wilkes, and that is where they are thought to have died, Elizabeth in 1805, and Thomas in 1806. A search of the older cemeteries in the area, including the Island Creek Church Cemetery, has failed to locate their graves, so the probability is that they were buried on the family property, and their graves long since lost.

Thomas and Elizabeth were the parents of eight children, perhaps more. They are thought to have had several daughters, whose records have not been found. Some others have been found, but are in question.

- One possible daughter is Martha Seale (1754-1812) married in 1772 to James Turner, a Revolutionary soldier, who was born in Orange County, Virginia in 1752 and died in Franklin County, Georgia in 1804.

- Another possible daughter: One Sarah Seale was married to William Benson in Prince William County, Virginia on September 7, 1786. In 1793, they were living in Wilkes County, Georgia. Their daughter Elizabeth married Daniel Buckner, who is thought to have been a son or grandson of Mary Elizabeth Seale, daughter of Anthony Seale.

Thomas Sr.'s and Elizabeth's known children were:

(a) Ann Seale, born about 1760 in Prince William County, Virginia, married John James, son of Francis James, who owned the plantation adjoining that of Thomas Seale on Overton Road in Cumberland County, North Carolina. Thomas Seale deeded his plantation to John and Ann James in 1782, when he was getting ready to leave North Carolina. John James sold this property in 1784, and they do not appear on the 1790 census for North Carolina, and are thought to have moved southward also.

(b) Benjamin Seale, born about 1761 in Cumberland County, North Carolina. He first appeared in the public records in 1785, when he was named as a member of a work crew to do work on Overton Road. This was the road on which the old Thomas Seale Sr. plantation was located in Cumberland County. In 1800 he was in the census for Edgecombe County, North Carolina, his age given as over 26 years. In 1802 he was on the tax list for Wilkes County, Georgia. That same year he died in Wilkes County, Georgia, leaving a wife and two daughters. He had married Elizabeth Crawford in Johnston County, North Carolina on March 2, 1797 (Record #5601191, bond #69700). I have not been able to trace Elizabeth Crawford after Benjamin's death, so she is thought to have remarried and disappeared from the records under the Seale name.

(c) Thomas Seale, Jr., born 1764 in Cumberland County, North Carolina, died 1850 in Perry County, Alabama, married twice, first to Ader (Ada) Elkins, daughter of Johnston Elkins, a Revolutionary soldier, and secondly to Jane Jameston Dorse, daughter of Isaac Jameston, a native of Kentucky. (See further)

(d) David Seale, born 1766 in Cumberland County, North Carolina, died before 1850 in Pontotoc County, Mississippi. David and his brother Thomas Seale, Jr. were very closely associated throughout their lives. They were together in Georgia. Then for a time, David went to Tennessee, where he owned six hundred forty acres in Williamson County. By 1806 he had abandoned this land and migrated to Marion County, Mississippi. He was cited in the Williamson County court records for not paying the three dollars and ninety-five cents in taxes that accumulated after the land was abandoned. Three years later he was joined in Mississippi by his brother Thomas Jr., and three years later they were joined by their cousin, Joshua Seale, son of Charles Seale. In the 1816 territorial census, David and Thomas were living next door to each other.

The name of David's wife is not known. The one fact that is known about her is that she was born in Ireland. On the Mississippi territorial census, she and David are shown with eight children, all under 21 years of age, of which five were girls and four were boys. Some information is known about the boys, but efforts to trace the girls have not been fruitful.

About 1820 David and Thomas, Jr. moved eastward into Alabama and settled in Butler County near their cousin James Seale, son of Charles Seale, and remained there for about fifteen years. About 1835, they moved north into the Shelby, Bibb, and Perry counties area. At that time the county lines were not firmly established, and they lived in the area where all these counties come together, so they might be shown in one county on a certain census and another county on the next, without having moved. David's wife had died by this time and David was living in the house with his son William. By 1840, they had moved to Itawamba County, Mississippi. That is the last census on which David appeared. His children, as many as are known, are as follows:

(da) Martin Seale, born about 1793 in Georgia, died before 1850 in Mississippi. He may have descendants.

(db) John J. Seale, born 1797 in Georgia, married in Alabama about 1834 to Nancy ____, born 1798 in South Carolina. Settled in Pontotoc County, Mississippi between 1840 and 1850. Died there between 1880 and 1890. He was the father of five:

>(db1) Sarah A. Seale, born 1835 in Alabama, unmarried in the 1870 census, but not listed with her parents in 1880.
>
>(db2) Nancy Seale, born 1837 in Alabama, married before the 1860 census.
>
>(db3) John Milton Seale, born 1839 in Alabama, married in Mississippi in 1861 to Mary____ in 1838, three children:
>
>>(db3a) Mary, born 1862, married J. B. Haney.
>>
>>(db3b) George.
>>
>>(db3c) Nancy.
>
>(db4) William A. Seale, born 1840 in Alabama, was a Confederate soldier from Mississippi. Married in 1874 to Matilda J. _____, born July 1855. He died in Pontotoc, Mississippi on December 10, 1892. Six children:
>
>>(db4a) Martha A.
>>
>>(db4b) John.
>>
>>(db4c) Mattie.
>>
>>(db4d) Willie.
>>
>>(db4e) Tishy.
>>
>>(db4f) Floy.
>
>(db5) Robert W. Seale, born 1841 in Alabama. Was with his parents in the 1860 census for Pontotoc County, Mississippi. Nothing known of him after that. He may have died in the Civil War.

(dc) William D. Seale, born 1799 in Georgia, married in Alabama about 1835 to Harriet _____, born 1814 in Tennessee. They lived in Alabama until about 1839. In 1840 they appeared in the census for Itawamba County, Mississippi, and in 1850 and 1860 in the censuses for Pontotoc County. He died in Pontotoc County before 1870. He was the father of eleven children:

(dc1) Martha Seale, born 1837 in Alabama.

(dc2) George Seale, born 1838 in Alabama, married Elizabeth _____, had three children:

(dc2a) John C., born 1858.

(dc2b) Ann, born 1860.

(dc2c) Jane, born 1862.

George died in the Civil War.

(dc3) William H. Seale, born 1840 in Mississippi, married Terissa and had six children:

(dc3a) Robert A.

(dc3b) Laurence E.

(dc3c) Flaurence.

(dc3d) Madena.

(dc3e) Hester.

(dc3f) Estelle.

(dc4) Eli D. Seale, born 1841 in Mississippi.

(dc5) John Seale, born 1842 in Mississippi.

(dc6) James Seale, born 1844 in Mississippi.

(dc7) Finias Seale, born 1846 in Mississippi.

(dc8) Mary Seale, born 1849 in Mississippi.

(dc9) Elmos P. Seale, born 1850 in Mississippi, married Lizzie and had four children:

(dc9a) Henry.

(dc9b) Icey.

(dc9c) Clyde (a daughter).

(dc9d) Thelma.

(dc10) Joan Seale, born 1852 in Mississippi.

(dc11) LaMinta Seale, born 1856 in Mississippi.

(e) Hopkins Seale, the fourth known son and fifth known child of Thomas Seale, Sr. was born in the year 1770 in Cumberland County, North Carolina. Most of his adult life was spent in central South Carolina on the fertile plains along the Wateree River in Sumter and Richland counties, where he became a wealthy planter and slave owner.

He was married about 1808 to Rebecca Watson, daughter of William and Sarah Watson, who owned a plantation bordering on Dry Swamp on the road between Camden and Stateburg. His first child John was born about 1809, but died young. He died between 1819 and 1836, since his name is not included with Hopkins' other children in his will.

There is on record in Sumter County, South Carolina (Deed Book FF p.256) a deed whereby his grandmother in 1819 gave John "a roan filly going on two years old." According to family historians, the filly that Sarah Watson had given to John was a racehorse that won several races at the Stateburg track, and after John's death, she wanted the horse back.

Hopkins was on the census for Sumter County in 1810 and 1820, but was absent from it in 1830. In that census, however, there was an H.M. Seale on the census for Gadsden County, Florida, on page 130, with three sons, one daughter, and no wife shown. Twenty years later, in 1850, this same H.M. Seale witnessed a deed for Hopkins' son, William T. Seale in Sumter County, South Carolina, so the probability is that it was the Hopkins in question.

He was back in Sumter County at least by 1833 and in that year sold his interest in the old Watson homestead in right of his wife, Rebecca, who evidently was no longer living. (Deed Book HH, p.448). Three years later, in 1836, he made a deed of trust to Robert E. Yates, the husband of his daughter Mary, in which he named his surviving children (Deed Book II, p.214.)

On February 6, 1850, Hopkins witnessed a deed, as before mentioned, for William T. Seale in Sumter County, signing himself H.M. Seale, and the following February 7, made affidavit (Deed Book NN p.146). On August 8th of that year, his name appeared on the public record for the last time, when his name was written into the census for 1850 for Richland County, his age given as 80. At this time he was living in the house with his son William T. Seale, who was thirty-seven years old and unmarried at the time. Hopkins Seale, Jr., age thirty and unmarried, was also in the household and their sister, Sarah Elizabeth Green, by then a widow, lived next door. At the time of the 1860 census, Hopkins was no longer living.

In his younger days, Hopkins had been an influential man in South Carolina, being a neighbor and close friend of Elliott Huger, the first senator from South Carolina, as well as a wealthy landowner and planter.

Hopkins and Sarah were the parents of six children:

>   (ea) James Seale, born 1808 in Richland County, South Carolina. Migrated to Alabama, then most of his family moved to Florida. Not much is known of him.
>
>   (eb) Mary Seale, born about 1810, married Robert E. Yates and migrated to Hinds County, Mississippi.
>
>   (ec) Sarah Elizabeth Seale, born 1811, married William H. Green, with whom she migrated to Florida. Sarah Elizabeth was cut out of her father's will according to family historians because William H. Green had borrowed money and slaves from Hopkins and never returned either. Sarah Elizabeth has descendants living in Plano, Texas.
>
>   (ed) William Thomas Seale, born 1813, died 1879. He lived his entire life in Richland County, South Carolina, where he became a prominent landowner. He married Frances Leonora Thompson, and became the father of nine children:
>
> >   (ed1) Elizabeth, who married first Bruce Lyman and secondly Napoleon P. Lenoir.
> >
> >   (ed2) William Henry Seale, who married Mary Alice Myers.
> >
> >   (ed3) Leonora Virginia Seale, who married John William Harvin.
> >
> >   (ed4) Elliott Huger Seale, a female, who married Marion Percival Moore.
> >
> >   (ed5) Laura Scott Seale, who married James T. Flowers.

(ed6) Anna Rivers Seale, who married Richard Manning Moore.

(ed7) John Arthur Seale married Bessie Call, and migrated to Coosa County, Alabama. He was employed for many years by the Birmingham Hide and Tallow Company in Birmingham.

(ed8) Rebecca Watson Seale, died young.

(ed9) A daughter, who died as an infant, unnamed.

(ee) John Seale, born about 1816, died before 1830, unmarried.

(ef) Hopkins Seale, Jr., born in 1820, never married. He migrated to Louisiana and became a very wealthy man, raising horses on a plantation he owned. Most of his estate went to his servants, with the residue being divided among his siblings.

(f) Rev. William Seale, the fifth known son and the sixth child of Thomas Seale, Sr., was born in 1777 in Cumberland County, North Carolina, and died on March 28, 1851 in Shelby County, Alabama. He was a Methodist minister all his adult life, having come under the influence of his father-in-law, who in turn had come under the influence of Bishop Asbury when he came to America to introduce the new religion of Methodism to the American colonies.

During William's life, and through his influence and that of his son Rev. David William Seale and others who shared the new faith, he saw Methodism spread throughout South Carolina, and from there all across the country as the colonists migrated.

He was married for the first time about 1801 to Temperance Crossland Pearce, born in 1774, the daughter of Edward Crossland and the oldest of his fourteen children. Edward Crossland had been a Revolutionary soldier under Gen. Francis Marion in the swamps of South Carolina. Besides being a preacher, he was a planter and a cattleman. Temperance's mother's maiden name was Ann Snead, a daughter of Samuel Snead and Temperance Buford. Edward Crossland was from a noble English family. I have seen a picture of the old Crossland manor house in England, and it is quite impressive. The state flag of Maryland is a combination of the Crossland and Calvert arms, and they were related to Alicia Crossland, wife of Lord Calvert, who was a nephew of Charles I, and mother of the first Lord Baltimore.

In the Jacobean rebellions following the regicide of Charles I, Edward Crossland's mother and father were murdered, the family home burned, and Edward captured and brought to America, where he was sold into an apprenticeship in Virginia. After his release from the apprenticeship, or his running away from his bondsman, (I'm not sure which) he went to the Marlborough District of South Carolina about 1800 and settled on the Great Pee Dee River, near Gardiner's Bluff.

Following his marriage to Temperance, who was the widow of Arthur Pearce, with a young son Arthur Pearce, Jr., William was given 100 acres of land by his father-in-law on the old Baltimore-to-New Orleans road, and there he operated a stagecoach stop and a place to rest the horses. William also received a grant of 264 acres in 1814, which would seem to indicate that he fought in the War of 1812, but no record of this has been found. Among the various other land records relating to this family in the Marlborough District is a deed dated May 14, 1823 in which William and some other trustees purchased from the estate of Peter Bowyer an acre of land on which their Methodist meeting house was located. (Deed Book N, p. 505).

Temperance Crossland Pearce Seale died sometime before 1819. William then left his children with the Crosslands and went to Marion County, Mississippi, where his brothers Thomas Jr. and David had settled. He was the bondsman when Thomas Jr.'s daughter Elizabeth was married in 1819. He seems to have remained in Mississippi for some time, probably until his brothers left there and moved to Alabama.

Upon returning to South Carolina, he met and, in 1832, married his second wife, Rachel Corloss, born in 1798, widow of Robertson Corloss, a prominent landowner and justice of the peace. Rachel, beautiful and accomplished, was the daughter of Baron De Poelnitz, a Polish nobleman who had settled in Marlborough District after the Revolution and purchased a large tract of land. William and Rachel remained in South Carolina for some years. William was granted a 703-acre tract on Reedy Creek in Marion County on Sept 14, 1833. (Grant Book 40, p. 353), which they sold on November 25, 1834 to J. B. Billingsley. (Deed Book O. p.108).

By 1840, William's children were all grown, and he and Rachel migrated to Shelby County, Alabama, where he lived near his brothers Thomas Jr. and David, and the Busby families, Meridith and several of Meridith's sons. These families were all closely intertwined both by kinship and the Methodist religion of which they were all staunch followers. According to Busby researchers, the Busbys were so-called "Black Dutch," the name given to a colony of European Protestants who had settled in the "Dutch Fork" of South Carolina—the Dutch Fork being the triangle of land in between the Broad and Saluda Rivers, in the 1700's.

From there, many of the Black Dutch migrated to Shelby County, Alabama, and settled in what is now the Wilsonville area. The Busbys, however, settled near William Seale in the Montevallo area. Twelve Busby families had organized and built their own Methodist meeting house in South Carolina. The name of William Seale appears on many records in Shelby County, when he performed marriages or helped establish a church. He died in Shelby County in 1840 at age 74, leaving a will.

The record of the settlement of his estate indicates that in addition to being a preacher, William owned and operated a fairly large farm and owned horses, cows and hogs. He also owned four slaves, three men and one girl. A field hand at that time was valued at nine hundred dollars, and a house girl at seven hundred dollars. William was the father of seven children, all by Temperance Crossland Pearce. They were:

> (fa) Ann Seale, born May 5, 1802 in the Marlborough District of South Carolina, and died in 1899 in Troy, Alabama. She married Dr. Peter McIntyre, born May 7, 1801 in Laurenburg, South Carolina, died February 1854 in Montgomery, Alabama, and is buried there, in the Oakwood Cemetery.

Dr. McIntyre was a man of many talents, being a prominent physician, educator, and lecturer, and dean of the Southern Botanical College, located in Macon, Georgia. He practiced holistic medicine. He and Ann spent some years in Sea Island, Georgia, where he was employed as a tutor for the sons of the rich planters, preparing them for entrance into prominent universities in the north.

In 1849, Peter and Ann moved into Alabama and he began practicing medicine in the Montgomery area, having studied medicine during his years of teaching and lecturing. They were the parents of four children:

> (fa1) Edward Legare McIntyre, born September 1829 In Bennettsville, South Carolina. He became an attorney in Alabama, and was senator from Pike County, Alabama.

(fa2) Archibald Charles Crossland McIntyre, born August 31, 1832 in Wayne County, Georgia. He married Mattie Goode, the daughter of a judge in Montgomery, Alabama. Archibald was an artist and a pioneer in the photographic industry, owned a gallery in Montgomery, and promoted the careers of other artists. He died in Selma, Alabama in 1890.

(fa3) Hamilton McIntyre, born August 1837 in Macon, Georgia. He attended law school in Montgomery, Alabama, married a Miss Mastin, and practiced law with his brother Edward in Pike County, Alabama. His daughter, Annie Lou McIntyre, married William Dana Taylor, Jr, born September 20, 1899 in La Grange, Georgia. William Dana Taylor Jr. was a son of the well-known engineer, William Dana Taylor, Sr., who rebuilt the first steel river bridge ever built, which was over the Missouri River. Hamilton's other child, a son named Peter Mastin McIntyre, married Janna Brown, and nothing further is known of him.

(fa4) Ann Page King McIntyre (called Hannah) born Sea Island, Georgia, married Wiley Cozart of Atlanta, Georgia, and became an author.

(fb) Elizabeth Seale was born about 1804 in South Carolina. She married first, Fernando Lowe and secondly a Mr. Taylor. The names of her children are not known.

(fc) Eliza Seale was born about 1805 in South Carolina. She died young. She married a Hines and had at least two children, Ann Hines, and M. Hines. Ann and M. are found living with their grandfather Rev. William Seale, in Shelby County, Alabama, in the 1840's, and their names appear on the probate records there.

(fd) Rev. David William Seale, born in 1806 in South Carolina, ordained as a Methodist minister in 1825, and died in 1895. He was married three times, first to Caroline J. Stokes, daughter of J. T. Stokes, on November 26, 1839, by Rev. S. Armstrong. She died at the home of her father on September 6, 1844, at age 29.

David married secondly Elizabeth Adeline Lawes, daughter of Salem Lawes, Esq. of Salem, Sumter District, South Carolina, on Tuesday evening, November 14, 1848, by Rev. N. Tolley. She died at the home of Robert J. Moorer of Cypress Circuit on July 15, 1861, at age 38.

His third wife was Anna Maria Graham, daughter of James Graham. The date of the wedding is not known. She died on August 15, 1868. The names of David's children, if any, are not known.

David was in the South Carolina conference throughout his career, which spanned some sixty years, and forty-five years of that time was spent riding various circuits, which meant thousands upon thousands of miles on horseback, preaching thousands of sermons. To get an idea of how great his dedication must have been, one only need look to how little he was paid. There is a record that in the 1840's, when he was riding a circuit in Fayetteville, North Carolina, his salary was $150.00 per year, assessed among the twelve churches in the circuit. Later in his career, he was given stationary assignments. He is known to have served charges in Laurensville, Sumter, and Wilmington, and in 1845 he was pastor of St. John's Methodist Church, the oldest Methodist church in Anderson, South Carolina.

I have seen a picture of David, which was published with his obituary, and can be found in the University of South Carolina Library at Columbia. He was quite a handsome man, with dark hair and a stocky build. His obituary said that he was a fiery preacher, raining fiery words on sinners, and evidently his congregations loved it; the fires of revival followed wherever he went.

When David died in 1895, a very touching tribute appeared in the minutes of the annual meeting of the South Carolina Methodist conference beginning with "Rev. David W. Seale did not answer roll call at conference this time". He had led a life of complete dedication, and his fellow preachers seemed genuinely saddened to have lost this old champion who had nurtured the fledgling religion of Methodism and seen it come into full flower in South Carolina.

> (fe) Rev. Jesse Seale, the fifth child of Rev. William Seale, was a Baptist minister. Born in 1808 in Marlborough District, South Carolina, he began his preaching career at a very early age in South Carolina. His wife's name was Ann.

About 1832, Jesse migrated to Alabama and settled in Shelby County, and began preaching there. He became pastor of the Shoal Creek church for a time. About 1834, he became pastor of the Helena Baptist Church. This church was destroyed by a tornado in 1933, and all church records up until that time were lost. In 1836 he was appointed to travel as a missionary for nine months within the bounds of the Canaan Association of United Baptists, based in Jefferson County, Alabama. I am assuming that the headquarters for this association was at the old Canaan Baptist church, which still is in existence today a few miles south of Bessemer, Alabama. It is one of the oldest Baptist churches in Alabama.

In his capacity as domestic missionary, Jesse traveled untold hundreds of miles on horseback and preached hundreds of sermons to the backwoods settlers wherever he could find them and all at his own expense. Then, having finished his missionary appointment, in 1837 elder Jesse Seale, with Elder H.H. Rockett established the Mud Creek Baptist Church in Jefferson County with sixteen charter members. This church is still in existence today. Sometime about 1840 Jesse moved into north Alabama and became pastor first, of Round Island Baptist Church, which was located about twelve miles west of Athens, in Limestone County, and then Wofford's Section, which was five or six miles northeast of Huntsville in Madison County. He seems to have been highly regarded wherever he went.

In 1842, he bought land from A.B. Gilbert to build a church in Limestone County, where he remained for about ten years. Sometime after 1850 he left Alabama and moved to Upshur County, Texas. According to other researchers, what prompted this move was the controversy that existed in the Baptist Association at this time, between the Missionary Baptists and the Primitive Baptists. Jesse opted out of the situation and moved to Texas. He died in Upshur County, Texas sometime before the 1870 census. He was the father of six children:

> (fe1) Rebecca, born 1828 in South Carolina.
>
> (fe2) David, born 1833 in South Carolina.
>
> (fe3) Sara Jane, born 1843 in Alabama.
>
> (fe4) Jesse, born 1845 in Alabama.
>
> (fe5) Alexander N., born 1845 in Alabama.
>
> (fe6) Elvie H., born 1848 in Alabama.

(ff) Edward Crossland Seale, the sixth child of Rev. William Seale was born in 1810 in the Marlborough District of South Carolina, and lived there until about age 28. He became the owner of the hundred acres of land at Gardiner's Bluff, which had belonged to his father and before that to his grandfather Edward Crossland, where they had operated a stage station and a resting pasture for horses on the Old Baltimore to New Orleans Road (Deed Book P, p.73). He sold it to his uncle William Crossland, and sometime before December of 1837, migrated to Shelby County, Alabama, accompanied by his brother Daniel Thomas Seale and their cousin Edward Crossland.

Edward Crossland became a schoolteacher in Shelby County, and on January 8, 1852, married Elizabeth Wooley, the marriage performed by John Faust, M.G. (Shelby County Marriages 1850-59, p.45). Edward Crossland Seale became a wealthy planter in the Montevallo area of Shelby County and a justice of the peace. His plantation was near his father, his uncles Thomas Seale, Jr., and David Seale, and his cousins, Charles and Felix Seale, and the Busbys: Meredith (also called Maraday in some records) Busby and his sons.

Edward was married twice, first to Desdemona Mahan, daughter of James and Susannah Mahan of Bibb County, on December 11, 1837. His second wife was Caroline Seale, born 1828 in Alabama, daughter of Felix Seale.

Edward Crossland Seale died in 1894, and is buried in the Sessions Cemetery. There was once a church there, but it is long since gone and the cemetery neglected, with some of the tombstones fallen and partly covered with dirt. This cemetery is on the Shelby-Chilton County line, about a half mile inside Shelby County, off a dirt road.

Edward Crossland Seale was the father of eleven children, all by Desdemona. They were:

> (ff1) George W. Seale, born 1841.
>
> (ff2) Elizabeth A. Seale, born 1844.
>
> (ff3) Susan M. Seale, born 1845, married George Moody October 1, 1861 (Marriage Book 4, p.76).

(ff4) James A. Seale, born 1849, married Mary E. Eddings December 28, 1868 (Marriage Book 4, p.90). Of James A., more follows below.

(ff5) William A. Seale, born December 21, 1849, died June 13, 1903.

(ff6) Mary J., born October 3, 1853, died November 30, 1921, married William Johnson April 20, 1866 (Marriage Book #1, p.326).

(ff7) Rachel, born 1853.

(ff8) Bertha, born 1854.

(ff9) Edward F., born 1856.

(ff10) Desdemona, born 1858.

(ff11) Oliver, a son who died at about age 25, unmarried, and is buried in the Sessions Cemetery near the old homestead.

The only one of these children that I know anything at all about is James, child #4. One of his descendants in Texas contacted me seeking information on the earlier generations of this family. She said that James had entered the Confederate Army in Shelby County, that he was an officer in a very elite cavalry unit, and that he had to furnish his own horse and equipment. He survived the war, and migrated to Texas, where some of his descendants still live.

I suspect that several others of Edward Crossland's children, maybe most of them, also went to Texas. I have never found any evidence of any of his descendants still living in Shelby County, Alabama.

(fg) Mary Seale, the seventh child of Rev. William Seale and Temperance Crossland Pearce, was born in South Carolina about 1815. She married John Neely. Nothing else is known of her.

(fh) Rev. Daniel Thomas Seale, the eighth and youngest child of Rev. William Seale, was born in 1819 in the Marlborough District of South Carolina. By the time of the 1840 census, he was in Shelby County, Alabama. He was a farmer, carpenter, and a Baptist preacher. He married Emeline Seale on November 9, 1845 (Marriage Book 1, p.203).

For a period of about thirty years Rev. Daniel Thomas Seale preached and performed marriages in Shelby County. He was pastor of the Limeville Baptist Church in 1860-61. I am not sure where this church was located, but think it may have been in the vicinity of the lime works at Saginaw. In 1867, he was pastor of Providence Church, which was eight miles south of Montevallo.

In between these two assignments he was one of the early domestic missionaries sent out by the Baptist Association to preach in the destitute areas of the Shelby County, traveling on horseback, knowing that little or no remuneration would be forthcoming. Mr. Ray M. Atchison, in his book "Baptists of Shelby County" describes these early missionaries as "giants among God's men," as surely they were.

During all these years, Daniel Thomas also traveled to Butler County, where some Seale cousins lived, and preached there, in the Shackelville community. These were evidently "cottage" services, held in people's homes, barns, or wherever there was space, since no Baptist church was there at the time. About 1870 he left Shelby County and moved to Butler County, and in 1872 established the Shackelville Baptist Church. It was through Daniel Thomas and the Shackelville church that I was finally able to establish once and for all that Rev. William Seale and Thomas Seale, Jr. were brothers. In a church publication there, Daniel Thomas Seale is referred to as a "a son of Rev. William Seale and a nephew of Thomas Seale."

In 1880, Daniel Thomas Seale appeared on the census for Butler County at age sixty-one. Sometime after this, he and Emeline migrated to Arkansas with their daughter, Martha Jane Sirmon. Both Daniel Thomas and Emeline are buried in Arkansas, but in different cemeteries. Emeline is buried in Howard County, and her grave is marked. It is not known where Daniel Thomas is buried. Daniel Thomas and Emeline were the parents of eight children. They were:

> (fh1) Henry Thomas Seale, born 1846 in Shelby County, Alabama, married twice. First wife's name Lucinda, second, Annie. He was a carriage and wagon maker at Shackelville, in Butler County, Alabama, and the father of four:
>
> (fh1a) Henry C. (1870).
>
> (fh1b) Minnie (1872).
>
> (fh1c) Annie (1876).

(fh1d) Benjamin (1880).

(fh2) Edward Seale, born 1847.

(fh3) William Seale, born 1849.

(fh4) D.A. Seale, a male, born 1853.

(fh5) M.D. Seale, a female, born 1855.

(fh6) Phillip P. Seale, born 1856, married Allie M. Saucer January 17, 1877.

(fh7) Martha Jane Seale, born 1857, married a Sirmon and later migrated to Arkansas.

(fh8) Charles H. Seale, born February 18, 1860, died May 17, 1939, in Perry County, Alabama. Married twice, first wife Marietta, second wife unknown. Charles became owner of and lived on the old Thomas Seale, Jr. homestead in Perry County after Thomas Jr. died and his youngest son, Isaac Hopkins Seale, migrated to Texas. Charles and his family are all buried in the Mount Olive Church Cemetery near Thomas Seale, Jr.'s grave. Charles was the father of nine children:

(fh8a) Jesse D. (1883-1938).

(fh8b) Sidney Miron (1885-1944).

(fh8c) Benjamin (1887).

(fh8d) John Comer (1888-1942).

(fh8e) Ermon O. (1890-1956).

(fh8f) Brooks C. (1892-1932).

(fh8g) Marvin (1894).

(fh8h) Naomi (1896).

(fh8i) Charles (1898).

(g) John Seale, the sixth known child of Thomas Seale, Sr. was born in Prince William County, Virginia, about 1765. He moved with the family to Cumberland County, North Carolina as a child. As a young man, he seems to have been very active in the Baptist church in that area, helping establish at least one church. He later followed his brothers, Thomas Jr. and David, first to South Carolina, and then to Wilkes County, Georgia, where he became Sheriff of Wilkes County. His wife's name is not known, but it is known that he had several children. After his brothers, David and Thomas, Jr., left Wilkes County, John seems to have remained for some time in Georgia, then settled in South Carolina for some twenty years, where he lived near his brother Hopkins. After this he disappeared from the records. The name of only one of his children is known, a son:

(ga) William. Little is known of him. His wife's name was Martha, and they had five children:

    (ga1) Anna Eliza.

    (ga2) Charles.

    (ga3) Elizabeth Seale Mooney.

    (ga4) James Pinkney.

    (ga5) Mahalia Seale Thomas.

This completes the list of children of Thomas Seale, Sr. and his wife Elizabeth. We now return to Thomas Seale, Jr., third child on the list, who was the Alabama pioneer. We will continue the line beginning with him.

As already stated, Thomas Seale, Jr. was born in Prince William County, Virginia in 1764. The family moved to Cumberland County, North Carolina when he was a small child, and he grew up there. Whether from his parents, or elsewhere, Thomas received a very good formal education for that day, as evidenced by later records.

The first record of him as an adult was in Camden County, South Carolina, in 1788, when he received a grant of one hundred acres as an assignee of Johnston Elkins, a Revolutionary soldier. Thomas had married Elkins' daughter, Ader Elkins. That same year Thomas Jr. enlisted in the militia, serving as an assignee of (in the place of) Johnston Elkins.

When the Revolutionary War began, Thomas had been too young to join the military. However, the state militia was maintained for many years after the war, and each landowner was expected to serve some time in the militia, or provide someone to serve in his place. It is not clear why

Johnston Elkins had to send an assignee when he had already served in the Revolution. Thomas Seale, Jr. served as an assignee of Johnston Elkins, and for this service he received a bounty grant. This is recorded in the *South Carolina Historical and Genealogical Magazine*, Vol. 7, page 76, and on the land grant itself (South Carolina State Grants, Vol. O, p 94). The tract, granted on March 4, 1793, was in Camden District, on Saxton's Branch of Swaine's Creek, waters of the Wateree River.

He sold this land in 1794 to his cousin, Elijah Seale, son of Charles Seale. By 1796, he was in Hancock County, Georgia, where he owned property on Town Creek, near his father, Thomas Seale, Sr., and his brother, David Seale. His brother, John Seale, was also living in the area at this time and later became Sheriff of Wilkes County. Thomas began selling his property off in parcels in 1804. In 1805, he sold another parcel, and in 1806, he sold the last two parcels.

By this time he was living in Baldwin County, where he owned 202 1/2 acres on Little River and five slaves. He may have cleared the land and raised cotton, but I somehow doubt this. I think it more likely that he, along with his oldest sons and his slaves worked the forests for turpentine on the tracts he owned. This was a very lucrative business at the time.

His father, Thomas Seale, Sr., died in Baldwin County in 1806. By this time his brother David had abandoned his 600-acre plantation in Williamson County, Tennessee, and headed for the Mississippi Territory. Thomas Jr. remained in Baldwin County until after his fourth child, who was my great-grandfather John Seale, was born. By the time his fifth child, David, was born in 1810, the family had migrated to Marion County, Mississippi, and joined his brother David.

What an incredibly difficult journey that must have been for my great-great-grandmother, although they had the slaves to help with the really hard work of the trip, driving the teams, fording the streams, and maneuvering around the Indian tribes. To get from Georgia to Mississippi at that time, it was necessary to travel between or around several Indian tribes in western Georgia and the Alabama Territory.

In the east were the Creeks and Cherokees, and in the West, the Choctaws and Chickasaws. To cross this territory, the settlers had to go far south, on what was called the "Three-Chop Way," so named because the trailblazers had marked it with three ax-chops on the trees. They would then come in below the Creek nation, or go north and travel the Great Trading Path, which had long connected the tribes of Georgia and the Carolinas with those further west; These early settlers usually had to secure a passport before traveling between the Indian tribes. Most of the settlers took the northern route, then crossed the Alabama Territory diagonally toward the southwest, avoiding the Choctaws and Chickasaws. David was born soon after the family arrived in Mississippi.

Thomas Seale, Jr. remained in Mississippi for about fifteen years. In 1811, he signed a petition to Congress for Mississippi to become a state. His brother Rev. William Seale joined him in Mississippi for a time, after the death of his wife in South Carolina.

Thomas Jr.'s daughter Elizabeth was married there on February 3, 1817, to Elias Cassels, son of Henry Cassels. The Cassels and Seale families had been closely associated in Georgia, before moving to Mississippi. Rev. William Seale was bondsman, and since Elizabeth was under legal age (thought to have been about 15), her father had to sign for her. Before 1820, Elizabeth was deceased after having given birth to a daughter, Margaret Cassels. Margaret was thereafter raised in the home of Thomas Jr. and Ader, later moving with them to Butler County, Alabama, where she married James Moore.

About 1820, Thomas Jr. and his brother David moved east into Butler County, Alabama, where some cousins were living. The Butler County courthouse was destroyed by fire in later years, so records of Thomas Jr.'s years there are scarce. What is known is that after he moved north to Bibb County, about 1835, James and Margaret Moore lived on his place in Butler County for a time. They eventually moved to Nacogdoches County, Texas.

Upon arriving in Bibb County, Thomas Jr. secured a tract of land through the Tuscaloosa Land Office. Located in the lush valley of the Little Cahaba River, the area eventually came to be called "Six Mile." The story goes that one of the settlers lost his milk cow and couldn't find her for several days. When he did find her and someone inquired as to where he had found her, he said, "about six mile," and so the place has been called "Six Mile" ever since. Thomas Seale Jr. was one of the first seven settlers at Six Mile; the other six being Jonathan Newton Smith, a Georgia native, who had a woolen mill, a grist mill, and probably a flour mill at Six Mile; George Leith; Jerry Hayes; W.P. Thompson; Samuel Glen Wilson; and John T. Wilson.

By 1840, Thomas Seale Jr. was living in Shelby County, alone, his wife Ader being no longer living by this time. His brother, Rev. William Seale, moved there about the same time, as did his brother, John Seale.

Thomas Jr., his brothers John and William, William's sons David Thomas Seale and Edward Crossland Seale, all lived near each other in the western part of the county, near Montevallo. There were other Seales families in Shelby County at this time, descendants of Charles Seales, and first cousins to Thomas Seale, Jr., but this group always seemed to stick together.

In 1847, Thomas Jr. was back in Bibb County, where he was married on October 27, 1847, to Jane Jameston Dorse, daughter of Isaac Jameston, formerly of Kentucky. Jane was a widow with a young son, George Washington Dorse. The ceremony was performed by Rev. David Ward, a young minister who was pastor of the Antioch Baptist Church in the historic community of Antioch. David Ward had been ordained there, and is buried in the church cemetery.

Thomas bought land in nearby Perry County (certificate #24288, Deed Book 1, page 145), and he and Jane settled there, in the Pinetucky Beat. A year later their son, Isaac Hopkins Seale was born. Thomas Jr. was 84 years old at the time. Then in 1850, when Isaac Hopkins was only two years old, Thomas Seale Jr. died. He is buried in the Mount Olive Church cemetery, near his old homestead.

Nearby Thomas Seale Jr.'s grave are the graves of Charles Seales, a great-grandson of his brother William through William's son Daniel Thomas Seale, and his son Phillip Seale. Charles was Phillip's youngest son. He and most of his children are buried at Mount Olive. Charles had bought the old homestead from Jane after Thomas Jr.'s death and her remarriage. In the settlement of the estate, Jane had been allowed to keep the homestead, but the slaves were sold and the amount of nine thousand dollars which they brought was divided among his children. His son David and his wife were both deceased by this time, and David's share of the money was turned over to his brother, my great-grandfather John B. Seale, in trust for the children. A guardian was appointed for the youngest child, Isaac Hopkins Seale, and was discharged when Isaac Hopkins attained majority. (Perry County, Alabama, Probate Court Regular Term, April 14, 1870)

Thomas Jr.'s widow soon remarried. In the 1860 census for Perry County, page 17, Pinetucky Beat, household # 117, shows her married to John C. Vedle, a farmer, age 65, born in North Carolina. Jane was 55 years old at the time, and her father, Isaac Jameston, age 80, was still living with the family. Isaac Hopkins Seale was age 12, and George Washington Dorse was already married. I found him in later census records listed under the name Doss. He is thought to have migrated to Texas in the latter part of the century.

Thomas Seale Jr. was the father of six known children. There are thought to have been at least one or two others who died as children in Mississippi. Those who are known are:

- (I) Barnabas Seale, born in Fairfield County, South Carolina in the 1790's, died in 1858 in Bibb County, Alabama, leaving a will (Will Book 1, p.66). He was married twice, the first wife unknown, the second was Harriet Elizabeth Ann Gaskey, whom he married on April 18, 1854 in Butler County, Alabama. He moved north to Bibb County some time after that, and lived in the Antioch community, about nine miles east of Centreville, and not far from his brother John, who was living at Six Mile. He was the father of nine children, whose names have been taken from his will and from Probate Minutes Book F, p.592. After his death, his widow continued to live in the Antioch community with her three daughters. Barnabas' other six children were by his first wife, and were on their own by this time. None of this family are buried in the Antioch Baptist Church Cemetery, and a search of the Bibb County cemetery census indicates that if they are buried anywhere in Bibb County, the graves are not marked. Barnabas' nine children were:
  - (A) Mary Ann Seale, married Elihu Sims and lived in Butler County, Alabama.
  - (B) William Morgan Seale, born in 1832 in Butler County, Alabama, was married on April 28, 1832 in Pensacola, Florida, to Henrietta Stephens. He was an attorney. His name appears on the tax lists for Escambia County, Florida from 1857 through 1878, and his family was in the 1860 and 1870 census for Escambia County. In 1880, they were in the census for Clarke County, Alabama.

He and Henrietta were the parents of twelve children:

- (1) Sara Seale, born 1857 in Florida.
- (2) Charles Seale, born 1859 in Florida.
- (3) Susan Seale, born 1863 in Florida, married J. W. Gwynn on November 7, 1881 in Clarke County, Alabama.
- (4) Martha Seale, born 1865 in Florida, married Robert J. Dickenson on May 4, 1883 in Clarke County, Alabama.

(5) Barnabas Seale, born 1867 in Florida, migrated to Texas as an adult.

(6) Thomas Seale, born 1869 in Florida, married Cora, born 1883 in Alabama.

(7) William H. Seale, born 1870 in Florida.

(8) Elizabeth Seale, born 1871 in Florida.

(9) George Seale, born 1876 in Florida, married Minnie.

(10) Andrew Seale, born 1874 in Florida.

(11) Alice Seale, born 1877 in Florida.

(12) Jessie Seale, born 1881 in Florida.

(C) Elizabeth Ann Seale, born 1840, married Jesse Webb, born 1837, and lived out her life in Bibb County, Alabama.

(D) Nancy Jane Seale, married Noah L. Coker on October 2, 1855, and died prior to August 3, 1857.

(E) Barnabas Seale, Jr., went west as a young man. He stopped in Marion County, Mississippi for a time, where his grandfather, Thomas Seale Jr. had lived, and where his father had lived as a young man. He was married there in 1863 to Mary Ann Smart, his son William was born there in 1864, his son Allen in 1870, and his son Charles was born there in 1872, according to the LDS archives. Barnabas later went on to Texas, where he had other children and raised a large and illustrious family.

(F) Manerva Seale, Married Columbus Corley and lived out her life in Bibb County, Alabama.

(G) Martha Seale.

(H) Mary Seale.

(I) Rebecca Seale.

These last three were by Barnabas' second wife, Elizabeth Ann Gaskey, and were small children when Barnabas died.

(II) Thomas Seale III, the second child of Thomas Seale, Jr., was born in Hancock County, Georgia between 1800 and 1810, and died between 1840 and 1850 in Butler County, Alabama. His wife's name was Nancy (born about 1810), and they were the parents of seven children. They were:

(A) Elizabeth Seale, born 1826. It is not known whom she married. She lived in Butler County, Alabama, and was the administrator of her brother John A.'s will.

(B) Amanda Seale, married D. Washington Austin and lived her life in Butler County, Alabama.

(C) Mary (Polly) Seale, married Amos Jones and lived in Butler County.

(D) John A., never married. He was a Confederate soldier, and died in Mobile, Alabama in 1862.

(E) William Riley Seale, married Frances Jane Yates. He was a Confederete soldier, and settled in Nacogdoches County, Texas after the war.

(F) James Thomas Seale, was a Confederate soldier. He and his brother Wilson were captured in Arkansas, then released because both were very sick, and one not expected to live. Wilson died, but James Thomas survived and went to Nacogdoches County, Texas. (*War of The Rebellion*, Series I, Vol. 17, p.352)

(G) Wilson Seale, died in the Civil War in Arkansas.

(III) Elizabeth Seale, the third child of Thomas Seale, Jr. was born between 1800 and 1810 in Georgia. She migrated with the family to Marion County, Mississippi in 1809, and was married there in 1817 to Elias Cassels, and died about 1820. She was the mother of one, a daughter named Margaret Cassels, who was raised by her Seale grandparents. She later moved to Butler County, Alabama, where she married James Moore, and later migrated to Nacogdoches County, Texas. The Seale family had known both the Cassels and Moore families in Georgia. James Moore's family is thought to have gone on to Nacagdoches County, Texas also.

(IV) John B. Seale, the fourth child of Thomas Seale, Jr., was my great-grandfather. Born in Baldwin County, Georgia in 1809, he migrated with the family to Marion County, Mississippi that same year, where it is thought that the family may have raised horses. I say this because I somehow can't picture them as cotton planters—the males in this family always had an affinity for horses. I have found records in which several of them operated livery stables, and all of them were brilliant horse-traders.

In his teen years John moved with the family to Butler County, Alabama, and was married there sometime before 1840. Little is known of his wife except that her name was Matilda, since the courthouse in Butler County burned, and records are few. The young family appears on the census for Butler County in 1840, and this record show that Matilda was born in South Carolina in 1815, and that they had at that time one child, a son born in 1840. Soon after 1840, John and his family moved to Shelby County, where his brother David, and other relatives were living.

At this time, Shelby County was a crossroads for pioneers going west. Some stayed for a time and then moved on, while others stayed permanently. A thriving industry in Shelby County during this time was the Shelby Iron Works, at Shelby Alabama, a few miles from Columbiana. I have been told that my great-grandfather worked there, that he was known as a hard worker, and a strong, tough, independent man, and that he had a knowledge of horses and was a brilliant trader.

John B. Seale remained in Shelby County less than ten years. By the time of the 1850 census he was living in Bibb County, on the east side of Cahaba River, near the community of Six Mile, and near his father and his brother David. His mother was deceased by this time. His brother Barnabas lived not far away in Antioch.

I have visited the site of old Six Mile, and it is undoubtedly one of the most beautiful spots I have ever seen. I was there in the month of April. The woods were deep and quiet, white with dogwoods in places, pink with wild azaleas, and yellow with jasmine in others. The roadsides were a patchwork of pink and blue, with sweet williams, and wild pansies, which are known as "rooster heads" blooming in profusion. The river is wide, and flows unhurriedly, the banks shaded by large water oaks, poplars and whiteoaks. There are many deep holes for pole fishing, and many natural waterfalls spanning the river. My visit was some years ago, so it may not be the same now.

John B. and Matilda had five children at this time, the youngest being William Thomas Seale, my grandfather. They subsequently had two more.

When the Civil War came, John B.'s oldest son enlisted, and subsequently spent most of the war in a northern prison camp. The family had a very hard time during the war. I am not sure where their sympathies lay, but I do know there were many in Bibb County, including others of my relatives who did not sympathize with the southern cause, or so I have been told. Bibb County became a very violent place. Bands of marauders made up of renegade northern soldiers and southern scalawags roamed the countryside, stealing whatever they could, destroying property, and killing any male they could find. It didn't seem to matter how old a man might be, or how many children he had to support: just being of the male gender made him a target for killing.

John B. Seale barely escaped their deviltry once when a group of renegades came to his home. As it happened, he was down at the spring, which was some distance behind the house. Matilda told the marauders that her husband wasn't home and then whispered to one of the children to go and warn their father. On another occasion his son Barnabas was in the woods splitting rails for a fence, happened to straighten up and look around, and a man was standing over him with an ax raised over his head, ready to kill him. This violence continued after the war and grew to include blacks, the whites in many cases blaming them for the entire mess. Bibb County came to be referred to as "Bloody Bibb."

Matilda died soon after the war. In the census of 1870, I found John B. living alone and working as a wagon driver at the Briarfield Iron Works, which was not far from his home. He died about 1885, and his grave has never been found, which would lead one to speculate that he probably was buried on the old homeplace, the grave long since lost. He and Matilda were the parents of seven children as follows:

> (A) John Anderson Seale, born 1840 in Butler County, Alabama, died in Bibb County, Alabama in 1919. About 1869 he was married to Elizabeth Smith, who was born in Georgia in 1843 and died in Bibb County in 1911, daughter of Uriah Smith, who was born in Georgia in 1804 and his wife Nancy, born in Georgia in 1809.

John Anderson Seale enlisted in the Army of the Confederacy on October 12, 1861, in Bibb County, Alabama, and was a member of Co. D, 20th Regiment, Alabama Infantry. He was captured at Port Gibson, Mississippi on May 1, 1863 and sent to the military prison in Alton, Illinois. On February 29, 1864, he was transferred to a prison at Fort Delaware, Delaware, and remained there until the end of the war, and his release on June 14, 1865.

John suffered untold deprivation and exposure to deadly diseases such as smallpox while in prison, and upon his release, even in his weakened condition, he had to walk all the way back to his home in Bibb County.

In the days and months following the end of the war, it was a common sight to see a Confederate soldier making his way along some country road, on his way back home. Most people shunned these returning soldiers, not because of any lack of compassion, but because they didn't dare take a chance with all the contagions that had swept the prison camps.

On the day of John's return, his mother Matilda and one of his sisters was walking along the road at Six Mile when they saw a soldier coming along meeting them. Matilda immediately got out of the road and up on an embankment, and told her daughter to do likewise. The daughter hesitated, saying she thought it was her brother John. After several such interchanges, and as the soldier came closer, Matilda saw that it was indeed her son. She hadn't recognized her own son in his sick and ragged condition.

After the war, John farmed near the town of Blocton, which is now called West Blocton, the newer part of town having overshadowed the old. Sometime about 1880 he moved to Sipsey for a time, and while there several of his children died in a diptheria epidemic, and are buried in the cemetery at Sipsey, their graves marked. Only four of his children survived to adulthood. They were:

(1) Nancy Matilda Seale, born 1871, died 1942, married Robert McBride, and had seven children:

(a) William.

(b) Maylene.

(c) Patrick.

(d) Herbert Luville (called, "Hub.")

(e) Marie Imogene.

(f) U.L.

(2) Harriet Rodesta (Hattie) Seale, married James Dycus from Belle Ellen (a small coal-mining town not far from Blocton), and had one child:

(a) Birdie Mae Dycus. Birdie was married twice, first to a Dr. Glover, a dentist, and the name of her second husband is unknown. She had two children:

(aa) Carolyn, who lives in Jacksonville, Florida.

(ab) a daughter who died in infancy.

Birdie Mae died in 1981, and is buried in Jacksonville.

(3) John Anderson Seale, Jr., born about 1883, died 1938, married Lorene and had one child:

(a) Kathleen, who is deceased, but has decendants.

(4) Maude Elizabeth Seale, born 1885, died 1971, married September 4, 1904 at the family home at Blocton, Alabama, to James Newton Erasmus Hayes, and had four children:

(a) John Martin Hayes, born July 2, 1905, died January 26, 1981, married Esther Carroll about 1923, lived in Columbus, Georgia, and had one child:

(aa) Thelma Doris Hayes, born June 24, 1927, died 1969, married Edward Cummings and had one child:

(aa1) Linda Ann Cummings, who married a Davis, lives in Columbus. Georgia, and has one child:

(aa1a) Allen Davis, born 1971.

(b) James Claude Hayes, the second child of Maude Elizabeth Seale and James Newton Erasmus Hayes, was born April 14, 1908, married Lillie Deerman about 1923, lived in West Blocton, Alabama, and had three children:

(ba) Billy Claude Hayes, lives in Tuscaloosa, Alabama, married Vera Beasley, and had two children:

(ba1) Kenneth.

(ba2) Kay.

(bb) Betty Joyce Hayes, born about 1936, married Billy Tillery, lives in West Blocton, Alabama, and has two children:

(bb1) Wanda Tillery.

(bb2) Joan Tillery.

(bc) Peggy Hayes, who lives in West Blocton, is married to Rev. Charles Rice, and has one child:

(bc1) James Anderson Rice.

(c) Rasie Mae Hayes, the third child of Maude Elizabeth Seale and James Newton Erasmus Hayes, was born

November 27, 1910, married James William Sumner on December 25, 1927, and had seven children:

(ca) James Arthur Sumner, born 1929, lives in Nashville, Tennessee, married Jean Dyson in 1974, and has 1 son:

(ca1) James Arthur Sumner, Jr.

(cb) Norma Jean Sumner, born January 27, 1931, lives in Pensacola, Florida, married Beverly M. Baisden in 1951, and has one child:

(cb1) Beverly Jean Baisden, who married first Mike Pulley and secondly Roger Gaddy, and has one child:

(cb1a) Bryan Pulley.

(cc) Carol Max Sumner, their third child, born December 4, 1933, lives in Dallas, Texas, married Claudine Stubbs in 1955 and has three children:

(cc1) Carol Ann Sumner, married Phil Wheeler, lives in Tampa, Florida, and has one child:

(cc1a) Tyson Wheeler, born 1976.

(cc2) Barbara Diane Sumner, born 1958, lives in Tampa, Florida, married Stewart Lanier and has no children.

(cc3) James William Sumner, born 1959.

(cd) Joyce Elaine Sumner, the fourth child of Rasie Mae Hayes and James Sumner, married Earl Morrow, was born 1935, lives in Jacksonville, Florida and has two children:

(cd1) Patricia Lynn Morrow, born 1955, lives in Jacksonville, Florida.

(cd2) Deborah Paige Morrow, who married Gareth Ray, lives in Manitou Springs, Colorado, and had two children:

(cd2a) Christopher Ray, born July 17, 1976.

(cd2b) Jennifer Ray, born November 14, 1979, and died in infancy.

(ce) Shirley Ann Sumner, the fifth child of Rasie Mae Hayes and James Sumner, was born in 1938, lives in Jacksonville, Florida, married Jack McCart in 1956, and has four children:

    (ce1) Tracy Elaine McCart, born 1960, married Greg Cohen, 1980.

    (ce2) Terry Russell McCart, born May 21, 1962.

    (ce3) Jacqueline Ann McCart, born 1964.

    (ce4) Mark Edward McCart (who is adopted), born April 29, 1972.

(cf) Nancy Louise Sumner, the sixth child of Rasie Mae Hayes and James Sumner, was born October 23, 1942, married Jerry Michael Pope in 1959, and had 3 children:

    (cf1) James Michael Pope, born July 15, 1960, married Maureen Heath and has one child:

        (cf1a) James Michael Pope, Jr.

    (cf2) Lisa Louise Pope, born March 17, 1964.

    (cf3) Stephen Sumner Pope, born April 28, 1970.

(cg) Wayne Hayes Sumner, the seventh child of Rasie Mae Hayes and James Sumner, was born November 7, 1946, died November 10, 1946.

(d) Marguerite Elizabeth Hayes, the fourth child of Maude Elizabeth Seale and James Newton Erasmus Hayes, was born May 18, 1919, lives in Dothan, Alabama, married Marion Michael Shaw in 1934, and had three children:

(da) Marion Faye Shaw, born May 1, 1936, married Dewey Deason and had three children:

    (da1) David.

    (da2) Douglas.

    (da3) Denise.

(db) Mildred Yvonne Shaw, born December 2, 1942, married David Daugherty, and had three children:

    (db1) Michael.

(db2) Scott.

(db3) Dale.

(dc) Ronald Wayne Shaw, who married first Sandra Kirby, second Tessie, and had three children:

(dc1) Jennifer.

(dc2) Michael.

(dc3) Bradley Paul.

(B) Sarah Seale, the second child of John B. Seale and his wife Matilda, was born in 1842. She married a McCollum and is buried in the Brierfield Cemetery in Bibb County. Nothing further is known of her.

(C) Mary Seale, the third child, was born in 1844. She married Flemming Gentry in Bibb County, Alabama. Nothing further is known of her, but it is thought that this couple migrated to Arkansas.

(D) Barnabas Bass Seale, the fourth child of John B. and Matilda Seale, was born in 1846 in Bibb County, Alabama. He was married about 1870 to Nancy Ashworth, born in 1845, a widow with a young son, Linzy Ashworth, born in 1866. They lived in Bibb County, and raised a family there. Nancy died about 1910, and in 1913, Barnabas went west, first to Pontotoc County, Mississippi, where he had cousins, and then on to Texas where he joined his son, Barnabas, Jr.

No one knows for sure where Barnabas died, since to my knowledge, no one in Alabama ever heard from him again. I have been told that both he and his son, Barnabas, Jr., are buried in the Seale-Hayes Cemetery on the Texas side of the Red River, somewhere along the strip where Texas and Oklahoma are separated by the Red, but I have not been able to find this cemetery, or anyone who knows anything of it.

I never knew "Uncle Barney," as he was called, but feel that I missed a great deal in not knowing him. He left Alabama some time before I was born. He used to come and visit my parents for a week or two at a time, and according to my mother, he was a good and kind man, very good with animals, loved horses, and like all the other males of this family, was a brilliant horsetrader. She said my father had told her stories of how as a boy he had gone coon hunting or fox hunting in the Cahaba River bottom in Bibb County, and how Uncle Barney always had such good hunting dogs, and how good he was with them, taking the trouble to train them just right. He always used a hunting horn, and the dogs knew to drop everything and hurry on back when they heard the horn.

Barnabas and Nancy were the parents of five children:

(1) Mary, born 1871.

(2) Nancy, born 1872 (In the 1900 census, she was in Clarke County, Alabama, in the household of William Morgan Seale, her father's first cousin).

(3) Martha, born 1875.

(4) Barnabas Bass, Jr. (called "Bassy"), born 1878.

(5) Ida, born April 16, 1888, died August 1, 1966, married a Creel.

(E) William Thomas Seales, the fifth child of John B. and Matilda Seale was born in 1848 in the Cahaba River Valley of Bibb County Alabama on the eastern side of the river, near the area that is now the Talladega National Forest. He was known throughout his life as "Billy" Seales, and he was my father's father.

Billy was married on July 4, 1870, at age 23, to Elizabeth Tabitha Smith, born 1848 in Alabama, a daughter of James Riley Smith, born in Georgia in 1805, and his wife Mary, born in North Carolina in 1808. Elizabeth was a first cousin to the Elizabeth Smith who earlier had married Billy's brother, John Anderson Seale. The ceremony was performed at the home of John Anderson Seale, and one of the witnesses was Barnabas Bass Seale, Sr., previously mentioned here.

Billy and Betty lived their entire lives in the Blocton-Smith Hill area of Bibb County. He worked in the coal mining industry, as did most people in that area during those years. It was the era in which the vast coal deposits beneath the hills of Bibb County were being exploited. The Smiths had been the first, or one of the first settlers in the area, and had acquired large tracts of land, which had now become immensely valuable because of the coal.

Betty's brother, Rufus Smith, was an important man in the area during this period. Being the owner of several coal mines, he was said to be a millionaire several times over, and was elected mayor of Blocton in 1910. The town of Smith Hill, which was the original settlement in the area, before Blocton came into being, was named for the Smith Family. Rufus Smith married Emeline Wheeler, a relative of Gen. Joe Wheeler, whom some military historians consider to have been the best tactical general in the history of the world.

It was in Billy Seale's generation that the Seales form of the name came into use. I blame this on the fact that they lived in a remote area of the state, where schools were few and not very good, and on public officials and mine bosses who were not well educated and tended to spell the names phonetically. I imagine that when you see your name spelled a certain way enough times, one would tend to give up and go along. Whatever the reason, from here on the name has been Seales, not Seale.

As a hobby, Billy Seales was a horse-trader who had few equals. This trait became more pronounced in this family after the Civil War, when times were hard and trading was a quick way to make a few dollars. Later, I think they traded just for the pure enjoyment and love of the sport and art of barter, and the thrill that came from besting someone in a trade.

Besides attending all the "trade days" in Bibb County, he and his brothers, sons, and father often made trips to Pontotoc County, Mississippi, where they had relatives, and attended the trade days there. A "trade day" was usually held one Saturday a month, always on the same Saturday, and it was a time when the farmers, miners, whoever, would bring in any horses or mules they wanted to sell or trade, and stood around the town square until someone made them an offer. It was said of the Seales men that they could go to a trade day, trade all day, go home with a pocket full of money, and still riding their favorite horse, which was the same one they had ridden to the affair.

The story is told of my grandfather's encounter with some gypsies. Everyone knows that gypsies in olden days were smart traders, and in this case, this band of gypsies had been traveling around Bibb County making some very lucrative trades. Then they encountered my grandfather riding one horse and leading another, in one of the small mining towns near Blocton, and engaged him in some horse-trading, some rather reckless horse-trading, on my grandfather's part, it seems to me. When it was over, my grandfather started for home, still riding his own horse and leading two more. It wasn't long before he heard the gypsies coming after him along the dirt road, their horses at a gallop and screaming what that they were going to do to him. Knowing the Bibb County woods well, he simply left the road and cut through the woods back to his home.

In the latter part of his life Billy Seales worked in the timber woods in Bibb County, for a man named Tom Hill. I found him on the census for 1900, working as a lumberman. His son, James Riley Seales, was listed as a teamster.

Billy and Betty both died within a short time of each other, about 1902. The exact dates are not known. They are buried in the Mount Carmel Cemetery at West Blocton, and the graves have markers, but no death dates. The graves are near the Frederick and McElroy plots in the central part of the cemetery.

Billy and Betty were the parents of seven children, six of whom lived to adulthood:

> (1) Rufus B. Seales, the oldest child of William Thomas Seales and Elizabeth Tabitha Smith was born on May 21, 1871 in Bibb County, Alabama, and died on April 24, 1945. He married Evie McBride, born 1875, died 1939. Both are buried in the Mount Carmel Cemetery at West Blocton, and the graves are marked. Rufus and Evie lived their entire lives at Blocton, and Rufus was the sheriff of Bibb County. They were the parents of three sons:
>
> (a) Herman Seales.
>
> (b) Hubert Seales.
>
> Herman and Hubert spent all their working lives in Detroit, Michigan, where they worked for a railroad, and neither ever married. After retirement, they moved to Miami, Florida, where they both died and were buried there.
>
> (c) Glen Ralph Seales was born on July 3, 1901, in West Blocton, Alabama, and died on November 30, 1941 in the same place and is buried in the Mount Carmel Cemetery near his parents. The grave is marked. He married Estelle Frederick, who was nicknamed "Dodge," perhaps because her father was an automobile dealer who sold that make of automobile. She is buried beside Glen Ralph in the Mount Carmel Cemetery. Glen Ralph and Estelle were the parents of two sons:

(ca) Ralph Frederick, Called "Freddy, " was born July 18, 1932 in West Blocton, Alabama, and died on June 14, 1973 in Oneonta, Alabama, and is buried there. He married Elizabeth Lavell Hathcock, born 1931, in Locust Fork, Alabama. They had no children.

(cb) Robert Glen, called "Bobby," born November 11, 1935, in West Blocton, Alabama, married Vicky Kathryn Harkins, born November 23, 1940 in West Blocton, Alabama. Robert Glen is a land surveyor, and Vicky holds a master's degree in special education. They have one child:

(cb1) Richard Glen Seales, married Suzy Farnham, and they have one child, a son:

(cb1a) Richard Clinton, "Clint," Seales, born July 15, 1993.

(2) James Riley Seales, the second child of Billy Seales and Betty Smith, was born on December 6, 1875 in Bibb County, Alabama, and died on May 15, 1934 in the same place. He never married, and was a farmer in Bibb County all his life. At least part of that time he worked for Cap and Candy Nelson. He is buried in the Mount Carmel Cemetery beside his parents, and the grave is marked.

(3) Anna Lu Seales, the third child, was born on April 30, 1876 in Bibb County, Alabama, died in 1960 at Smith Hill, near Blocton, and is buried in the Mount Carmel Cemetery at West Blocton. She married Isaac Thrasher, and they had five children:

(a) Hobert Thrasher, the oldest child of Isaac and Anna Thrasher was born in 1904, and is buried in the mount Carmel Cemetery. He married Lydia McCool and they had six children:

(aa) Emma Lou, who married George Ferue.

(ab) Charles Thomas, who died young.

(ac) Annette.

(ad) Bobby, who married a Hunt.

(ae) Mary Sue.

(af) Preston.

(b) Henley Thrasher, the second child of Isaac and Anna Thrasher, was born in 1906 and is buried in the Mount Carmel Cemetery. He was married twice, first to Martha Eddins, by whom he had two children, and secondly to Eloise Segal, by whom he had three children. They were:

(ba) Anna Frances.

(bb) Rosella.

(bc) Wesley.

(bd) Henry Wayne.

(be) a daughter whose name is not known.

(c) Hersery Thrasher, the third child, was born in 1910 and died in 1968 in Tucson, Arizona, and is buried in the veterans plot of the South Park Cemetery there. The name on the grave marker is "Herschel Thrasher," but the marker was ordered by a friend, and the friend evidently made a mistake. I definitely remember his mother telling me that his name was Hersery. He had always been called "Buster," and not many people knew his real name. He was never married.

(d) Lenna Thrasher, the fourth child of Isaac and Anna Thrasher, married Reynolds Jones, and had two children:

(da) Betty Jean Jones, who married first Tim Grammar, and had one child:

(da1) Jimmy Dale Grammar.

Betty Jean then married Charles Hudgins and had one child:

(da2) Charles Richard Hudgins.

(db) Freda Jones (called "Johnnie") was Lenna's second child. She married first, Cecil West and had two children:

(db1) Connie West.

(db2) Eugene West.

Freda married secondly Thomas Gann, and had one child:

(db3) Bradley Gann.

(e) Elizabeth Thrasher, the fifth child of Isaac and Anna Thrasher married Howard O. Jackson and had one child:

(ea) Jacqueline Jackson, married first George Lacey, and had three children:

(ea1) George Wesley.

(ea2) Julie Lynn.

(ea3) Michael Howard.

Jacqueline married secondly Melvin Horton, and had one child:

(ea4) Brandy Michelle.

(4) John Robert Seales, the fourth child of Billy and Betty Seales was born on February 20, 1878 in Bibb County, Alabama, and died in 1912 in the Bluff Ridge community near Bessemer, Alabama. He is buried in the Arnold's Chapel Cemetery at Bluff Ridge, and the grave is unmarked. He married Mattie Holley, daughter of John Holley of Bibb County, and they had one son:

(a) Harold Seales. Harold was born in 1908 in Bibb County, Alabama, and died about 1979 in Mobile, Alabama. He married Bertha Cole, and they had no children. Harold and Bertha died within three weeks of each other. Neither left a will, and the estate reverted to the state of Alabama. They are buried in the Pinecrest Cemetery in Mobile, Alabama.

(5) William Martin Seales, the fifth child of Billy and Betty Seales, was born on March 29, 1881 in Bibb County, Alabama. As a young man he worked in the timber woods in Bibb and Jefferson Counties. About 1913, he left Alabama, going to join his uncle Barnabas Seale in Texas, and was never heard from again, except word that drifted back that he had reached where Uncle Barney was.

He was not married when he left Alabama, and since he was past the usual marrying age at that time, it is doubtful that he ever did. He no doubt died in Texas, and is buried wherever his uncle Barnabas Bass Seale and his cousin Barnabas Bass Seale, Jr., are buried, and as already written, they are said to be in the Seale-Hayes Cemetery on the Red River, on the Texas side, but I have never been able to locate this cemetery.

    (6) Joseph Horace Seales, the sixth child of Billy and Betty Seales, was born on January 20, 1886 in the Cahaba River valley of Bibb County, Alabama. He was my father, and he never spent a day in school.

His parents died when he was about sixteen, and he went on his own, apprenticing himself to a Mr. Holland, who was a butcher in the town of Blocton. He would get out before daylight, even on the coldest mornings, riding a mule and delivering meat to the hospital, restaurants, and markets in the town of Blocton. He did, however, learn the trade of butchering, and this proved to be a good thing, because, whatever else he was doing for the rest of his life, he always did butchering on the side, and there were times when this came in very handy, especially during the great depression.

After leaving Mr. Holland, he tried mining for a while. His uncle, Rufus Smith, owned several coalmines in the Blocton vicinity. But coal mining was not for my father. He said at times the shaft was so narrow, he had to lie on his stomach to work. Then there were times that the overhead would "work," and there was danger that the whole overhead would come down on top of the miners. This was in the days before the present-day mining laws were enacted. At any rate, my father longed to be out in the sunshine and working with animals. He had already saved enough money to buy a small herd of cattle, which he ran on the free range near Blocton. These were later sold, but he always retained his love of animals.

Early in 1912, Joseph Horace Seales left Bibb County and moved to Jefferson County, where he spent the rest of his life. He worked in the timber woods for Tom Hill. He and his brother Martin worked as partners, and it was said that they made more money than anyone else in the woods. The two of them could fell a very large tree and in the course of a day, remove the branches, saw it into lengths of about five feet and split the lengths into mining props. These were used to prop the mine overheads so they didn't fall in on the miners.

Soon after moving to Jefferson County, he met my mother, Margie Eugenia Porter, daughter of John William Porter and Margaret Fatima Thomas. Her mother had died when she was very small, and at the time my father met her, she was living in the house with her father, his second wife, and their brood of six, which eventually grew to nine, and she was the unpaid help.

After about a three-month courtship, they were married on August 21, 1912, the ceremony performed by my mother's uncle, Rev. William Harrison Sturdivant, who was living at Bamford and had his own church there. He had the couple stand in front of the huge fireplace in the parlor, facing in the direction that the boards in the floor ran, for good luck, he said. My mother's stepmother had gone with them and served as a witness, the other witness being Rev. Sturdivant's sister-in-law, who was living with them and helping in the house, since his wife, Cynthia Ray Sturdivant was an invalid confined to a wheel chair. The marriage was to last for a lifetime, and the couple was to prosper far beyond their expectations.

During the first year of their marriage, my parents lived on the old Elijah Cost place at Bamford, not far from her uncle William, and their first child was born there. It was a prosperous year for them. They farmed, and my father would sell what they raised in the small towns in Shelby County. My mother said that times were good, and they could sell anything they had with no trouble. After one crop-year, however, they moved back to Genery's Gap, where she had grown up, and bought ten acres from Tom Hill, the timber man my father had worked for, with a small weatherboard house where the timber workers had lived. They improved the land and farmed, and in a matter of a few years built a much larger and better house further down the hill, and that is where we all grew up.

The original house was enlarged and made into a dairy barn, and the fields were turned into pastures, and for a few years they ran a dairy, with my father selling the milk and butter in Bessemer. Their next venture was chicken farming. This was when I was very small, but I can remember the little white biddys and the brooders we had to keep them in to keep them warm, the hatchers, feeders, and the big chicken house that was built to house them. They were all White Leghorns, and the hill where we lived was always white with chickens. Later on, I had to gather the eggs, and what a job that was. We would pack them into crates holding thirty dozen each, which my father would sell in Bessemer.

I suppose any reader of this account will have gotten the idea by now that my parents did whatever it took to make money, as long as it was honest, and that is the way it was. Sometime during the Depression they started getting out of the chicken and egg business and started buying cattle. They had bought property in Shelby County, and ran the cattle there. For about ten years while the Depression held the country in its grip, we also reverted to dirt farming in order to survive. We raised corn, peas, tomatoes, and many other kinds of vegetables and my father sold the excess in Bessemer. He always butchered for the markets in Bessemer, as well as for our own use, so we bought very little for the kitchen except flour, sugar, salt and coffee.

They also, during the Depression, bought up various tracts adjoining the small original tract. We survived the ordeal of the Depression, and came out better off than before. My father helped many people who had been unable to feed their families. Some would ask, but a few just went in the fields and took what they needed, but these incidents were few. Most people were very honest. With the cattle, it seemed that my father had found his true calling, and from then on, he lived the life of a cattleman, attending auctions, wheeling and dealing, for the rest of his life. He died on October 27, 1967, and my mother died on April 4, 1982. Both are buried in the Genery's Cemetery, a short distance from their home, and the graves are marked. They were the parents of eight children as follows:

> (a) Velma Elizabeth Seales, born May 19, 1914, in Shelby County, Alabama, graduated University of Montevallo, B.S. degree. She spent her career as a teacher in the Jefferson County schools. She was married on August 21, 1936, to Walter Dean Carter, born September 6, 1912, in Shelby County, Alabama, son of Reuben Green Carter and Viola Baker. He died on January 20, 1979, and is buried in the Genery's Cemetery at Genery's Gap. He was a veteran of WWII, and spent his career with US Steel. They had two children:
>
>> (aa) Elizabeth Lou, born March 16, 1938, in Jefferson County, Alabama, married Joseph E. Weeks, born May 3, 1937, son of Clarence and Virginia Hereford Weeks. They have three children:
>>
>> (aa1) David Shane Weeks married Tammy Jean Wingard, and they have two children:
>>
>> (aa1a) Shane Weeks.
>>
>> (aa1b) Tamara Weeks.
>>
>> (aa2) Dawn Marguerite Weeks married Troy Curtis, and has two children:

(aa2a) Crystal Curtis.

(aa2b) Kasi Curtis.

(aa3) Michael Kavell Weeks married Tammy Gail Smith, and they have one child:

(aa3a) Alex Weeks.

(ab) Margaret Ann Carter, the second child of Walter Carter and Velma Elizabeth Seales, was born on February 25, 1943, in Jefferson County, Alabama. She married Wayne Dunkin, and has two children:

(ab1) Derrick Wayne Dunkin married Suzanne Stanton and they have one child:

(ba1a) Devin Dunkin.

(ab2) Randall Lee Dunkin.

(b) Hazel Jane Seales, the second child of Joseph Horace Seales and Margie Eugenia Porter, was born on October 4, 1916, and died on November 24, 1918, in the flu epidemic that swept the country and the world that year.

(c) Mary Madge Seales, the third child, was born on March 4, 1920, in Jefferson County, Alabama, and graduated from Birmingham-Southern College. She married William Francis Pettit of Los Angeles, California, a veteran of World War II and the Korean conflict. They have one daughter:

(ca) Holly Frances Pettit, born January 19, 1962, in the state of Washington. Holly is a graduate of Florida State University, with a MDiv. Degree from Harvard University. She married Laurence Lutton, a native of Massachusetts, and lives near Boston. She is a novelist and poet.

(d) Joseph Horace Seales, Jr., the fourth child, was born on March 26, 1924, in Jefferson County, Alabama. He is a veteran of WWII, Eighth Air Force. He was married on February 28, 1947, at Bessemer, Alabama, to Dorothy Nell Stephens, born September 23, 1926, and they had three children:

(da) William Joseph Seales, called "Little Bill," born April 7, 1948; drowned in Cahaba River on June 1, 1957 at age 9; buried in Genery's Cemetery.

(db) Horace Dale Seales, born February 19, 1950, in Jefferson County, Alabama; married Becky Wilson of Orange County, California; two children:

(db1) Charity Lynne.

(db2) Jason Dale.

(dc) The third child, Michael Glen Seales, was born on March 29, 1956, married Rita Jones, of Shelby County, and has two children:

(dc1) Jennifer Michelle.

(dc2) Christy.

(e) Eugene Thomas Seales, the fifth child of Joseph Horace Seales and Margie Eugenia Porter, was born on July 26, 1926, in Jefferson County, Alabama. He is a veteran of WWII, Navy. He was married on July 16, 1951 in Columbus, Mississippi, to Gladys Theo Garner, born April 26, 1930 in Shelby County, Alabama. His career was with the Pullman-Standard Car Co., in management. He is also a cattleman, and is active in community affairs. They have two children:

(ea) Brenda Gale, born December 12, 1955, married first to Charles Beck, one child:

(ea1) Kevin DeWayne.

Brenda married secondly Ivey Warren.

(eb) Thomas Jeffrey Seales, the second child of Eugene Seales and Gladys Garner was born March 3, 1960, never married.

(f) William Sturdivant Seales, the sixth child of Joseph Horace Seales and Margie Eugenia Porter, was born on July 6, 1929 in Jefferson County, Alabama. He is a veteran of the Korean War, in which he was in anti-aircraft. His career has been in insurance and investments. He was married on July 18, 1958 to Billie Jean Sides, born

September 19, 1932 in Walker County, Alabama. She spent her career in teaching. They have two children:

    (fa) William Keith Seales, born December 25, 1959, in Bessemer, Alabama.

    (fb) John Scott Seales, born May 14, 1965.

(g) Evie Lorene Seales, the seventh child, was born on October 2, 1931 in Jefferson County, Alabama. She is a graduate of Birmingham-Southern College, with a masters degree from Samford University. Her career has been in teaching and business. She was married on December 20, 1952 in Birmingham, Alabama, to Rev. Samuel Allen Balch, Jr. He is a graduate of Birmingham-Southern College, with an MDiv. from Emory University. They have four children:

    (ga) Hilda Carol, born April 4, 1955.

    (gb) Barbara Lynne, born October 28, 1956, died in 1983.

    (gc) Anne Marie, born August 8, 1958.

    (gd) Dawn Elizabeth, born November 17, 1966.

(h) James Riley Seales, the eighth child of Joseph Horace Seales and Margie Eugenia Porter, was born on October 31, 1932, in Jefferson County, Alabama. He is a veteran of the Korean War, Naval Advisory Group, Tiawan and Formosa. His career was with Eastern Air Lines. He was married in September, 1964, to Betty Bailey of Tampa, Florida, and they have one child:

    (ha) Julie Christine Seales, born March 15, 1966. Julie has two children:

        (ha1) Brandon Michael.

        (ha2) Christopher.

(7) Jessie Mae Seales, the youngest child of William Thomas Seales and Elizabeth Tabitha Smith, was born on July 11, 1890, and died on April 20 1901. She is buried in the Mount Carmel Cemetery at West Blocton, Alabama, and the grave has a marker.

This is the end of the line of William Thomas Seales, so now we revert to the line of his parents, John B. and Matilda Seale, and begin with his sixth child.

(F) Mahala Seale, the sixth child and third daughter of John B. Seale and his wife Matilda, was born in Bibb County, Alabama in 1855. In 1870, she was living in the home of her brother, Barnabas Bass Seale. It is thought that she migrated to Arkansas, as there is no further record of her in Alabama.

(G) Matthew Seale, their eighth child, was born in Bibb County, Alabama in 1857. As a young man, he migrated to Arkansas. I remember hearing as a child that he had established a trucking business in the town of Little Rock, and that he had sons who were carrying on the business. I also remember my father speaking of a trip he and some of his brothers had made to Little Rock on horseback when he was a teenager, to visit their uncle Matthew, for whom they had a very great affection. However, I have not been able to trace Matthew or his descendants.

This completes the John B. Seale family, so now we revert to the family of his father, Thomas Seale, Jr., which we complete with these entries for David Seale and Isaac Hopkins Seale.

(V) David Seale, the fifth child of Thomas Seale, Jr. and his wife Ader, who survived to adulthood, was born in Marion County, Mississippi in 1810. He was married in Wilcox County, Alabama on January 1, 1832, to Mary Parrott, who was also called "Polly."

David died between 1851 and 1853, and Mary died between 1852 and 1853. They were on the 1850 census for Bibb County, Alabama together; their seventh child, Mortimore was born in 1852, so Mary was still living at that time. By October 1853, when Thomas Jr.'s estate was settled, they were both deceased. At that time, a sum of money was settled on David's children, and John Seale, David's brother, was named administrator. David and Mary were the parents of eight children. Their names and what is known of them follows:

(A) Susan J. Seale, born 1833, married Gilbert Mason on June 24, 1852 in Bibb County, Alabama.

(1) James A. Seale, born 1835 in Bibb County, Alabama. He served in the Confederate Army, Co. C, 10th Alabama Infantry, captured at Talladega, Alabama on April 22, 1865, signed an oath and was released. Nothing further is known. He may have died soon after the Civil War, or he may have gone west, as many Alabamians did during reconstruction, but no record has been found.

(B) Elizabeth Seale, the third child of David Seale and Mary Parrott, was born in 1837 in Bibb County, Alabama. She married David Adams on January 15, 1858, in Shelby County, Alabama. These two are buried in the "Adams Monument" in the Randall-Richardson Cemetery in Calera, Alabama.

I found this landmark quite by accident one day, just poking around in what I knew to be a very old Shelby County Cemetery. It is a very large man-made mound, resembling an Indian mound, and is located on the exact geographical center of the state of Alabama. There's no way these graves could ever be lost, as long as the state of Alabama is in existence.

I was told by locals that the monument was built by a grieving relative (a son?) who had moved the graves there from elsewhere, then carried the dirt for the mound from quite some distance away, by using a yoke, which he fitted over his shoulders. From the yoke was suspended two buckets, in which he carried the dirt, obviously making uncountable trips. When the mound was finished, a grave marker was placed on top. On one side is "Elizabeth Seale 1833-1890", and on the other side, "David Adams (1822-1891)."

(C) David Seale, Jr., the fourth child of David Seale and Mary Parrott was born in 1838 in Bibb County, Alabama. He was not included in the list of David and Mary's children in the 1850 census, so he probably was living with relatives in Pontotoc County, Mississippi or elsewhere, doing farm work. In the 1880 census, he was in Yazoo County, Mississippi census, page 32, line 12; his age given as 42, his wife Mary, 37, and three children, Anne W., age 13, Emma J., age 10, and Mattie L., age 5, all born in Alabama.

(E) Martha Seale, the fifth child of David Seale and Mary Parrott, was born in 1840 in Bibb County, Alabama. Nothing further is known of her.

(F) Sara F. Seale, the sixth child of David Seale and Mary Parrott, was born in 1843 in Bibb County, Alabama. In the 1860 census, she was living in the home of Thomas Gayland, working as a domestic, her age given as 16. (Bibb County census, page 86, household 582, family 576). Nothing further is known of her.

(G) Lucinda C. Seale, the seventh child, was born in 1850, in Bibb County, Alabama. In the census of 1860, she was living in the home of Palmore Kendrick in Bibb County. Nothing further is known of her.

(H) Mortimore Seale, the eighth child, was born in 1852 in Bibb County. In the census of 1860, he was living in the home of Palmore Kendrick and listed as age 8. Nothing further is known of him.

(VI) Isaac Hopkins Seale, the only child of Thomas Seale, Jr. by his second wife, Jane Jameston Dorse, was born in 1848 in Perry County, Alabama. On October 14, 1850, following the death of his father, his name appears in the court records of Perry County, when Drury Muse was appointed his guardian. This guardianship was later transferred to Wiley W. Fowler. In 1860 he appears on the census for Perry County with his mother and her new husband, John C. Vedle, and her father, Isaac Jameston, then age 80. Isaac Hopkins' age was given as 12. On April 14, 1870, Isaac Hopkins discharged his guardian, W. W. Fowler. He was married soon afterward to Martha Caddell. Beginning in 1875, which is as far back as the church records have been kept, his name appears in the history of Bethlehem Church, where he served as church clerk. This church is located not far from the old Thomas Seale, Jr. homestead. In 1880, the family appears on the census for Perry County, and In 1885, he received a land patent there. Sometime between then and

1900 he migrated to Houston County, Texas, after selling the old homestead to his cousin, Charles Seale, of Butler County, grandson of Rev. William Seale. Charles' descendants still live in the area. As for Isaac Hopkins, he and Martha became the parents of nine children, and I understand from other researchers that he has approximately 400 descendants living in the area of Maud, Texas today. Their nine children were:

(A) Drusillah (1871).

(B) Geneva (1875).

(C) Helen (1877).

(D) Nancy Jane (1878).

(E) Mary L. (1879).

(F) Thomas Jefferson (1882).

(G) H. M. (1885).

(H) Alma E. (1891).

(I) H. H. (1894).

Information on the Seale family is from my own research, with help from other researchers so numerous I couldn't name them all. Of special help to me were Mr. Wright Seal of Salt Lake City, Utah, Joyce Jones Seal of Picayune, Mississippi, and Nancy Keuhl of Nacogdoches, Texas. The Seale family is probably as well documented as any family in America, with numerous histories in print, most notably Seals From All Around, *by Joyce Jones Seal, and* A Seale Anthology *by Nancy Keuhl.*

JOHN SMITH

John Smith was one of the very first white men to enter the area that later became the old county of Cahawba and later Bibb County. According to his records with the Revolutionary War pension board, he settled in the area in 1797. He had been a private in the regiment of Col. William Thompson in the South Carolina Continental Line, service no. 32526. His name was placed on the pension roll on May 29, 1832, and he was paid retroactively from March 4, 1831, at the rate of eighty dollars a year. He evidently did not draw his pension for very long, since on October 17, 1832, he made declaration in Bibb County, Alabama saying he had been stricken from the pension roll because of property. He had applied under the act of June 17, 1832, his age at that time given as 73.

The Smiths did become fabulously wealthy in Bibb County, owning large tracts of land, and later developing the coal resources on these lands. Some of his property may have been from inherited wealth that he brought from the Carolinas. His ancestors had all owned large plantations and many slaves there, and he no doubt had received a land grant for his Revolutionary service. By this time, also, John had been in the area for thirty-five years, and likely had acquired considerable wealth on his own.

John Smith was born in Halifax County, North Carolina in 1759, died in Bibb County, Alabama in 1833, and was most likely buried on the home place, this being in the vicinity of what is now called Smith Hill, a part of West Blocton, Alabama. He was a brother to my great-great-great-grandfather, Uriah Smith, both being the sons of Peter Smith, who died in Halifax County in 1794, three years before John's migration to Alabama.

Sometime before the Revolutionary War, John and his brother Zachariah moved to the old Ninety Sixth District of South Carolina, and he joined the Continental Line there. There was one John Smith, a Revolutionary Soldier from South Carolina who earned such a fierce reputation during the war that he came to be called "Hell Nation Smith," or "Hellstone Smith," but there is no proof that this was the same individual.

After the war, John served on the jury in South Carolina in 1789. His wife was Mary Long, whom he married in Santee, South Carolina in 1782. Mary Long must have been a hardy soul, for it was extremely rare for a pioneer, in 1797, to bring his family into the wilderness that would one day become Bibb County, and live among the Indians. The white settlers didn't begin coming in any appreciable numbers until about 1815.

In the census of 1850 for Bibb County, Alabama, Mary Smith, age 87 was living in the household of her daughter Frances and her husband, Noah Foshee. The 1830 census was the last time John appeared. Beyond this, little is known of John Smith. However, the land on which he and his brother Uriah (who eventually joined him) settled and produced large families eventually came to be called "Smith Hill."

As time went on and the coal fields of Bibb County came to be exploited, Smith Hill became a section of a much larger place called Blocton, supposedly named for a block of coal weighing a ton that was taken from one of the mines there. Later, as the coal fields were exhausted, Blocton faded, and a part of town called West Blocton gained in prominence. Today, this is the name that is on the maps, and "Blocton" and "Smith Hill" are rarely heard, but there was a time when it was different: Smith Hill was a place of some import, and the name "Smith" was one to be reckoned with in Bibb County. John Smith is known to have had a large family, but since he left no will, the names of all his children are not known. The names that are known are:

- William.
- Wiley.
- Samuel.
- James.
- Frances.

This Smith line is said to have come originally from Scotland, where they were a sept of the McGowan clan. The name itself is one of the oldest in the world, being an occupational name and having been in existence three thousand years ago when the Israelites fought the Philistines and lost, and thereafter were not allowed to have any smiths, that is, workers in metal who might forge swords and other armaments. That, one might imagine, is why David in the Biblical story had to resort to a slingshot as a means to kill the giant Goliath.

The first Smith of this line to come to America was:

(I) Alexander Smith, son of Joseph Smith.

Born about 1620 in Scotland, he died about 1690 in Middlesex County, Virginia. His wife was Anne Cox, who was born in England, and whom he may have married in England before sailing from the port of Bristol. He is known to have had a brother John Smith. On September 1674, he received a grant of 110 acres in Middlesex County, adjoining land he already owned, for bringing three persons into the colony: Elizabeth Royland, Phillip Powell, and John Day. In 1797 one Alexander Smith (a grandson?) witnessed a deed for Mitchell Dooley in Edgefield County, South Carolina.

Although there probably were others, Alexander and Anne had only one child whose name is known to us:

    (A) Nicholas Smith.

Nicholas Smith was born about 1680 in Middlesex County, Virginia, and died on October 12, 1757 in Essex County. His wife was Anne Cox, and they were the parents of six children:

    (1) Francis.

    (2) Nicholas, who was one of the very first settlers in the ceded lands of Wilkes County, Georgia. At the time he had a wife and five daughters. He settled on one hundred acres on Fishing Creek, and lived in a cabin that had been built by John Dooley, who was murdered by Creek Indians.

    (3) Samuel.

    (4) Susannah, who married James Medley, son of James Medley, Sr. and his wife Eleanor and had a son John Medley and a daughter Ann Medley.

    (5) Ruth, who married a Saile.

    (6) Lucy, who married a Dunn.

The only one of these about whom anything further is known is child #1, Francis Smith, who was born in 1720 and died on March 15, 1762 in Essex County, Virginia, leaving a will in which he divided his land and eighty slaves among his children.

He was married first to Lucy Meriweather and secondly to Ann Adams, and had six children:

    (a) Francis.

    (b) William.

    (c) Meriweather.

    (d) Ann.

(e) Mary, married James Webb and had a son, Francis Webb.

(f) Elizabeth, married William Young.

The line descends through child #3, Samuel Smith.

Samuel Smith, who was known as Captain Samuel Smith, was born about 1700 in Middlesex County, Virginia, and died about 1775 in either Middlesex or Essex counties. His wife was Anne Amis, and they had four known children as follows:

(a) Samuel Smith II, who was known as Col. Samuel Smith, was born on December 3, 1729 in Essex County, Virginia, and died on October 6, 1800 in Granville County, North Carolina, where he was a planter and a justice of the peace in the area of Adam's Plains.

His wife, whom he married in May 1761, was Mary Webb, born October 21, 1740 in Essex County, Virginia, died November 20, 1827 in North Carolina, the daughter of James Webb, born in Essex County in 1705 and his wife Mary Edmondson.

Samuel and Mary were the parents of eleven children. They were:

(aa) Anne Smith, born May 9, 1762, Essex County, Virginia.

(ab) Mary Smith, born September 18, 1762, Essex County, Virginia, married William Williamson in February 1800, died March 21, 1814, Adams County, Ohio.

(ac) Samuel Smith III, born September 25, 1763 in Virginia, died June 4, 1816 in Caswell County, North Carolina, married Elizabeth Harrison on May 15, 1792, who was born February 20, 1772, died December 17, 1838 in Caswell County, North Carolina.

(ad) Elizabeth Smith, born April 7, 1767 in North Carolina, died September 17, 1804, Granville County, North Carolina, married James Downey.

(ae) Jane Smith, born October 7, 1768 in North Carolina, died June 1813 in Caswell County, North Carolina, married Alexander Murphy.

(af) James Webb Smith, born May 18, 1770, Granville County, North Carolina, died after 1850 in Jackson County, Tennessee, married first Polly Downey and secondly Polly Webb.

(ag) John Granville Smith, born March 5, 1772, in Granville County, North Carolina, died October 2, 1828, same place, never married.

(ah) William Smith, born June 2, 1774 in North Carolina, died June 4, 1818 in Warren County, North Carolina, married Lethy Eaton and had a son, William Smith, Jr., born October 1, 1817, died June 10, 1827. Lethy Eaton married secondly Maj. Pugh. She died in May, 1831 in Granville County, North Carolina.

(ai) Maurice Smith, born May 6, 1776, Granville County, North Carolina, died May 21, 1835, married first Frances Goodwin, born December 1, 1788 in North Carolina, and secondly Amy Webb on April 10, 1829. She was born on August 31, 1794.

(aj) Thomas Smith, born February 9, 1779, Granville County, North Carolina, died September 27, 1794.

(ak) Alexander Smith, born February 11, 1781, Granville, North Carolina, died December 25, 1827, married Anne Alexander Beasley on September 12, 1811 in Granville County. They had only one child, Sarah Pomfret Smith who married her first cousin, Samuel Smith Downey, son of Elizabeth Smith and James Downey.

Samuel Smith Downey had married first Jane Harrison, half-sister to Elizabeth Harrison, who married Samuel Smith, another first cousin of both. Sarah and Samuel Downey had only one child, Anne Alexander Downey. She married Hilliard Davis. (from *Genealogies of Virginia Families*, Vol.III by Pinkethman-Tyler, Pages 295-301.)

(b) William Smith, second son of Samuel Smith and Anne Amis, was born about 1740, settled in Moore County,

North Carolina. He was living there before the Revolution, and died there sometime after 1790.

He had four known children:

>(ba) William, a Revolutionary soldier, born 1763 in Moore County.
>
>(bb) Zachariah.
>
>(bc) John.
>
>(bd) Mary, called "Polly," who married a Patterson.

(c) Nicholas Smith, who settled in Moore County, North Carolina.

(d) Peter Smith, born about 1720, who lived out his life in Halifax County, North Carolina. The line descends through child #4, Peter Smith.

Peter Smith was born about 1720, and died on September 25, 1799 in Halifax County, North Carolina, leaving a will. (Will of Peter Smith, Halifax County, North Carolina, Will Book 1, page 233, 1794 November Court.) His wife's name was Mary, and according to the will, they had eight children:

>(da) Uriah Smith. Born about 1750 in North Carolina, was in Alabama by 1820. His descendants will be delineated in the material on Uriah Smith.
>
>(db) Zachariah Smith, born about 1752 was a soldier in the Revolution, serving in the North Carolina Line. After the war he moved to Williamson County, Tennessee. In 1840 at age 81, he was living in the household of Charles S. McCall, according to a survey of Revolutionary pensioners in Tennessee in that year.
>
>His son:
>
>>(db1) Alexander Smith, was one of the Tennessee Volunteers under General Andrew Jackson, who came into Alabama and fought in the Battle of Horseshoe Bend, the final great battle of the Creek wars. (*Roster of Soldiers in the Battle of Horseshoe Bend*, National Archives, Washington D.C.)

(dc) Peter Smith, born about 1756.

(dd) John Smith, a Revolutionary soldier, born about 1759. John was the Alabama pioneer who is the subject of this piece. Refer to the beginning.

(de) Francis Smith, born about 1765.

(df) Anna Smith, who married a Guthrey.

(dg) Elizabeth Smith, who married a Parker.

(dh) Susanna Smith, who married a Rose.

This completes the John Smith line so far as it has been figured out. Many from this line went west, and little is known of the more recent generations. More is known of the descendants of his brother Uriah, who also settled in Alabama, and with John was a founder of Smith Hill.

Information on the John Smith line is from personal knowledge, and research by Madge Pettit.

URIAH SMITH

Uriah Smith, the oldest son of Peter Smith and his wife Mary, was born in Halifax County, North Carolina between 1740 and 1750.

The first record of him as an adult was in 1786, when he appeared on the census for Halifax County in January of that year, with his wife, two sons and two daughters. On September 24th of 1794, he was named in the will of his father, and identified as a son. (North Carolina Wills 1728-1824, Will # 492, p.233). On October 13th of 1795 he was one of the executors of the will of Richard Norwood of Halifax, North Carolina, who identified him as his brother-in-law. Since Richard Norwood was unmarried, this means that Uriah's wife was a Norwood. One Richard Norwood Smith was one of the executors of the will of Zachariah Smith in 1822, so Zachariah's wife may also have been a Norwood.

After 1795, Uriah migrated to South Carolina, but by 1820, he was in Limestone County, Alabama, and appeared on the census there. By 1830, he had joined his brother John in Bibb County, Alabama, where he appeared on the census, age 80-90, his wife age 60-70, with a young couple age 20-30 and a child under age 5 in the house with them. Next door was their son, William Smith, age 50-60.

In Limestone County, their son Uriah Smith, Jr., was on the census as he had been in 1820, now age 50-60, his wife age 40-50, four daughters and two sons, (Limestone County Census, page 32.) Living nearby was Joseph Norwood, possibly a first cousin, age 50-60, no wife, four daughters and two sons. Later that same year this same Uriah appeared on the census for Bibb County, age 50-60, wife age 30-40, two sons and one daughter, and an elderly male, age 80-90 in the household. This was Uriah Smith, son of Peter Smith, his wife having died since the census began earlier in the year and his son Uriah having moved from Limestone to Bibb.

In 1840, Uriah Smith, son of Peter Smith, did not appear on the census. He would have been 90-100 years old at this time, had he been alive. By 1846, his son Uriah, Jr. had also died and the settlement of his estate was recorded in Limestone County, Alabama. He died intestate, and Alexander Smith, probably a grandson, was one of the administrators, the widow having relinquished her right to administer in favor of him, Paul Robbins, and George W. Miller.

Uriah is thought to have had nine children, but since he left no will, this list is subject to errors. The nine are thought to have been:

SOME ALABAMA PIONEERS

(I) Mary Smith, born 1790-1800, married William R. McElroy on December 19, 1825.

(II) Uriah Smith, born in 1804 in Georgia, died 1860-70, Bibb County, Alabama, married Nancy Meadows, born 1809 in Georgia.

(III) Riley Smith, born 1802 in Georgia, died 1860-70 in Bibb County, Alabama, and married Mary Tillery.

(IV) Archibald Smith, born 1800-1810, married Sara Reach.

(V) Joshua Smith, married Rebecca Hamilton January 28, 1829, Bibb County, Alabama.

(VI) Senah Smith, born about 1800, married Elisha Jones.

(VII) Samuel Smith, born 1790-1800, died before 1840.

(VIII) Peter Smith, born 1790-1800.

(IX) Wiley Smith, born 1800-1810.

In the nineteenth century, the Smiths from this line probably numbered in the hundreds in Bibb County. They all had very large families and all tended to give their children the same names. There are Uriahs, Elizabeths, Johns and Archibalds in numbers that are confounding to researchers. For this reason I decline to sort them all out, but will stick to the two that I do know, that is, Uriah III and his brother Riley. Riley's daughter Elizabeth married my grandfather William Thomas Seales, and Uriah's daughter Elizabeth married his brother, John Anderson Seales. As you can see, they did tend to give their children the same names. Since Riley was the older of the two, his family will be given first.

Riley Smith was born in Georgia in 1802, the son of Uriah Smith. He died during the Civil War era, and it is not known whether he died from natural causes, or from some of the violence that was rampant in Bibb County, Alabama at this time, from southern scalawags and renegade northern soldiers turned marauders. It is not known where he was buried, but it probably was on the home place, as Mount Carmel Cemetery had not been established at that time. He was married to Mary Tillery, daughter of Wiley Tillery, who had migrated to Alabama with the Smiths. Mary was a midwife, born in North Carolina in 1808. She died at a very advanced age and is buried in Mount Carmel Cemetery, where she was one of the very early burials. She is buried very near Charity Holland, who was the very first burial. On her tombstone she is identified as the wife of Riley Smith.

They were the parents of nine children:

(A) John R. Smith, born 1829. Nothing further is known. He is thought to have died in the Civil War.

(B) William R. Smith, born 1832, married Kissiah Reach on February 22, 1852.

(C) Theresa M. Smith, born 1834, married William Lawrence on June 16, 1843.

(D) Uriah Smith, born December 6, 1838, married Martha J.; Uriah died in the woods near Blocton, and was buried where he died. The town of Blocton later grew up around his gravesite, and today his grave is in a residential area of Blocton.

On the day he died, he was hunting in the woods accompanied by his dog, which was always with him. The family thought at the time that what happened was that the dog had made a sudden move or somehow frightened Uriah, who lost his balance, fell backward, became wedged between two trees and stayed there and died. He has descendants, but their names are not known.

(E) Mary Jane Smith, born 1840, married Levin Stewart. He died in the Civil War, scalded to death in a kitchen accident. They had one child, a daughter, Nancy Jane Stewart, who married William Henderson, who became a wealthy farmer in Shelby County, had large herds of hogs and cattle, and was an excellent blacksmith. He died of typhoid fever.

They had seven children, but all died young but two daughters. Four daughters died of tuberculosis and their only son was shot by a Miller boy in Shelby County, and died 24 hours later. For more on the Henderson descendants, see the material on the Ammons family.

After the death of Levin Stewart, his wife Mary Jane married John Redd and had several more children, plus John had some before they were married. Not being sure which children came from which of John Redd's marriages, I have listed them together here:

- William.

- Bud (who became a member of the Bart Thrasher gang which terrorized Bibb County in the 1880's).

- Al.

- John (a preacher, he married Minnie Lawley. He lived for years in Detroit, Michigan after everyone in Bibb County thought he was dead.)
- George.
- Joe (died young—never married.)
- Azalie (died in an Oklahoma prison, serving a life term for killing her son-in-law, thought to have been wrongly accused)

The preceding information on the Redd family is from a telephone conversation with Mae Ammons in 1981.

(F) Nancy A. Smith, born 1842, married a Cox.

(G) Rufus Smith, born 1846, married Emeline Wheeler, a relative of General Joe Wheeler of Civil War fame, thought by military historians to have been the greatest tactical general in history.

Rufus became a multimillionaire in Bibb County, owning large tracts of land, several coal mines, and buildings in the town of Blocton. He became mayor of Blocton in 1910. He and Emeline had four daughters and a son, and the son inherited the entire estate, the daughters each getting one dollar, this according to his great-granddaughter.

(H) Elizabeth Smith, born 1848. This lady was my grandmother. She married William Thomas Seales on July 4, 1870 at the home of his brother John Anderson Seales near Blocton. William Thomas Seales was a farmer, a cattleman, and a lumberman. A complete history of this family may be found in the material on the Seale family.

(I) Amanda "Polly" Smith, born 1850, married Lafayette McCully about 1872. After his death, she married secondly James Reach.

Uriah Smith, the son of Uriah Smith, the son of Uriah Smith, the son of Peter Smith of Halifax County, North Carolina, and a brother to the above Riley Smith, was born in 1804 in Georgia, and died 1860-1870 in Bibb County, Alabama. On September 1, 1826, he married Nancy Meadows in Bibb County, Alabama. They became the parents of twelve children as follows:

(A) Sylvania Smith, born 1829, Bibb County, Alabama.

(B) Greenberry Smith, born in 1830, was a Civil War veteran. He married Frances A. Brent and had two children, Jasper and Mary. Then Frances died and Jasper was brought up by Greenberry's twin brother Leeberry and Frances' sister Julia Ann. John Brent, Frances' and Julia Ann's brother, was also a Civil War Veteran.

(C) Leeberry Smith, born 1830, a twin to Greenberry, married Julia Ann Brent, Frances Brent's sister.

(D) Jasper Smith, born 1832, married Frances Green.

(E) Newton Smith, born 1837.

(F) Mary (Polly) Smith born 1839.

(G) Thina Ann Smith, born 1840.

(H) Nancy Ann Smith, born 1841, married James Mills.

(I) Elizabeth Smith, born 1843, married John Anderson Seales, son of John B. Seales and his wife Matilda. The history of this family may be found in the material on the Seale family.

(J) Mariah C. Smith, born 1845.

(K) Job R. Smith, born 1846.

(L) Uriah P. Smith, born 1849.

Information on the Smith families is from research in the DAR Library in Washington D.C.; the National Archives; The Jack Ladson Genealogical Library in Vidalia, Georgia; several LDS libraries; Hayden Burns Library, Jacksonville, Florida; Will of Nicholas Smith, Will Book II, Page 19; Essex County, Virginia; Will of Francis Smith, Will Book II, Page 413-416, Essex County, Virginia; Will of Peter Smith, Halifax County, North Carolina, Will Book 1, page 233; Will of Zachariah Smith, Halifax County, North Carolina, Will Book V, page 681; 1830-1880 census records, Bibb County, Alabama; Bibb County Marriage Books; "William and Mary College Quarterly," IX, page 46; Bibb County, Alabama Court Records; Early census records for Halifax County, North Carolina; Census records for Limestone County, Alabama; Edgefield County, South Carolina; Minutes of the County Court, by Brent Holcomb; Revolutionary Soldiers in Alabama by DAR; "Hunting For Bears," Salt Lake City Utah.

Help also came from Linda Davis of Macon, Georgia, a descendant of John Anderson Seales and Elizabeth Smith; from Richard Patton of Pittsburgh, Pennsylvania, a descendant of Uriah Smith; from Elaine Stewart Henderson of Montgomery, Alabama, a decendant of Rufus Smith and Emeline Wheeler; and from Mae Ammons, a descendant of Mary Jane Smith and Levin Stewart.

SHERROD AARON STURDIVANT

The Sturdivant family is a very old and highly respected one in America, the first ones having arrived on these shores only about a decade after the pilgrims. They came here from England, and though no research has been done on this family's sojourn in that country, it is thought that they most likely descended from a Dutch trader who settled there. In America, the earliest ones were planters, but by the third American generation, this family was producing teachers, lawyers, doctors, and community leaders. Members of this family have served in every war America has fought, and as a group, they probably have done as much to make America what it is today as any other colonial family.

Sherrod Aaron Sturdivant, the Alabama pioneer with whom this entry is concerned, came into Alabama near the middle of the nineteenth century. He was a fourth great-grandchild of Daniel Sturdivant, who was born in 1600 in England, and descends through Daniel's son, John Sturdivant. John was born about 1627 in England, and died about 1695 in Henrico County, Virginia. He owned land in Henrico County as early as 1652, and later became an extensive landowner, some of it in partnership with one Christopher Robinson (probably a cousin), when the two of them received 600 acres for bringing 12 new settlers into the colony.

John had a brother, Daniel Sturdivant, born 1625, who was overseer of a 1400-acre plantation in James City County, Virginia, for Francis Newton, a London grocer. John's wife was Sarah Hallom, and they had five known children. John left no will, so these names have been culled from several different sources, including the will of Mary Thompson (mother of Ann Thompson), the will of Henry Sturdivant, and various genealogies of Virginia families. The five were:

(I) Daniel Sturdivant, born about 1670 in Henrico County, Virginia, died about 1750 in Prince George County, Virginia.

(II) Matthew Sturdivant, born about 1672 in Henrico County, Virginia.

(III) Chichester Sturdivant, born about 1675 in Henrico County, Virginia.

(IV) Henry Sturdivant, born in Henrico County, Virginia.

(V) John Sturdivant, born about 1680 in Henrico County, Virginia, died after 1753 in the same county, married Ann Thompson.

From here, the line descends through child #2, Daniel Sturdivant. In 1725, he purchased 250 acres from Hall and Elizabeth Hudson on Second Swamp, Bristol Parish, Virginia, next to land he already owned in Prince George County. The name of his wife is unknown, and since he left no will, the names of all his children are not known, but he is known to have had sons named William, Robert, and Allen.

The line descends through William. He was born about 1700 in Prince George County, Virginia, and died about 1768 in Dinwiddie County, Virginia. His wife's name was Frances, and they were the parents of eight children, whose names are taken from his will, which was probated in Dinwiddie County on October 29, 1768, and from the baptismal records in Albemarle Parish. Their names were:

    (A) James Sturdivant.

    (B) Robert Sturdivant, born 1752 in Dinwiddie County, Virginia, married Elizabeth Turner. (This couple was my fifth great-grandparents).

    (C) William Sturdivant.

    (D) Joel Sturdivant.

    (E) Mary Sturdivant.

    (F) Martha Sturdivant, who married John Pegram.

    (G) Sarah Sturdivant.

    (H) Elizabeth Sturdivant.

The line descends through child (B), Robert Sturdivant. Robert was born in 1752 in Dinwiddie County, Virginia, and died on September 6, 1808 in the same county. He was married about 1777 to Elizabeth Turner, born February 14, 1755. Like most of the early Sturdivants, Robert was a planter. He and Elizabeth became the parents of nine children, all born in Dinwiddie County, Virginia:

    (1) William Sturdivant, born February 21, 1778, married Martha Chedz.

    (2) Susan Sturdivant, born March 13, 1780, married William Hargrove.

    (3) John Sturdivant, born December 4, 1782, married Martha "Patsy" Hill Bass.

(4) Mary Sturdivant, born March 29, 1785, married Richard Inge.

(5) Martha Sturdivant, born February 29, 1788.

(6) Robert Sturdivant, born March 21, 1790.

(7) Joseph Sturdivant, born October 1, 1792.

(8) Aaron Sturdivant, born March 21, 1795.

(9) Charles Sturdivant, born February 5, 1798, died after 1860 in Lowndes County, Mississippi. He was married on June 2, 1825 in Mecklinburg County, North Carolina to Lucy A. Burwell. Charles was a physician. In the census of 1860, he was in Lowndes County, Mississippi. He had one known son, Armistead Sturdivant, born 1826, who married Bettie Baskerville, a widow with two children.

The line descends through child #3, John Sturdivant. John, who was my third great-grandfather, migrated to Georgia as a young man and settled in Putnam County, where he became a planter and justice of the peace. On November 24, 1808, he was married in Hancock County, Georgia, to Martha Hill Bass, who was called "Patsy," who was born about 1779, the daughter of Edward (or Edin) Bass, and granddaughter of Aaron Bass. She had a brother named Hartwell Bass. She is thought to have died in Troup County, Georgia about 1840. In the 1840 census, an elderly female was living in the household of Sherrod Aaron Sturdivant, Patsy's son, and this conceivably may have been Patsy.

John Sturdivant died on November 4, 1824 in Putnam County, Georgia, leaving a will (Will Book B, p. 24). He was 42 years old. He and Martha Hill Bass were the parents of five children. They were:

(a) Elizabeth Mary Sturdivant, born November 4, 1809 in Putnam County, Georgia, married Carlton G. Smith, son of Ralph Smith of Putnam County. He died eight years later, in 1835, in Upson County, Georgia.

(b) Sherrod Aaron Sturdivant, born August 31, 1811 in Jasper County, Georgia. Sherrod is the subject of this entry, and there will be more about him later.

(c) Joseph Allen Sturdivant, born April 28, 1813 in Putnam County, Georgia, fought in the Creek-Cherokee wars in Georgia, then lived among the Cherokees of north Georgia and married Aerie Beck, a Cherokee, then removed to Arkansas with the Cherokees and finally went on to California in the gold rush of 1849. He filed survivor's application #3456 in California on May 25, 1894 for Creek War service with the Georgia Volunteers. A copy of his letter written to the board indicates that he was well educated as were all the members of this family, and we must assume that they were all home educated.

(d) Robert Sturdivant, born May 30, 1815 in Putnam County, Georgia, joined his brother Joseph when he went to California in the gold rush. In California, he worked in the San Francisco mint, and married Ann M. ____.

(e) Martha W. Sturdivant, married Hiram J. Smith, a brother to Carlton G. Smith, on October 30, 1833.

Now let us return to Sherrod Aaron Sturdivant, the one member of this family who eventually migrated to Alabama. He spent his early years in Putnam County, Georgia. When he was thirteen years old, his father died, and since Sherrod was the oldest son, he had to take on responsibilities far beyond his years. Two years after his father's death, he and his brother Joseph joined the Georgia militia, and fought in the wars against the Creek Indians. After their military service, the brothers went to north Georgia and lived with the Cherokees. This was the era in which gold was being mined in north Georgia, especially in the area surrounding Dahlonega. The Indians had mined gold there since time immemorial, but now the white settlers had begun mining and created America's first gold rush.

About 1834, Sherrod Sturdivant was married in Georgia to Elizabeth Dooley, a Cherokee. Elizabeth had been born in Edgefield District, South Carolina, in 1810, daughter of James Dooley, an Indian agent, and Mary Ray, whose family was also Cherokee. On her father's side, Elizabeth was descended from Major John Downing, a British army officer, who had come to Augusta County, Virginia, as a soldier of the British king, then "sent to Caroline" (South Carolina), according to one reference, to represent British authority in the area. There he settled among the Indian towns on the upper reaches of the Saluda River in the old Ninety Sixth District. Major Downing married a full blood Cherokee of the Wolf Clan, and had a very large family. Then according to *Old Cherokee Families and Their Genealogy* by Emmett Starr (University of Oklahoma Foundations, 1968), one of his daughters married a Dooley, and as best I can figure out, taking all the available references into consideration, this was William

Dooley, grandfather of Elizabeth Dooley. Her father, James Dooley, was murdered in Lincoln County, Georgia in 1834, by one John Ray, who probably was an Indian trader. The account of this murder is recorded in *The Black Book of Georgia* by Robert Scott Davis.

In the 1830's when the Cherokees were rounded up and removed to a reservation, the Dooleys did not go. I am not sure if they were among the Eastern Cherokees (and incidentally, the Wolf Clan is one of the seven clans included in this group), who hid in the Great Smoky Mountains and refused to go, or whether they were granted amnesty because they had fought on the side of the U.S. Government during the Creek Wars. Be that as it may, I could find no name of a Dooley on any of the Indian Rolls that were compiled at the time of the removal.

Sherrod Sturdivant and Elizabeth settled for a time in De Kalb County, Georgia, in the area near Stone Mountain, and some of their children were born there. By 1840, however, he had moved into Troup County, and was living near his cousin, Joel Sturdivant, who owned a large plantation there. By 1860, he had moved again, this time to Shelby County, Alabama, where he settled on the Cahaba River, at a spot that is today called "Stine's Bend."

They lived there until after the Civil War, and several of their children died there. They are buried in an old Sturdivant-Henderson cemetery which they shared with Michael Henderson and his family, their close neighbors. Today the cemetery is in deep woods and in very poor condition, being on privately-owned land and without any maintenance.

Sherrod and Elizabeth seemed to prosper in Shelby County. Their children all received a good education, all home taught. Their son, William Harrison Sturdivant, later wrote in his autobiography when he was serving in the Alabama Legislature, that he only attended school about six weeks.

In the meantime, Sherrod's brother Joseph had married Aerie Beck, a Cherokee Indian, in Georgia. About 1835, he traveled in an official capacity to escort a group of Cherokees to Arkansas. His younger brother Robert went along. This group of Cherokees included some who had fought alongside the Sturdivant boys in the wars against the Creeks. Dragging Canoe, the famous Cherokee warrior, was in the group, and his name appears in the account of this group which was found in the University of Tennessee Library. They settled in Going Snake District in Arkansas, and remained there for about 14 years. In 1849, when news spread across the country of a gold strike in California, this group, who were already familiar with gold mining, set out for the gold fields of northern California. Their route covered approximately 2500 miles, and crossed the most difficult part of the Rocky Mountains.

In California, they settled on the Trinity River, in Trinity County. Joseph had a large ranch, so large in fact, that his ranch was a separate census district. He also was a miner, and ran a trading post on the Trinity River at a place called Arkansas Bar. His brother Robert went to San Francisco and became employed in the San Francisco mint, sold real estate, and was the census taker. In 1860, he married Ann M. ____, born 1841 in Alabama, and had six children:

> (1) Joseph H., born 1863.
>
> (2) Lillie M., born 1866.
>
> (3) Isabel A., born 1868.
>
> (4) Benjamin B., born 1870.
>
> (5) John T., born 1873.
>
> (6) Paul H., born 1875.
>
> Nothing is known of this family after 1900. In the earthquake of April 1906, 503 people died in San Francisco, but it is not known if any Sturdivants were among this number.

Joseph Sturdivant's wife, Aerie Beck, was of the Cherokee Grant Clan, which descends from Ludovic Grant, an Indian trader in the old Ninety-Sixth District, and was of the same generation as Maj. John Downing, mentioned earlier. She was a daughter of Jeffrey Beck and Susannah Buffington, Susannah being the daughter of Ezekiel Buffington and Mary Emory. Mary was the daughter of William Emory and his wife, who was a daughter of Ludovic Grant.

Joseph Sturdivant and Aerie Beck had five children:

> (1) John Calhoun Sturdivant, who married Elizabeth McLaughlin.
>
> (2) Martha Sturdivant, who married Ezekiel Beck.
>
> (3) Martin Butler Sturdivant, who married Matilda Barnett.
>
> (4) Sabra Sturdivant, who married Weatherford Beck.
>
> (5) Robert Sturdivant.

Joseph's brother Sherrod Sturdivant continued living in Shelby County, Alabama until after the Civil War. The war had devastated Shelby County, and there was much unrest. Many residents chose this time to move on westward. The Sturdivant family moved as far west as Mississippi. I have never been able to prove just where in Mississippi they settled, but reason tells me that they probably went to Lowndes County, where Sherrod's uncle Charles Sturdivant, a physician from Granville County, North Carolina, had settled some years earlier. All I have ever heard from relatives is that their new home was "just over the line" in Mississippi.

Sherrod Sturdivant died there before the 1870 census. No one knows exactly where he is buried, and the grave is not marked. This is not surprising, since everyone had been left poor by the war, and tombstones were not a priority. Untold numbers of graves from this era have been lost forever. Elizabeth returned to Shelby County, Alabama, and lived with her son, William Harrison Sturdivant. She died there in 1900 and is buried in the Sturdivant Cemetery next to her son, William Harrison Sturdivant, who was the only child of hers that was still living at the time.

My mother said she never saw her great-grandmother Elizabeth but once. She was only five years old at the time, and what she remembered was a little old lady who always sat in her rocking chair in the corner, smoking a pipe, and always wore her bonnet, even in the house. I have heard from other relatives that all the years she lived in Shelby County, she practically lived in the Shelby County Woods, gathering roots and herbs from which to make medicines to use when there was illness in the family. I have an idea it was also because she just loved the woods, and felt at home there, as did my mother. I wish I could have known her.

Sherrod and Elizabeth had a total of thirteen children, but only six lived to adulthood. They were:

> (1) George W. Sturdivant, born 1835, married Sarah Estes Harmon, a widow. He was a soldier of the Confederacy, was killed in the battle of First Manassas in 1862 and was buried on the battlefield. Sarah is buried in the Shiloh Cemetery in Shelby County, Alabama, and the grave is marked.
>
> (2) Mary Sturdivant, born 1843 in Georgia. Mary was my great-grandmother. She was married four times, and had one child by each husband.

Her first husband, Wesley Hinton, died in the Civil War. They had a son, Thomas Hinton, who was brought up by her brother, William H. Sturdivant, and went to Texas as a young man.

Her second husband was my great-grandfather, John Abraham "Ibzan" Porter, a Confederate soldier, whom she married in Mississippi soon after his return from the war. They had a son, John William Porter, who was brought up by John Thompson of Genery's Gap, Alabama. Ibzan Porter had died when his son was just three years old, from the abuse and exposure to disease he had suffered in a northern prison camp.

Mary's third husband was a Mann, and they had a daughter, Beulah, who was brought up by William H. Sturdivant.

Her fourth husband was Henry Bailey, Sr., and they had a son, Henry Bailey, Jr. Mary died in Tuscaloosa County, Alabama in 1893, while visiting some Sturdivant relatives, who were descendants of Randolph Sturdivant, a Revolutionary soldier from North Carolina. She is buried in the Shiloh Cemetery in Shelby County, Alabama.

> (3) William Harrison Sturdivant, born June 15, 1845, at Stone Mountain, Georgia. He grew up in the backwoods of Shelby County, Alabama, but was given a very good education, evidently taught by his father. I have seen deeds, marriage licenses, and various official documents that are in his handwriting, and he obviously was a well educated man. He married Cynthia Ray, daughter of Isaac Ray, of Shelby County. They had only one child, a daughter, who died in infancy. When the Civil War began, William Harrison Sturdivant enlisted in the Confederate Army in Shelby County, was later captured at the siege of Vicksburg, and sent to a northern prison camp. Conditions in the camp were terrible, and southerners were dying every day from killer diseases such as smallpox and dysentery. He was given a chance to get out of prison, and perhaps save his life, by joining the Union Army, with the proviso that he would never be asked to fight against any southerners. He grabbed the chance, and was subsequently sent to Leavenworth, Kansas, to help guard the frontier against the Indians. He was one of the relatively few soldiers (about 2000 in all), who fought for both the North and the South during this conflict. They came to be known as "Galvanized Yankees." After the war, he settled in Shelby County, where he became a fabulously wealthy man. He owned a plantation at Bamford, where he also ran the post office, owned a store, was the justice of the peace, and was a Baptist preacher. He had built his own church near his home, and preached there

every Sunday. According to family tradition, his land holdings reached from Bamford all the way to Cahaba River, and most of it was fine timber land. He served in the Alabama Legislature, and in 1913 ran for the U.S. Congress. The one picture I have of William Harrison Sturdivant shows him to have been a tall (probably 6'4"), thin man, and very handsome. He was wearing a suit that featured a frock coat, and with it he wore what was called a "plantation hat," which was made of Panama straw and had a brim about five inches wide, slightly curled upward at the edges. He had had all his teeth crowned with yellow gold. His smile must have been blinding.

He died of pneumonia at his home at Bamford on March 22, 1926, and is buried in the Sturdivant Cemetery, which was near the church he had built, but now the church is gone, as is the railway station, the post office, his old home, everything, and the cemetery is in deep woods, with pine trees eight inches in diameter having grown up around the graves. The graves are well marked, and William Harrison's marker is engraved with this poem: Remember youth, as you pass by/ As you are now, so once was I/ As I am now, so you will be/ Prepare for death, and follow me. More than one hunter has been given reason to think of his mortality as he was tramping through the woods and stumbled upon these graves.

I have found in my research that this same anonymous poem has been found on at least one grave in North Carolina. Cynthia Ray Sturdivant died in the 1940's and is buried beside her husband. Her tombstone also features a poem, but it is more of a tribute than an admonition.

   (4) Rebecca A. Sturdivant, born 1847 in Georgia.
   (5) Elizabeth "Sis" Sturdivant, born 1851 in Georgia.
   (6) Sallie Sturdivant, born 1857 in Georgia.

During the time that Sherrod Aaron Sturdivant spent in Alabama, there were several other Sturdivants also living in the state. All were cousins, but their exact lineage has been difficult to trace, since the early Sturdivants all seemed to have such large families, and tended to use the same family names over and over. To avoid the possibility of getting someone's lineage wrong, I merely list them here, with a minimum of information. They are:

- Allen Cannon Sturdivant: Allen Cannon was a blacksmith from New Bern, North Carolina. As a young man he moved to Georgia, where he was in the gold lottery in 1832 in Walton County, Albertson's District. He was married in Walton County, Georgia on January 14, 1838 to Vicey Fielder, daughter of John and Sallie (Casey) Fielder, and they migrated to Shelby

County, Alabama about 1840. He died in Shelby County, Alabama on March 7, 1878.

Vicey, who was born in 1817, died in 1887 in Shelby County. They had a large family, but only one, Arnold Cannon Sturdivant, is known to have reached adulthood. Several of their children are thought to have been buried in the Beaver Creek Cemetery in Shelby County. Allen Cannon may have been the son of Matthew Sturdivant, son of Henry Sturdivant, son of Matthew Sturdivant Jr., son of Matthew Sturdivant Sr., son of Hollum Sturdivant, but this is not proven. His son, Arnold Cannon Sturdivant, was born in 1854 in Shelby County, Alabama. He was married on December 14, 1884 in Elmore County, Alabama, to Ida Elizabeth Rawls, daughter of Jabez P. Rawls and Emma Gunn. They had one known child, Russian Edward Sturdivant, born 1901 in Shelby County, Alabama. Arnold Cannon was foreman of furnaces at Shelby Iron Works, which is no longer in existence. Not much is left of it but the old smoke stack.

- Hon. Allen Dudley Sturdivant: Allen Sturdivant was a judge in Dadeville, Tallapoosa County, Alabama for 26 years. Born in Troup County, Georgia on January 29, 1819, he was the son of Joel Sturdivant and Melinda Cochran. Joel Sturdivant, born in 1786 in Sussex County, Virginia, was the son of John S. Sturdivant, and Caroline Martha Hobbs. John S. Sturdivant was a Revolutionary soldier who had commanded a company of Marines on a row galley in the war. In 1819 he was granted 2,666.66 acres for his service during the war.

Joel Sturdivant owned a large plantation in Troup County, Georgia, where he raised a family of twelve children.

- Allen Dudley Sturdivant married Jane Caroline Clark in Troup County, Georgia. They became the parents of seven children:

    (1) Mary Sturdivant, born 1842, married Henry Agnew.

    (2) Robert Sturdivant, born 1845.

    (3) Martha J. Sturdivant, born 1848.

    (4) Charles J. Sturdivant, born 1851.

    (5) Joseph A. Sturdivant, born 1854.

    (6) Commodore Sturdivant, born 1855.

    (7) Thomas S. Sturdivant, born January 29, 1854 in Dadeville, Alabama; married Mary Corpew, daughter of C.E. Corpew, a Dadeville merchant, who had migrated from North

Carolina. Thomas owned a bank and mercantile business in Dadeville, and also had farming interests. He and Mary had four children:

(a) Herbert C., who became president of the Sturdivant Bank.

(b) Fred F., who became the bank cashier.

(c) Raymond, who became a professional baseball player, a bank director, and had farming interests.

(d) Helen, who died young, unmarried.

- Dempsey Sturdivant: Dempsey Sturdivant was married in Putnam County, Georgia on December 10, 1810, to Matilda Foster. He appeared in Shelby County, Alabama in 1859, when he received two land patents from the St. Stephens land office. He received two more in 1860. Two more, one in 1886 and one in 1890, may have been for his son, Dempsey, Jr. He may have been a brother to Allen Cannon Sturdivant. Other speculation is that he was a son of the Revolutionary soldier William Sturdivant and his wife Elizabeth Denton. None of this is proven.

- Matthew Parham Sturdivant: This Sturdivant was the first member of the Methodist faith, which was very new at this time, to set foot in the Alabama Territory, which would later become the state of Alabama.

In 1808, Matthew Parham Sturdivant was a young Methodist preacher, and a member of the Virginia Conference. When the conference met that year, 58 members were present, but when Bishop Asbury asked for volunteers to go into the Alabama Territory and preach to the settlers, Matthew Parham Sturdivant was the only one who volunteered. He was then sent to the country along the Tombigbee River, where there were no Methodists, not even any churches, and a population with a preponderance of refugees from the law.

Obviously, he was in great danger, not only from the criminal element, as he rode the circuit between the settlements, but from wild animals—panthers in particular—and from the elements. There were few bridges, and a horse could get swept away crossing a swollen stream. All of this was in addition to the cold, fatigue, and the hostility of many of those to whom he was sent to preach. His circuit included

Tensaw Lake, Wood's Bluff, Choctaw Corner, Thomasville, St. Stephen's, Suggsville, Coffeeville, and other pioneer settlements.

In December of 1808, he traveled to Georgia, to attend the South Carolina Conference, which was meeting at Liberty Chapel that year, with Bishop Asbury presiding. In front of this gathering, he reported how he had camped in the Alabama wilderness, slept on the ground, forded swollen streams, been in danger from the Indians, the wolves, bears, and panthers. Nevertheless, he was reappointed to Tombigbee, and was given a helper in the person of Michael Burdge. In 1810 he was appointed to Fayetteville, North Carolina, in 1811 to Sparta, Georgia. In 1813, he rejoined the Virginia Conference, and was sent to Franklin Circuit, North Carolina.

He was married on November 24, 1813 in Halifax County, Virginia, to Agnes Kent, daughter of William Kent. In February of 1814, he ceased to ride circuits, and lived in Pittsylvania County, Virginia, then in Amherst County, where he ran the Poor House from 1826 to 1831. He finally settled in Nelson County, Virginia, where he died as an honored local preacher at Massies Mill between 1850 and 1860, and is buried in an unmarked grave at Massies Mill. He last appeared on the census in 1850, and his age at that time was given as 74.

- Randolph Sturdivant: This Alabama pioneer was a Revolutionary soldier from North Carolina, who migrated to Tuscaloosa County, Alabama. Born about 1740 in North Carolina, he is thought to have been a son of Matthew Sturdivant, Jr., son of Matthew Sturdivant Sr., son of Hollum Sturdivant of Albemarle Parish, Sussex County, Virginia, but this is as yet unproven. He had one known son, John Sturdivant, who married Sally Harrison on September 24, 1829 in Tuscaloosa County, Alabama. This may have been his only son, for in the 1790 census for North Carolina, Halifax District, Warren County, page 78, he is shown with one son under 16 years of age, and four daughters.

- Robert Sturdivant, Esq.: Robert Sturdivant was born on July 28, 1789 in Dinwiddie County, Virginia, and died at his plantation, "Summerfield", in Dallas County, Alabama on December 21, 1856. He was the son of John Sturdivant, a Revolutionary soldier, born December 14, 1757, who died on April 7, 1839 in Hancock County, Georgia, and is buried in the Old Sparta Cemetery in Sparta, Georgia, and the grave is marked with a box tomb.

Robert Sturdivant was married twice, first to Ann Norwood, whom he married on March 3, 1814, in Georgia. Ann was born on March 18, 1800, the daughter of James Norwood and Hannah Boston, of Maryland, Virginia, and Georgia. She was said to have been beautiful, gracious, and a social leader. She died on May 28, 1836, and is buried in the Childers Chapel Cemetery, six miles north of Selma, Alabama.

Robert's second marriage was on August 6, 1837, to Mrs. Harriett Rembert Hollis, who was born on December 9, 1796, died at age 53 on October 12, 1850, and is buried in the Childers Chapel Cemetery.

Robert Sturdivant had moved with his family to Hancock County, Georgia, when he was very young, and remained there until age 29, at which time he moved to Dallas County, Alabama, where he was one of the very early settlers. He had nine children, all by Ann Norwood. They were:

(1) James Norwood Sturdivant, born January 18, 1817.

(2) John Marion Sturdivant, born February 17, 1819.

(3) Jane Boston Sturdivant, born February 3, 1821.

(4) Martha Elizabeth Sturdivant, born January 20, 1823.

(5) Robert Daniel Sturdivant, born April 6, 1824, died October 28, 1883, he is buried in the Childers Chapel Cemetery in Dallas County. On September 23, 1847, he married Sophia Clark King, who was born on March 1, 1831 in Perry County, Alabama, the daughter of Judge George Clark King and his wife Elizabeth Downing Byrd. She died on February 8, 1904, and is buried in the Childers Chapel Cemetery.

Robert Daniel Sturdivant had been sent to Georgia for his schooling. He attended a school conducted by Rev. Nathan S. Beeman at LaGrange, Georgia. He was a captain in the Civil War, Co. B, 7th Alabama Cavalry. After the war, he served in the Alabama legislature. He and Sophia Clark King became the parents of twelve children, all born in Dallas County, Alabama.

In the town of Selma, Alabama, there is a museum called the Sturdivant Museum, which is located in a beautiful antebellum mansion, built in 1853, which was purchased in 1957 through a bequest from Robert Daniel Sturdivant, and is operated by the Sturdivant Museum Association. The building is said to be one of the finest examples of neoclassic architecture in the south, and was designed by Thomas Helm Lee. It is furnished with rare antiques from the home of Robert Daniel Sturdivant.

(6) Edmond Troup Sturdivant, born March 28, 1828. Edmond Troup was a general in the Army of the Confederacy. After the Civil War, he moved to Florida and settled in the area where Orlando is now. It took him six months to make the trip, since for a good part of the way he had to cut his own road. In Florida he planted orange groves and became very prosperous. However, in 1895, his groves were wiped out by a hard freeze, and Edmond Troup Sturdivant is said to have died of a broken heart shortly thereafter.

(7) Lewis LaFayette Sturdivant, born July 25, 1830.

(8) Roxanna Hollingsberry Sturdivant, born January 26, 1832.

(9) Susan Turner Sturdivant, born December 7, 1833.

Information on the Sturdivant family is from my own research, which was done in many places, using innumerable sources, including the National Archives, records for colonial Virginia, and the Military Archives. Of special help was the book "Notable Men of Alabama," by Thomas McAdory Owen.

ETHELRED WATSON THOMAS

Ethelred, a native of Georgia, came to Alabama as a young man, and settled in Tuscaloosa County, where on August 24, 1824, he married Verlinda McKinney, daughter of Harris McKinney and Jane Jensy Ivey. Ethelred Watson Thomas was a son of William P. Thomas, who was born in 1770 in Bertie County, North Carolina, and died in 1824 in Georgia, and his wife Dicey Ivey, who was born in 1792 in Virginia, the daughter of Peebles Ivey. William P. Thomas had a total of four children:

(I) Seaborn Jones Thomas, born November 23, 1794 in Georgia, was married in 1820 to Charlotte Ivey, and died on August 20, 1872 in Tallapoosa County, Alabama.

(II) Ethelred Watson Thomas, above.

(III) Patience Thomas, born in 1807 in Georgia, married Curtis Williams on October 19, 1825 in Tuscaloosa County, Alabama, then settled in Pickens County, Alabama. Curtis had owned the first cotton gin in Georgia before coming to Alabama.

(IV) Mary Thomas, born in 1808 in Georgia, married Lightfoot Williams, who is thought to have been a brother to Curtis, on August 28, 1826, and also relocated to Pickens County, Alabama.

Ethelred Watson was the grandson of Michael Thomas, who died in Georgia about 1792. Besides William P. Thomas, Michael's only other known child was Michael L. Thomas, born in 1785.

Ethelred Watson Thomas and Verlinda McKinney were the parents of eleven children:

(A) Charlotte Thomas. Nothing more is known.

(B) Mary Jane Thomas, born March 9, 1827 in Coosa County, Alabama, died February 19, 1885, married Stokely D. Massengale and is buried in the Socopatoy Cemetery, Coosa County, Alabama.

(C) William Horton Thomas, born 1830, at McCalla, Alabama, married Martha Frances Ford on April 1, 1849 in Coosa County, Alabama and died in the Civil War in 1862 in Georgia.

(D) Patrick Thomas, born in 1833 in Tuscaloosa County, Alabama, never married. A captain in the Confederate army, he was killed at Appomattox in April, 1865, and is buried in the Socopatoy Cemetery in Coosa County, Alabama.

(E) Frances Amelia Thomas, born April 11, 1835 in Tuscaloosa County, Alabama, married John Cobb Massengale on December 25, 1851 in Coosa County, Alabama, and died in Milam County, Texas on September14, 1870.

(F) Amanda S. Thomas, born in 1837 in Coosa County, Alabama, married July 26, 1853 in Coosa County to John D. Bell, and died in 1916 in Colorado City, Texas, but her body was brought back to Alabama for burial in the Socopatoy Cemetery in Coosa County, Alabama.

(G) Elverena Thomas, born July, 1840 in Coosa County, Alabama, Married on September 16, 1858 to John Chapman Goodgame. The date and place of her death are not known.

(H) Houston Thomas, born 1842 in Coosa County, Alabama, never married, and died in Coosa County on November 12, 1857.

(I) Julius Thomas, born in 1845 in Coosa County, Alabama, and died in Texas. Nothing further is known of him.

(J) Ethelred Watson Thomas, Jr. born December 5, 1847 in Coosa County, Alabama, married in 1870 to Nancy Elizabeth Maxwell in Coosa County, died on July 31, 1910 in Coosa County and is buried in the Socopatoy Cemetery in Coosa County.

(K) Seaborn Jones Thomas, born November 15, 1849 in Coosa County, Alabama, married Nancy E. Hastings in 1871 in Coosa County, and died on October 26, 1926 in Rosebud, White County, Arkansas.

Of these, the most is known of the family of William Horton Thomas, child #3 above. He died in the Civil War at age 32, but before that he had married Martha Frances Ford, daughter of Nathaniel and Ann Ford of Fairfield District, South Carolina, and had fathered three children. They were:

(1) Susan A. Thomas, born 1853 at McCalla, Jefferson County, Alabama, married Stephen Franklin Bryant, and died on November 12, 1881 in Coosa County, Alabama.

(2) Albert McKinney Thomas, born in February 1855 in Alabama and died in Texas, the date unknown. He had

married in Alabama, and his wife's name is thought to have been Matilda.

(3) William Houston Thomas, born December 8, 1857 in the Socopatoy Community, in Coosa County, Alabama, married on November 2, 1879 in Coosa County to Martha Ella Smith. He died on October 23, 1940 in Coosa County, Alabama and is buried in the Poplar Springs Cemetery there. Martha Ella Smith was the daughter of John and Martha Logan Smith of Rockford, Coosa County, Alabama. Born on October 15, 1857 in Rockford, she died on December 3, 1945 at Rockford and was buried in the Poplar Springs Cemetery.

Of these the most is known of child #3, William Houston Thomas. He and Martha Ella Smith Thomas became the parents of nine children. They were:

(a) Mary Etta Thomas, born October 18, 1880 in Coosa County, Alabama, married a Mr. Collins on February 6, 1902 in Coosa County, died June 27, 1961, and is buried in the Poplar Springs Cemetery in Coosa County.

(b) Nancy Scott Thomas, born September 14, 1882, in Coosa County, Alabama, died on October 24, 1952, and is buried in Albertville, Marshall County, Alabama. She was married on November 29, 1900, in Coosa County, but the name of her spouse is unknown.

(c) William H. Thomas, Jr., born in June, 1884, in Rockford, Coosa County, Alabama. Married on November 16, 1907, (spouse's name unknown) William H. died in June, 1971 in Birmingham, Alabama, where he is buried in the Forest Hills Cemetery.

(d) Annette Thomas, born on August 7, 1886, in Coosa County, Alabama, and died there on September 3, 1887.

(e) Arthur Patrick Thomas, born July 1, 1888 on Rural Route 2, Rockford, Alabama, and died on January 12, 1970 in Elmore County Hospital, Wetumpka, Alabama. He was married on March 3, 1917, in Coosa County, Alabama, to Evie Lee Murchison.

(f) John Sebron (Seaborn?) Thomas, born July 18, 1890, in Rockford, Coosa County, Alabama, died on June 23, 1986 at Alabaster, Shelby County, Alabama, and was buried at Clanton, in Chilton County, Alabama. He was married on November 2, 1910, at Rockford, in Coosa County, but the name of his spouse is unknown.

(g) Clara Thomas, born March 9, 1893, in Coosa County, Alabama, died on May 12, 1896 in Coosa County, and is buried in the Poplar Springs Cemetery.

(h) Martha Ester Thomas, born July 15, 1895 in Coosa County, Alabama, died on August 23, 1972, and is buried in the Shady Grove Baptist Cemetery in Coosa County, Alabama.

(i) Aaron Bartley Thomas, born February 28, 1898, in Rockford, Coosa County, Alabama, and died on March 4, 1974, in Cairo, Grady County, Georgia. He was married on October 24, 1917, in Rockford County, Alabama, but the name of his spouse is unknown.

Of these, the most is known of child #5, Arthur Patrick Thomas. Born on July 1, 1888, on Rural Route 2 in Rockford, Coosa County, Alabama, he died at age 82 in Elmore County, Alabama. He was married twice, but all that is known is that one of his wives was named Gertrude. His children were all by Evie Lee Murchison, a daughter of Rora McKeever Murchison and his wife Donna Adelia Jane Little, whom he married in 1917. She had previously been married to Adie Waites. Arthur Patrick and Evie Lee became the parents of five children. They were:

(ea) Albe Virgil Thomas, born January 18, 1918, in Equality, Coosa County, Alabama. He was married in Sparta, Georgia, date unknown. On April 13, 1961, he died in New Bern, North Carolina.

(eb) Marjorie Hazel Thomas, born September 3, 1921, in Montgomery, Alabama. Nothing further is known of her.

(ec) Ralph Waldo Thomas, born August 28, 1923, in Coosa County, Alabama, He was married on April 23, 1944 in Coosa County.

(ed) Arthur Lee Thomas, born May 4, 1929 on Route 1, Equality, Coosa County, Alabama, he died on May 29,

1997, at Wetumpka, Elmore County, Alabama. He was married on June 27, 1953 in Rockford, Coosa County, Alabama.

(ee) An unnamed son who was born and died on January 13, 1935.

Information contributed by Randy Thomas of Virginia Beach, Virginia, formerly of Coosa County, Alabama. Randy is a grandson of Arthur Patrick Thomas and Evie Lee Murchison.

JOHN THOMAS

John Thomas was born in Bertie County, North Carolina about 1767, and died about 1840 in Bibb County, Alabama. He came to Alabama some time before statehood, probably about 1815, and settled for a time in Clark County, then moved north to Tuscaloosa County. After Alabama became a state in 1819, the county lines were not firmly established for many years, so the records sometimes show him living in Tuscaloosa County and sometimes in Bibb County. He was a son of Maj. Joseph Thomas, an officer in the Revolutionary War from South Carolina, and his wife, Joyce Calihan. Joseph Thomas was born in Bertie County, North Carolina about 1740, and was married there about 1764, to Joyce Calihan. His father is thought to have been Ezekiel Thomas of North Carolina, but this is unproven. Joseph's ancestors had come from Wales and Joyce's ancestors came from Ireland. They are thought to have been the parents of seven sons, but not all of these are proven. Some may have been cousins. They were:

(1) Jeremiah Thomas, born about 1767.

(2) John Thomas.

(3) Joshua Thomas, born about 1768.

(4) George Thomas, born about 1769.

(5) William Callihan Thomas.

(6) Ethelred Thomas.

(7) Benjamin Thomas.

Of these, Jeremiah Thomas lived out his life in Edgefield District, South Carolina. George and Ethelred settled in Wilkes County, Georgia. William Calihan Thomas settled in Jasper County, Georgia. John and Joshua migrated to Clark County, Alabama, then moved to Tuscaloosa County. Benjamin died in Greene County, Georgia in 1794, unmarried.

Joseph Thomas drew land in the Georgia Land Lottery in 1804, in Oglethorpe County, #1397, one draw, and the records indicate that he may have lived in Georgia for a short time, then moved back to Edgefield District, South Carolina, where he died about 1815. Of his two sons who migrated to Alabama, a good and complete history of the Joshua Thomas line is included in a history of the Standley family by Florence and John Guttery.

The other son, John Thomas, the Alabama pioneer with whom this piece is concerned, had two known sons, John Thomas, and William Thomas. Nothing is known of William. John Thomas, son of the older John and grandson of Col. Joseph, was born in Edgefield District, South Carolina in 1793, and came to Alabama at about age thirty-seven. He lived for a time in Tuscaloosa County, but after the Creek cession and the opening of Coosa County for settlement, he moved there.

It is unclear how many times he was married. There is a record in the Coosa County Marriage Book, published by the Coosa County Historical Society, that a John Thomas was married at age 24 in Coosa County, to Ann Billingsley. This would put the date at 1817, and at that time the area that later became Coosa County was still Indian territory, although a few white people were living there, but this was not the same couple and the record obviously is in error.

According to my own research, John Thomas was married in Abbeville, South Carolina about 1820, to Matilda Pace, and they came to Alabama together between 1829 and 1830. At that time they were the parents of four children. Matilda was born in 1805 in South Carolina, a daughter of John Pace. She evidently died before 1859, since on September 30, 1859 John was married to Julia Ann Billingsly McClendon, born 1828 in North Carolina, a widow with a young son, J. McClendon, born 1855 in Alabama. John Thomas was the father of twelve children, all by Matilda Pace. They were:

(1) Allan J. Thomas, born September 13, 1820, in South Carolina, died on April 12, 1880 in Coosa County, Alabama. He married Mary Susan Tuck.

(2) Albert Thomas, born January 7, 1822, in South Carolina, died on June 2, 1886 in Coosa County, Alabama. He was married twice, first to Mahala W. Byland, and secondly to Sarah Robbins.

(3) William Houston Thomas, born in 1826, in South Carolina, died in Coosa County, Alabama. He married Martha Frances Ford.

(4) Selden Burtram Thomas (see further).

(5) A daughter born in Coosa County in 1830, who died in infancy, unnamed.

(6) George M. Thomas, born April 18, 1837 in Coosa County, Alabama, and died on April 28, 1917. He married Mary J. Morgan.

(7) Benjamin Thomas, born in 1838, married Mary Smith.

(8) John M. Thomas (see further).

(9) A daughter, born in 1840, who died in infancy, unnamed.

(10) Caroline Thomas, born in 1841. Nothing further is known of her.

(11) Henry C. Thomas, born April 6, 1843, in Coosa County, died on February 13, 1913, in the same place. He was married to Margaret F. Hill.

(12) Mary F. Thomas, born in 1848 in Coosa County, Alabama. Nothing further is known of her.

Of these twelve, more is known of Selden Burtram Thomas and John M. Thomas than of the others. First, Selden Burtram:

Selden Burtram Thomas was born July 26, 1828 in South Carolina, and died October 29, 1909 in Coosa, Alabama. He married (1) Clara Ann Wilkerson February 10, 1853, in Coosa, Alabama, she being the daughter of Sidney Wilkerson and Elizabeth Reid. He married (2) Mary Emeline Wilkerson on August 19, 1872, in Coosa, she being a sister to Clara Ann. He was the father of nine children, four by his first wife, and five by the second. They were:

(1) Edgar Thomas, who married Lila Brown.

(2) Elizabeth "Betty" Thomas.

(3) Sarah Matilda "Sallie" Thomas, who was born in 1853 in Coosa, Alabama and died in 1919 in the same town. She married Benjamin F. Crew, son of Robert and Lucinda S. Crew, on December 17, 1874 in Coosa, Alabama. They were the parents of three children:

(a) Lillie Belle Crew, born November 7, 1879, died August 24, 1962, in Goodwater, Coosa County, Alabama; married Seaborn V. Thomas in Coosa County.

(b) Marcus Eugene Crew, born July 27, 1882, in Coosa, died September 17, 1899 in Goodwater, Coosa County, Alabama.

(c) Morton Harrison Crew, born in 1888, died in 1961 in Coosa County, Alabama.

(4) John Seldon Thomas, born in 1856, in Coosa, Alabama, died in 1939 in Coosa County, Alabama. He married Molline Forbes in Coosa, Alabama, and became the father of four children:

(a) Carl Thomas, born 1889 in the town of Coosa, Alabama, and died in 1939 in the same place.

(b) W. Ed Thomas, born 1890 in Coosa, died in 1969 in the same place.

(c) William B. Thomas, born in March, 1900.

(d) Coy Thomas, born 1908 in Coosa, died in 1939 in the same place.

(5) Willie C. Thomas, married Ada Nicholson, and had the following children:

(a) Carrie, born April 14, 1896 in Mississippi, died April 1, 1983 in Mississippi. She married Ernest Guy.

(b) Sudie Thomas, born July 20, 1898 in Mississippi, died May 12, 1964 in Mississippi.

(c) Vera Mae Thomas.

(d) Ruby Thomas.

(6) James H. "Jim" Thomas, born January 21, 1881, in Coosa. Alabama, died May 22, 1962 in Neshoba County, Mississippi, buried in the Morrow Cemetery. He married Mollie Nicholson and had six children:

(a) Seldon Bertrand Thomas, born in Mississippi, married Lorena Dorsey and they lived out their lives in Baltimore, Maryland.

(b) Ina Lois Thomas, born 1901 in Mississippi, died 1924 in Neshoba County, Mississippi, buried in the Morrow Cemetery.

(c) Lucille Thomas, born December 21, 1904, died as an infant and is buried in the Morrow Cemetery.

(d) James Rufus Thomas, born December 28, 1909.

(e) Ruth Thomas (a twin to James Rufus) born December 28, 1909.

(f) Cullen Thomas, born July 30, 1915 in Mississippi.

(7) Albert Reed Thomas, born June 5, 1874, in Coosa, Alabama, died February 21, 1948 in the same town. He married Ada Robbins and had nine children:

(a) Ethel Inez Thomas, born November 13, 1894 in the town of Coosa, died June 13, 1971, at Kellyton, Coosa County, and is buried in the Kellyton Cemetery.

(b) Seldon Robbins Thomas, born 1896 in Coosa, Alabama.

(c) Emmie Thomas, born 1897 in Coosa, Alabama, died in Mt. Dora, Florida.

(d) Verna Blanche Thomas born 1900 in Coosa, Alabama, married Richard McCain.

(e) Carrie Mae Thomas, born 1902, Coosa, Alabama, married Theo Waldrop.

(f) Raymond Thomas, born 1904, Coosa, Alabama, married Elizabeth Ferguson.

(g) Carey T. Thomas, born 1908, married Florence Thornell.

(h) Joseph Carey Thomas born October 27, 1908, Coosa, Alabama, died March 5, 1958 at Kellyton, Coosa County, Alabama, buried in the Kellyton Cemetery.

(i) Herbert Thomas, born December 20, 1915, died November 9, 1936.

(8) Carrie Thomas, born in January 1878 in Coosa, Alabama, died January 27, 1933 in Neshoba County, Mississippi, buried in the Mt. Bethel Cumberland Presbyterian Church Cemetery. She married John Cooper and had two children, Amci Cooper and Mary Emma Cooper.

(9) George Duncan Thomas, born January 25, 1885, Coosa, Alabama, died October 21, 1965, in Sylacauga, Talladega County, Alabama. He married Eva Clara Corley on December 24, 1916 in Kellyton, Coosa County, Alabama. Eva was the daughter of William Corley and Mary Monk.

George Duncan and Eva Clara lived on 123 acres, which they farmed. They had a small farmhouse with three small bedrooms, an entry hall, a place for the dining table, and a kitchen. They had an outhouse, and had to carry their water from a nearby spring. Duncan raised chickens and vegetables which he peddled in town. They also had plenty of fresh butter and buttermilk. They were the parents of four children:

>(a) Mary Eleanor Thomas, born October 30, 1917 in Coosa County, Alabama, died September 12, 1980, Alexander City, Tallapoosa County, Alabama.
>
>(b) Fred Duncan Thomas, born April 3, 1920 Coosa County, Alabama, died November 16, 1987, in Dallas, Texas.
>
>(c) William Aubrey Thomas, born June 4, 1921, Coosa County, Alabama.
>
>(d) Claude Lewis Thomas, born February 8, 1923 in Coosa County, Alabama. He married Evelyn Doris Crawford, daughter of Edward Crawford and Ora Connell, on August 24, 1946 in Talladega, Alabama, and they are the parents of three children:
>
>>(da) Claude Lewis Jr. born in 1951, Atlanta, Fulton County, Georgia.
>>
>>(db) George Braxton born in 1955, Atlanta, Fulton County, Georgia.
>>
>>(dc) Yvonne Marie, born in 1961 in Bisbee, Arizona, where the family now lives.

Selden Burtram Thomas's younger brother, John M. Thomas, is the other member of this family about whom more than a minimum of information is available. He was the seventh son of and the eighth child of John and Matilda Thomas of Abbeville District, South Carolina and Coosa County, Alabama. Born in Tuscaloosa County, Alabama on March 29, 1839, he moved with his family to Coosa County as a child.

On August 18, 1859, he was married at Elyton Village (now the city of Birmingham) to Margaret Emeline Horton, daughter of James Horton and Violetta Patterson of a neighboring plantation in Coosa County. Margaret was born in Coosa County on October 20, 1846, so she would have been only thirteen years old at the time of the marriage. They apparently eloped to Elyton, and were married there by Reuben Phillips. The records do not indicate whether Mr. Phillips was a minister of the gospel or a justice of the peace. The young couple then stayed for a time in the home of John Horton, Margaret's uncle, who lived in Elyton. They lived in Elyton until the beginning of the Civil War, and Margaret continued living there until John returned from the war in 1865.

When the war broke out in 1861, John enlisted in the infantry and was sent to Mississippi, where he was captured at the siege of Vicksburg. Before being captured, he was severely wounded, losing one hand entirely, two fingers off the other hand, and having one elbow and one knee shattered. He was sent to the prison camp at Rockford, Illinois, where he remained until the end of the war.

After the war ended, most of the prisoners had to walk the hundreds of miles back to their homes in the south. Because of his severe wounds, however, John Thomas was afforded transportation by train back to Jefferson County, Alabama. Shortly thereafter, and possibly because of a breach with Margaret's family, they settled in Tuscaloosa County near John's grandfather and other Thomas relatives. The place where they settled is now called Vance, but at that time it was called "Eight Acres of Rocks," because of a large area of glacial-exposed sandstone formations nearby. Today it is a tourist attraction.

After settling in Tuscaloosa County, John and Emeline farmed, but life was very hard, with John being handicapped as he was. To make matters worse, he lost another two fingers when a muzzle-loading shotgun that he was loading exploded and blew away his fingers. This meant that a great part of the farm work fell on Margaret and later on the children, particularly on the older ones. They were very devout people, and never missed a service at the Union Cumberland Presbyterian Church where John was a deacon. They became the parents of nine children. They were:

(1) Mary Jane Thomas, born about 1865 in Tuscaloosa County, died about 1930 in the same place, buried in the Thomas plot in the Union Cumberland Presbyterian Church Cemetery. She married Joshua Vining.

(2) Margaret Fatima Thomas (see further).

(3) John Thomas, born about 1869 in Tuscaloosa County, Alabama, died about 1950 in Atlanta, Georgia. His wife's name was Ethel.

(4) Robert Thomas, born about 1871 in Alabama, died on November 17, 1913 in Bessemer, Alabama. He married

Viola Crider. Both are buried in the Cedar Hill Cemetery in Bessemer, Alabama.

(5) Martha Thomas, born November 12, 1874 in Alabama, died September 20, 1885 in Tuscaloosa County, Alabama, unmarried, buried in the Union Cumberland Presbyterian Cemetery.

(6) George Thomas, born about 1876 in Tuscaloosa County, Alabama, died April 16, 1960 in Bessemer, Alabama, and is buried beside his wife in the Cedar Hill Cemetery in Bessemer. He married Mariah Wilson and became the father of two daughters and a son:

   (a) Ruby.

   (b) Lennie.

   (c) William.

(7) Missouri E. Thomas, born about 1878 in Tuscaloosa County, Alabama, died 1941 in Bessemer, Alabama, and is buried in the Cedar Hill Cemetery in Bessemer. She married Starling Whaley and had five children:

   (a) Otto.

   (b) Paul.

   (c) Clarence.

   (d) Irene.

   (e) Leona.

(8) Emeline Thomas, born about 1880 in Tuscaloosa County, Alabama, she married Roman Vining. Roman Vining was born February 19, 1882, died August 25, 1945 and is buried in the Green Pond Cemetery in Bibb County, Alabama. If Emeline is buried there she does not have a marker.

(9) Coleman Thomas, born February 25, 1882 in Tuscaloosa County, Alabama. He died at age 24 on August 13, 1906 from food poisoning, probably botulism, but back then they didn't have a name for it. The day he died, it was extremely hot, and when he got off work, hot and tired, he bought and ate an ice cream cone, hoping to cool off. By the time he

arrived home he was very ill, and died during the night. He was married to Josephine Wright and had one daughter:

> (a) Colie, was brought up by the Wrights. Colie married a man named Gray, and died in May, 2000, in Bessemer, Alabama. She had one known daughter.

Margaret Fatima Thomas was my grandmother, so my knowledge of her is slightly more than of the others. Although even in her case, my knowledge is not extensive, since she died at age thirty-two, when my mother was only five years old. Furthermore, my mother was subsequently brought up in the home of John Thompson, a foster grandfather who lived at Genery's Gap in Jefferson County, and had little contact with the Thomas family. She passed along to me what she remembered of her mother, but it wasn't much. All of the dates are from tombstones in the Cedar Hill Cemetery in Bessemer, Alabama and the Union Cumberland Presbyterian Church Cemetery in Tuscaloosa County. I also have visited the site of the old Thomas homestead and talked with the then pastor of the Union Cumberland Presbyterian Church, where the Thomas family worshipped and where John was a deacon.

Margaret Fatima Thomas met John William Porter, my grandfather, in 1893, and they were married that same year. John William Porter was the son of John Abraham (Ibzan) Porter, a Confederate veteran, and Mary Sturdivant, daughter of Sherrod Sturdivant and his wife Elizabeth Dooley, who was a full blood Cherokee. John William's father had died soon after returning home from the war, a good part of which was spent in a northern prison, and probably as a result of the deprivations suffered there. The couple met when he traveled from the home of his foster father, John Thompson, in Jefferson County to Tuscaloosa County to visit his mother who had been living there with her then-husband, and who was in her last illness. Margaret Fatima Thomas, a neighbor, was taking care of her. His mother died soon after, but John William continued to travel to Tuscaloosa County to visit Margaret Fatima, and they were married within a few months, and settled on a farm near her parents.

The property where they settled had previously been occupied by William Thomas, who probably was a relative, but the relationship has not been proven. There was a huge sink hole not far from the house. When William Thomas had been living there, there had been a huge chestnut tree in the yard. One night they heard a very loud noise and the next morning the chestnut tree was gone along with a good part of their yard, having been replaced by the sink hole. My mother said that when she was small, she wasn't allowed to go near the sink hole. They told her that if she did, the earth might swallow her up. Sometimes the hens would hide their nests down in there and my grandfather would go down in to the hole and get the eggs.

The only other thing I remember that my mother told me about that period was that the water was very bad at the place where they lived. There was, however, a good spring of water up a hollow and through the woods a mile or so from the house, and once in a while she would accompany her mother as she walked to this spring to get a good drink of water. They didn't go very often, since there were some blacks living between them and the spring, and my grandmother was afraid of them. The bad water where they lived was probably what caused my grandmother's death. She died of typhoid in 1899. She had given birth to her third child just three months before her death, and the child, Samuel David Porter, suffered from what probably today would be diagnosed as polio, but then it was called "brain fever." It left him a hunchback. My mother said that when her mother died she went outside and sat down in the chimney corner and cried for hours. Her five-year old heart was broken.

John William Porter and Margaret Fatima Thomas were the parents of three children. They were:

(1) Margie Eugenia Porter, born July 16, 1894 in Tuscaloosa County, Alabama, died April 4, 1982 in Jefferson County, Alabama, and is buried in the Genery's Cemetery, Genery's Gap. Alabama. She married Joseph H. Seales, and was the mother of eight children. For more information on this line, please see the entries for the Seales and Porter families.

(2) John Monroe Porter, born December 8, 1896 in Tuscaloosa County, Alabama, died August 28, 1963, and is buried in the Genery's Cemetery, Genery's Gap, Alabama. He was married twice, first to Ruby Howard and had one son, William Porter, and secondly to Lessie Jordan, and had six children, whose names are unknown.

(3) Samuel David, born April 14, 1899 in Tuscaloosa County, Alabama, died June 30, 1973 in Jefferson County and is buried in the Genery's Cemetery. He is buried beside his sister and her husband. He was never married.

Information on the John Thomas family is from personal knowledge, conversations with family members, census records, land records, probate records, conveyances, and other records in Coosa County, Alabama and Tuscaloosa County, Alabama. Information on the Selden Burtram Thomas family was contributed by Evelyn Thomas of Bisbee, Arizona. Some information on Maj. Joseph Thomas was taken from a history of the Standley family by Florence and John Guttery.

JOSEPH THOMPSON

Joseph Thompson was a Revolutionary soldier from Virginia who had settled in Clarksville, Tennessee after the war. Born about 1760 in Hanover County, Virginia, he died on December 2, 1834 at Thompsontown, Alabama, which he founded, and which later became part of the larger town of Bessemer, Alabama.

His wife's name was Elizabeth. Born in Virginia, she died on September 13, 1849 at Thompsontown. Joseph, Elizabeth, and eight other members of this family were buried in the family burying ground on the plantation between 1834 and 1883, and the place, which eventually came to be called Glen Springs, remained as it was until 1928.

At that time the property was in the ownership of a descendant, who sold it to a developer, with permission to remove the graves and re-inter the remains in the Cedar Hill Cemetery. This was done, but with the odd twist that all the remains were put into one grave, and the small stone which marks the spot gives no indication of who is interred there. This seems rather shabby treatment for a man who fought in the Revolution, and later founded (not far from the old Indian trail known as the Great Trading Path) the settlement called Thompsontown which was the beginning of the town of Bessemer, Alabama.

The names of the people buried in the common grave have been obtained from the Cedar Hill Cemetery records. Their names and burial dates are:

- Joseph Thompson, December 2, 1834.
- Elizabeth Thompson, September 13, 1849.
- Emily W. Thompson, September 28, 1861.
- William Thompson, January 17, 1862.
- Whitmill Thompson, June 5, 1873.
- Nancy Thompson, August 19, 1873.
- James William Thompson, 1860.
- Dock Thompson, 1880.
- J. W. Thompson, 1883.
- Jessie Thompson, an infant.

They were all buried in the same grave on January 3, 1928.

Joseph Thompson was the son of an older Joseph Thompson, a planter of Hanover County, Virginia, and his wife Mary Waddy, daughter of Anthony Waddy. The elder Joseph Thompson, born about 1710, was a son of Samuel Thompson of Hanover County, Virginia, who was known as "Samuel of Hanover." His son Joseph was in the records of the Virginia militia as having fought in the Revolutionary War in Frederick County, Maryland, under George Washington.

Including the aforementioned younger Joseph Thompson, the elder Joseph Thompson's children were:

(I) William, who settled in Bedford County, Virginia. Born about 1720, he died on May 24, 1753. His will was written on the previous May 15th, and mentions his wife, but does not give her name. William was the father of four children, Mary, Samuel, Thomas, and William.

(II) James, who settled in Augusta County, Virginia. Born about 1730, he died on August 20, 1776, in Augusta, now Rockbridge, County, Virginia. His will was written on March 26, 1773, and names his wife Mary and eight children:

(A) James, who married Elizabeth.

(B) John, who married Catherine Steele. John was a Revolutionary soldier in Captain Long's company, Augusta County.

(C) Margaret, who married Andrew Hall.

(D) William, who married Rosanna Davis and was in the Revolution in Captain Given's company, Augusta County, Virginia.

(E) Joseph, who was a Revolutionary soldier in the same company.

(F) Elizabeth.

(G) Mary.

(H) Catherine.

(III) Josiah, who settled in Cumberland County, Virginia and married Mary Ann Swann. They became the parents of three children:

(A) William Morris Thompson.

(B) John Thompson, who married Elizabeth_____. His will was written in Cumberland County, Virginia in 1785. He had one son:

    (1) John Daniel Thompson.

(C) Waddy Thompson, who was a prominent planter in Hanover County, Virginia. He married Jane Lewis, daughter of Colonel Robert Lewis of Belvoir, Albemarle County, Virginia. His son:

    (1) The Honorable Waddy Thompson, Jr. was Chancellor of State for South Carolina, then a member of Congress from South Carolina, and Minister to Mexico under President Harrison. He was a descendent of Henry Patillo of colonial and Revolutionary fame. His son:

        (a) Waddy Thompson III, settled in Mobile, Alabama before the Civil War, according to page 470, of *Virginia Genealogies.*

(IV) Joseph Thompson, as mentioned above, born around 1760, died 1834.

Josiah and Mary Ann Thompson had a granddaughter, Maria Swann Thompson, who married in South Carolina Dr. Richard Harrison, son of Major Richard Harrison, a Revolutionary hero from James River, Virginia. According to *American Ancestry.*

Mary Ann Swann, Josiah Thompson's wife, was daughter of Thompson Swann, son of Thomas Swann Jr., son of Captain Thomas Swann and Elizabeth Thompson, daughter of William Thompson of Nansemond County, Virginia, according to the Cumberland County Records and *Hennings Statutes,* Vol. 6, p. 466.

Samuel of Hanover, father of the older Joseph Thompson, was the son of Rev. William Thompson, Jr. and his wife Martha. Born about 1690, he died about 1750. He was the father of three children:

    (1) William: A deed from Samuel in 1742 proves his sonship. William was born about 1710 and died in 1788, leaving a will which was probated in Woodford County, Virginia, with Rhodes Thompson as trustee. His wife's name was Ann, and they were the parents of eleven children, namely

        (a) Rhodes.

(b) William, who was the father of Elizabeth Thompson who married Captain Thomas Swann, sheriff of Louisa County in 1787.

(c) Clifton.

(d) Asa.

(e) John.

(f) David, who was the father of Waddy Thompson, Sr., (will 1801). This is a different Waddy Thompson from the one who married Jane Lewis.

(g) Ann.

(h) Margie.

(i) Eunice.

(j) Lydia.

(k) Sarah.

(2) Joseph, who was the father of the Joseph Thompson who migrated to Alabama.

(3) Thomas, who lived out his life in Virginia, but his son Samuel migrated to Alabama and settled at Elyton, where he had a large plantation a few miles from his uncle Joseph. Samuel, born about 1765 in Surry County, Virginia, died in 1839 at Elyton, in Jefferson County, Alabama, leaving a will (will book 1818-1840, p. 218).

He was married twice. His first wife was Ann Eliza Camp, daughter of John and Eliza Camp, born April 24, 1834, died September 16, 1858, according to her tombstone in the Old Elyton Cemetery in Birmingham. After her death, Samuel married Mary Prescoat, who brought three Prescoat children into Samuel's already large family, and then they had three more. Mary's children were:

- Martha.
- Thomas.
- Jane.

Samuel's eleven children, eight by his first wife and three by the second, were:

(a) Thomas.

(b) Fleming.

(c) Nancy.

(d) Julia.

(e) Rhoda.

(f) Elizabeth.

(g) Samuel, Jr.

(h) Josiah.

(i) Katherine.

(j) Caroline.

(k) Waddy.

The oldest son, Thomas, settled in Walker County, Alabama, as did the seventh child, Samuel Jr. Thomas had ten children by two wives.

His first wife, Clarissa Hood, was the mother of

(aa) Oliver (1830).

(ab) Joseph (1833).

(ac) John (1835).

(ad) Eliza (1838).

(ae) Susan (1840).

(af) Rhoda (1844).

(ag) Clarissa (1845).

(ah) Margie (1847).

(ai) James (1848).

His second wife, Salina _____, was the mother of:

(aj) Martha.

Of the others, these facts are known:

One Fleming Thompson was in the Revolution, but was in the wrong time frame to have been Samuel's son; He was probably an uncle or great uncle.

(c) Nancy married a Gilcrease.

(d) Julia married a Freeman.

(e) Rhoda married a Ramsey.

(f) Elizabeth, born 1811 in South Carolina, married first David Carmichael on December 4, 1824, and had four children. He died on September 27, 1834. Thomas Thompson was administrator of the estate.

(g) Samuel, Jr. died in 1842 in Walker County and Thomas Thompson was administrator of the estate. His will is recorded in Will Book A, p.293, Jefferson County, Alabama.

(h) Josiah, born in 1783, married Mary E. ____, and had only one known child,

(ha) Ophelia.

Josiah was living in Jefferson County, Alabama in 1860, his age given as 77.

With his second wife, Mary Prescoat, Samuel had the following children:

(i) Katherine.

(j) Caroline.

(k) Waddy.

Of these three, nothing is known. Samuel and Mary Prescoat also had another daughter who died unnamed in infancy on August 18, 1856, and is buried in the Old Elyton Cemetery in Birmingham.

Rev. William Thompson Jr., who was the son of Rev. William Thompson, Sr., was born in 1665 and died in 1732, leaving a will, which names his four children:

(1) Samuel, who was known as Samuel of Hanover, as already mentioned.

(2) John, who was Justice of Halifax County, N.C. in 1768. This according to the *North Carolina Colonial Records*.

(3) Katherine.

(4) Hannah.

The will also mentions two grandchildren, Samuel and Mary. Rev. William was a minister in Westmoreland County. He also owned several thousand acres in Surry County. This according to the *William and Mary Quarterly*, Vol. 2, p. 261, the *Land Book*, and general court records.

Rev. William Thompson Sr., born 1613 in Ireland, came to America in 1635 on *The George*. He was twenty-two years old. This according to *Early Settlers of Alabama*, page 469. According to *Burke's Landed Gentry*, Rev. Thompson is assumed to have come from Ireland because the "p" in the name indicates that. He probably came from County Antrim or Longford, as Thompsons were numerous there, and were intermarried with the Drury, Waddy, Lowe, and Manning families as they were in Virginia. In 1660 Rev. Thompson was minister of Lawne's Creek Church, Surry County, Virginia. According to the *William and Mary Quarterly*, he was still there in 1673. He was the father of three children:

(1) Samuel, whose wife's name was Mary. His will named his nephew Samuel, his son, William and two cousins, William Mosely and Robert Payne and his wife Mary, and a daughter Elizabeth, who married Captain Thomas Swann. They were parents of Thomas Swann Jr., who was the father of Thompson Swann, who was the father of Mary Ann Swann, who married Josiah Thompson. They were the grandparents of Marie Swann Thompson who married Dr. Richard Harrison in South Carolina. This from *American Ancestry, The Georgians,* and the *Virginia Gazette*.

(2) Rev. William Thompson Jr., already discussed.

(3) David: The line of Waddy Thompson descends through him.

Now to return to Joseph Thompson, the Alabama pioneer, son of Joseph Thompson, son of Samuel of Hanover, son of Rev. William Thompson, Jr., son of Rev. William Thompson, Sr., son of Rev. William Thompson, born 1613 in Ireland. Joseph, a Revolutionary soldier from Hanover County, Virginia, came into the Alabama Territory about 1817, two years before statehood, from Clarksville, Tennessee, where he had settled after the Revolution.

A good guess would be that he came at the urging of his twin sons, William and John, who had come into the territory about 1813, with Andrew Jackson and his army of Tennesseeans to wage a final campaign against the Creeks, in pursuit of which they were joined by the Cherokees. They engaged in battles and skirmishes from Burnt Corn to the final great battle at Horseshoe Bend on the Tallapoosa River in the eastern part of what later became the state of Alabama.

According to the records at Horseshoe Bend Military Park, William was something of a hero. He was a private in the artillery under the command of Capt. Joel Parrish, and was a cannoneer in the great battle, pounding away at the log ramparts the Creeks had erected. He was commended by Col. Andrew Jackson on March 1, 1814, and again on March 16, 1814. At the time of the battle, Col. Jackson and the Tennessee Volunteers had just suffered through the very trying winter of 1813-14. Supplies had been slow in coming, and they had no food or winter clothes.

After the final defeat of the Creeks the Tennessee Volunteers had returned home with glowing accounts of the land to the south, the beautiful streams, rolling hills, and great virgin forests, and many of them had returned to settle, along with many others who had been influenced by their accounts. It was at this time in history that the Thompsons came into Alabama.

According to his grandsom, John Thompson, the family arrived in Alabama by raft down the Cumberland River to Nashville, then overland to the Tennessee River in north Alabama. There they forded the river at a shallows near Huntsville, and then overland to their final destination.

Joseph settled his family near the old town of Jonesboro, not far from the Great Trading Path, which cut a swath through Alabama, connecting the tribes of Mississippi and Alabama with those of Georgia and the Carolinas. Jonesboro is now part of the much more recent town of Bessemer.

Where Joseph settled came to be called Glen Springs. Glen Springs later became an upscale section of Bessemer.

Joseph's wife's name was Elizabeth, and besides the twin sons, William and John, they had only one more known child, a daughter, Mary, who married a Nickson, but there may have been others. According to the Orphans' Court Records of Jefferson County, on June 5, 1826, Joseph Thompson was appointed guardian of Melissa and Minerva Phillips, twin infant children of Bennett Phillips. These may have been his grandchildren. (*Orphans' Court Book 1824*, p.116). According to an entry in the 1830-37 *Orphans' Court Book,* dated May 26, 1835, Joseph Thompson is deceased and his only heirs at that time were William Thompson and Mary Nickson. His son John had died some time before.

William Thompson settled his family where Fairfax Avenue in Bessemer is now. He had a farm, a store, and various enterprises, and the place came to be called Thompsontown. Thompsontown was well known by the people of my grandparents' generation, as it was the place where the farmers and settlers in the area bought their supplies. It was eventually swallowed up by Bessemer, which came into being in the late 1800's when the iron ore deposits in nearby Red Mountain began being mined.

William's wife was Whitmill Sullivan, whom he had married in Tennessee before migration to Alabama. Born on February 11, 1789 in Virginia, William married Whitmill on June 9, 1816, in Clarksville, Tennessee. William died on January 17, 1873 at Thompsontown, and was buried at Glen Springs. His remains later were removed to Cedar Hill Cemetery. Whitmill was born in 1794 in North Carolina, and died on June 5, 1862, most likely from grief, as she and William lost three of their family in the Civil War, which was well into its second year at that time. They were the parents of eight children:

(1) John, born 1818, died 1907, buried in the Genery's cemetery at Genery's Gap, Alabama. More on John follows below.

(2) Emily, born 1820, died 1861, Thompsontown, buried at Glen Springs.

(3) Joseph, born 1822, was killed in the Civil War.

(4) Nancy, born 1825, died 1873 at Thompsontown, Alabama, buried at Glen Springs, never married.

(5) Jesse W., born 1828, died 1891, married Melissa Caldwell on June 13, 1857. Wallace Thompson, mayor of Sylvan Springs, Alabama, is a great-grandson of Jesse and Melissa.

(6) Margaret, born 1832, married an Armstrong, who was killed in the Civil War.

(7) William, born 1834, died 1880, at Thompsontown, married Bazie Dailey.

(8) Whitmill, a son, and a twin to William, born 1834, was killed in the Civil War.

In his old age, William Thompson ran the store at Thompsontown with the help of his daughters, Nancy and Margaret.

John Thompson, the oldest of William Thompson's children, is the one about whom the most is known by this writer. He was my foster great-grandfather, and was dearly loved by my grandfather and his twelve children, one of whom was my mother. He died thirteen years before I was born, but according to all I have ever heard about him, he was a good and kind man such as is rarely seen. My mother and her siblings spoke of him with almost reverence. Indeed, my research has revealed that these seem to be traits that run all through the Thompson generations.

John was born in Clarksville, Tennessee on February 23, 1818 and died at Genery's Gap on April 1, 1907, and is buried in the Genery's Cemetery. His wife was Mary Thompson, a cousin, whom he married on November 17, 1840. Mary was born in Alabama in 1822, and died suddenly at Genery's Gap on October 22, 1887.

When he was eighteen years old, John Thompson participated in the roundup of the Creek Indians for relocation to Oklahoma. In 1880, when a census was taken of the men who had participated in that operation, John Thompson was the only one of the group of 300 still living in Jefferson County, the others having died or moved westward, according to an article in *The Birmingham News* at the time. In 1840, he received a land grant of 160 acres for his services. He and Mary moved onto the property as newlyweds, lived out their lives there, and my family still lives on the property.

John and Mary Thompson had no children of their own, but raised two orphan foster children. The oldest was Jane Smith, an orphan from Bibb County, who was born on February 25, 1847 and died on November 23, 1921. She is buried beside John and Mary in Genery's Cemetery, having never married.

On the day Jane came to the Thompsons as a ten-year-old, there was deep snow on the ground. She had walked from Bamford, accompanied by a man who was taking a day off from farm work because of the snowstorm, so he had time to walk the seven miles or so with her. Someone had given her a pair of shoes that were much to big for her, and when she arrived at the Thompsons, snow had collected in them and was frozen hard around her feet. One might wonder why the man didn't wait for more favorable weather to bring her to the Thompsons, but in the hard lives of the pioneer farmers of the area, good weather days were for farm work, and bad weather days were for other things.

The second child that John and Mary took was John William Porter, who was my grandfather, son of a Civil War veteran who had died soon after the war, from the poor treatment he had received in a Yankee prison. Born on May 2, 1866 in Lowndes County, Mississippi, he died on May 9, 1946 in Jefferson County, Alabama.

John and Mary Thompson were the very first settlers in the part of Jefferson County where Genery's Gap later came into existence. It was some twenty years before another settler moved into the area. They built what was called a double log house on the property, cleared the land and farmed, with the help of their foster children. By the 1890's, they had become quite prosperous, lost quite a lot in the panic of 1893, but still remained fairly well off.

John was known for his fine saddle horses. During the Civil War he had visited the Yankee encampment on Cahaba River at night and traded horses with the soldiers. He would trade them a farm horse that was in good shape for a thoroughbred that had been stolen from the plantations along the Tennessee River in northern Alabama and ridden to exhaustion. He would then take his thoroughbreds home, feed and nurture them, and end up with fine horses. It was a dangerous business, going to the Yankee camps at night, but remember John, like his father before him, had been an Indian fighter and knew a few things about how to survive.

Stories abound in our family of the Thompson family encountering bandits many times on the journey from Clarksville, Tennessee to Jefferson County, Alabama, and barely escaping without having their throats slit. John told of crossing the Tennessee River on horseback, of being swept off his horse by the flood and having to hang onto a bit of brush all night until he could be rescued. A man who had experienced so much of life would not frighten easily.

Jane Smith cared for John Thompson in his old age. When he died in 1907, his estate was divided equally between his two foster children. Then when Jane Smith died childless, her part of the estate was divided among John William Porter's children, so the original land grant of 1840 has remained in the hands of his family for well over 150 years. (Further information can be found in the histories of the Porter and Seales families of Genery's Gap, Alabama.)

This history of the Thompson family is mostly from personal knowledge of your writer, with some research on the earlier generations at the Georgia Room of the Marietta Public Library, the Georgia State Archives, the National Archives and Records Administration, and the archives of the Church of Jesus Christ of Latter Day Saints.

ENOCH TYLER

Most of the Tyler families in the present-day Alabama counties of Shelby, Bibb, and Jefferson are descendants of Enoch Tyler, who migrated to Alabama from Georgia in 1855. Their family roots are in England.

The first one of this line came to America about 1735 with a Church of England congregation that came over as a group, settled in the South Carolina colony and founded the town of Britton's Neck. Their minister, Dr. Robert Hunter came with them. One of their first acts in South Carolina was to build a church, which in later years became a Methodist church, probably following the death of Dr. Hunter.

The Tyler who brought his family over with this group was Benjamin Tyler, born about 1700 in England. Little is known of him or his family. He is known to have had a son, Benjamin Jr., through whom the Alabama line descends, and is thought to have had a son named Thomas. A George Tyler, who was a ship's master working up and down the East Coast in the 1700's may also have been his son. George was master of the sloop *Free and Easy* and the schooner *Elizabeth,* and made his home in Georgetown, S.C.

Benjamin Tyler, Jr. was born in England about 1728 and came to South Carolina as a small boy. He died there about 1800. No will has been found for him, so a complete list of his children's names is not known to exist, but the records seem to indicate that he had four sons who fought in the Revolution, mostly with Francis Marion, the "Swamp Fox," in the swamps of South Carolina. They were:

(I) Benjamin: He was born about 1750 in Britton's Neck, South Carolina, and married Jane ____. She died as his widow at age 84 on September 2, 1857, according to a notice in the *Pee Dee Times.* In the Revolution, Benjamin served as sergeant under Captain Thornley, Colonel Irwin, and General Marion. During 1781 he was wounded while looking for a party of forty Tories. A musket ball went through two ribs and out the backbone, this according to File # AA7982A in the Revolutionary records. His only known child was named William, and it is through him that the Alabama lines descend. More about him later.

(II) John: From March 2 to May 22, 1780, John served in the Britton's Neck Regiment under Captain Joseph Greaves. He was at the fall of Charleston. He served in the South Carolina militia on horseback and on foot during 1781 under Captain Baxter, and was sergeant under General Marion during 1782, and was six months in the Continental Line in 1783, according to files AA7983, X205, Y1033, and a yearbook published in 1897. It is not known if he married or had a family.

(III) Lewis: Died in the Revolution, according to Revolutionary File #AA7983A. He married Mourning____. In the 1810 census Mourning was still alive in Marion County, South Carolina and was drawing a widow's pension.

(IV) Samuel: He was a sergeant in the South Carolina militia under General Marion, according to files AA7984 and Y414. Nothing further is known of him.

William Tyler, son of Benjamin, was born about 1775 in Georgetown District, South Carolina and died about 1850 in Jasper County, Georgia. He is thought to have migrated to Georgia about 1800, at a time when a good part of Georgia was still Indian lands. He was married in Jasper County, Georgia in 1804 to Betsy Goolsby, and lived out his life there. He was in the 1832 Gold Lottery in Jasper County. Through him the Tylers became very numerous and very prominent in Jasper County. They were prominent Methodists, farmers, and businessmen.

An old Tyler Settlement, Tyler's Cross Roads, is on Clay Road between Gladesville and Smith's Mill. In Monticello, there existed a Tyler's Barber Shop and a Tyler's Insurance in the late 1800's, although none of these are in the direct line of Enoch Tyler of Alabama. The court records reveal that they also tended to be litigious, with numerous cases in the court records where one or another of the Tylers were in court either suing or being sued.

No will has been found for William, so the list of his children is derived mostly from how they were associated in the records. He is thought to have had eight sons. No names of any daughters are known. His sons were:

(A) William: Was on the census in Jasper County, Georgia in 1830 as head of a household, along with his father. He was in the 1832 Gold Lottery. On April 2, 1837 in Meriwether County, Georgia, he married Emily Smith.

(B) Britton C. was in the 1820-21 Land Lottery and the 1832 Gold Lottery in Putnam County, Georgia. On February 22, 1833, he married Mary Lewis in Jasper County.

(C) Wiley: Was on the 1820 Land Lottery and the 1832 Gold Lottery in Meriwether County, Georgia. On March 26, 1829, he married Elizabeth Shackelford in Upson County, Georgia. In 1830 he was on the census in Upson. In 1842 he witnessed the will of George Powell in Upson County.

(D) Enoch: Was on the 1830 census for Meriwether County, Georgia, and in 1832 he was in the Gold Lottery there. He was not on the census in 1840, so it can be assumed that he had already migrated to Alabama. On March 12, 1826 he had married Comfort Lewis (probably a sister to Mary Lewis mentioned above) in Jasper County, Georgia. The Alabama line descends through him. See further.

(E) Owen: He was on the 1830 census and the 1832 Gold Lottery in Jasper County.

(F) Thomas: Was on the 1830 census in Jasper County.

(G) Asa: On December 18, 1831 he married Mary A. Kelly in Jasper County, and in 1832 he was in the Gold Lottery there.

(H) Alexander G. He was on the 1830 census in Putnam County, also the Cherokee Land Lottery in Putnam and the 1832 Gold Lottery in Jasper County.

Enoch Tyler, son of William Tyler, was born in Georgia in 1809, and died about 1880 in Shelby County, Alabama. He had migrated to Alabama from Meriwether County, Georgia before 1840. His wife was Comfort Lewis, whom he had married in Jasper County, Georgia on March 12, 1826. He received a patent for land in Shelby County, Alabama, near present day Montevallo, on January 10, 1855. Henry N. Tyler (his son), Ezekiel Arnold (Henry's father-in-law, who had previously lived in Carroll County, Georgia), and Richard Tyler (another son) all received nearby tracts on the same day. Samuel S. Tyler and William Tyler received land five days later, on January 15, 1855: Samuel in Shelby County, and William in Jefferson. Enoch and Comfort were the parents of twelve children, as follows:

(1) Henry Newton: Born in Jasper County, Georgia in 1827, he died in 1909 in Jefferson County, Alabama, and is buried in the Arnold's Chapel Cemetery at Bluff Ridge. On December 12, 1850, in Coosa County, Alabama, he married Lucy Ann Valinda Arnold, daughter of Ezekiel Arnold, born 1810 in South Carolina, and his wife Sara, born 1815 in Georgia.

Henry Newton and Lucy were the parents of ten known children. They were:

(a) Pauline: Born 1855.

(b) Parthenia: Born 1857.

(c) William Andrew Jackson: Born 1859, married Susan Lee Ann Kimbrel, daughter of Ransom Kimbrel and Rachel Heflin. They were the parents of twenty-one children, whose names are listed in the material on the Kimbrel family.

(d) Elizabeth Ann: Born 1864, died 1864, buried Arnold's Chapel.

(e) Henry Newton: Born 1865.

(f) Ann: Born 1867.

(g) Sarah Jane: Married John W. Doss on December 4, 1870 in Shelby County, Alabama.

(h) David Y.B.: Married Puseyline Pell on March 10, 1871, in Shelby County, Alabama.

(i) Alabama: Born 1872.

(j) H. Alonzo: Born March 13, 1873, died April 27, 1966, buried Arnold's Chapel.

The remainder of Enoch and Comfort's twelve children were:

(2) Samuel: Born 1830 in Georgia, married Martha____ in 1854 in Shelby County.

(3) William: Born about 1832 in Georgia.

(4) Richard: Born about 1834 in Georgia.

(5) Mary: Born about 1840. On May 4, 1855 she married John Blankenship in Shelby County, Alabama.

(6) Daniel: Born 1842.

(7) Isabel: Born 1844.

(8) John: Born 1846, married Martha Jane Baxley on January 15, 1868, Jefferson County, Alabama.

(9) Homer T.: Born 1848.

(10) Susan: Born 1850.

(11) James: Born 1852

(12) Thomas: Born 1853.

(Information on the Tyler family is from History of the Old Cheraws, *by Alexamder Gregg. D.D.,* South Carolina Immigrants 1760-1770, *by Jones and Warren, Records of Jasper County Georgia, Georgia State Archives Soundex, LDS Microfiche, Tombstones in Arnolds's Chapel Cemetery, Shelby County, Alabama Marriage Books, and* Old Tuskaloosa Land Office Records and Military Warrants, *by Barefield).*

SIDNEY WILKERSON

Sidney Wilkerson came to Alabama about 1837, and settled in Coosa County. Born on December 23, 1800 in Greene County, Georgia, he was the son of Robert Thomas Wilkerson and Celia McIntosh. He married Elizabeth Reid who was born January 20, 1809 in Georgia. Sidney died on October 10, 1853 in Coosa County and Elizabeth died on December 8, 1885 in Coosa County, Alabama. Both are buried in the Old Shiloh Cemetery in Coosa County. They raised a family of eight children:

(I) Amanda F. Wilkerson, born August 15, 1827 in Coweta County, Georgia, she died in Coosa County, Alabama on March 6, 1893. She was married on May 3, 1844 in Coosa County to Adam J. Hill.

(II) Clara Ann Wilkerson, born January 9, 1830 in Coweta County, Georgia, she died on November 20, 1871 in Coosa County, Alabama. She was married on February 10, 1853 in Coosa County to Seldon Bertrand Thomas, son of John Thomas and Matilda Pace. They had four children:

(A) Edgar Thomas who married Lila Brown.

(B) Elizabeth "Betty" Thomas.

(C) Sarah Matilda "Mattie" Thomas born 1853, died 1919, married Benjamin F. Crew.

(D) John Seldon Thomas born 1856, died 1939, married Molline "Lilla" Forbes.

After Clara Ann's death, Seldon Bertrand Thomas married her sister, Mary Emeline F. Wilkerson, widow of Thomas R. Ogletree who had been killed in the Civil War, leaving her with three small children. The names of these Ogletree children are not known. Mary Emeline and Seldon Bertrand Thomas had five more children:

(E) Willie C. Thomas who married Ada Nicholson,

(F) James H. "Jim" Thomas, born January 20, 1881 in Coosa County, married Mollie Nicholson, died May 22, 1962 in Neshoba County, Mississippi, buried in the Morrow Cemetery,

(G) Albert Reed Thomas, born June 5, 1874, married on December 27, 1892 to Ada B. Robbins, died February 21, 1948 in Coosa County.

(H) Carrie Thomas, born January 1878, died January 27, 1933, married John Cooper.

(I) George Duncan Thomas, born January 25, 1885 in Coosa County, married on December 24, 1916 at Kellyton, Coosa County, Alabama to Eva Clara Corley. Died on October 21, 1965 in Sylacauga, Talladega County, Alabama.

(III) Sarah Ann Wilkerson, born 1832 in Georgia, married James Hill on December 30, 1856 in Coosa County, Alabama.

(IV) Thomas Wilkerson, born 1834 in Georgia.

(V) Joseph B. Wilkerson, born August 1, 1836 in Georgia, married on April 28, 1865 in Coosa County to Luanne Lauderdale, died on August 8, 1904 in Coosa County, Alabama.

(VI) James R. Wilkerson, born 1838, married Lucinda Elizabeth Goodgame on August 16, 1859, in Coosa County, Alabama.

(VII) Mary Emeline F. Wilkerson, born August 1, 1840, in Campbell County, Georgia, died May 14, 1903 in Coosa County, Alabama, married first Thomas R. Ogletree and secondly Seldon Bertrand Thomas.

(VIII) Benjamin Wilkerson, born 1843 in Coosa County, Alabama.

Material on the Wilkerson family contributed by Evelyn Thomas of Bisbee, Arizona. Her husband Claud is a grandson of Seldon Bertrand Thomas and Mary Emeline F. Wilkerson through their son George Duncan Thomas.

Fullname Index

ABERNATHY, Emeline 92
ABRAM, Ulysses H 50
ADAMS, Ann 159 David 154
  Elizabeth 154 Mr 4 Viney 4
AGNEW, Henry 178 Mary 178
ALEKSEW-ADAIR, Marie 10
ALEXANDER, Ann 27
ALPHIN, Nancy 29
AMIS, Anne 160-161
AMMONS, 166 Alice Agnes 2
  Allen 1 Annie Marie 1 Bessie
  May 2 Bobby Jean 2 Cecil
  Clayton 2 Charles Edward
  (Pike) 2 Clara Belle 2 Eliza 1
  Ellen 1 Felix 1 Florence 2
  George Washington 2 Hannah 1
  Harold Anderson 2 Harry
  Henderson 2 Henley 1 Henry
  Clayton 2 Jack Madison 2 Jake
  1 James Edward 1 James
  Emmett 2 James Madison 1
  James Thomas (Dude) 2 James
  Wallace 2 Jesse 1 Jesse Daniel 1
  John Roy 2 Josiah 1 Mae 167-
  168 Martha 1 Mary Elizabeth 2
  Maryann 1 Minnie Lee 1 Minnie
  Lou 1 Nancy 1 Nancy Ida 2
  Nettie 1 Orell 2 Roxie Mae 2
  Sarah 1 Sidney Emma 1 Stephen
  1 Troy Lee Madison 2 William
  Allen 1 William Allen (Buster)
  2
ANCELL, Edward 17-18 Elizabeth
  18 John 18 Mary 17-18 Thomas
  17
ANDERSON, Mary 50 52 Melisha
  44 Susan Elizabeth 84 Thomas
  44 William 50 52
ARCHER, George 13 Mary 13
ARMISTEAD, Elizabeth 22
  Rebekah 71 William 71
ARMSTRONG, Margaret 207 Rev
  S 120

ARNOLD, Ezekiel 212 Lucy Ann Valinda
  212 Sara 212
ASBURY, Bishop 117 179-180
ASHBY, Adeline 95 Andrew J 95
ASHWORTH, Linzy 140 Nancy 140
ATCHISON, Alice Faye 10 Alto Sue 10
  Amelia 6 Ann 4 B F (Frank) 25 Basel
  (Bass) 4 Bennett 3 Betty 3-4 Betty
  Delois 10 Beulah 5-6 Brenda Darlene
  10 Carol Virginia 9 Carolyn Sue 10
  Catherine 6 Charlene Cecilia 10
  Charlotte 4 10 Christine 4-5 Dewitt D
  6 Donald Olen 9 Donna Hope 10
  Doyle Lee 10 Edgar C 6 Edmond 3
  Edward Earl 10 Edward Harrison 4
  Effie Dee 7 Eliza 3 Elizabeth 3 Emma
  Rosella 4 Emma Victoria 7 Eritta Jane
  3-4 Estelle 25 Ethel Margaret 7
  Florence 25 Frances Lucille 7 9
  George B 5 Goldie Earnestine 8
  Harvey Longshore 7 Higdon 3 Hilda
  Carol 10 Homer Longshore 6 Irene
  Walker 11 Jackson 3 5 Jackson
  Franklin 4 James Clinton 7 James H 3
  James Howard 6 James T 3 James
  Taylor 4-5 28 Jessie Coburn 6 Joel
  Andrew 10 Joel Fisher 7 John Henry 6
  John Littleton 7 Judia 3 Julia Mary
  Ann 7 Laura 4 Lela 6 Lena Kate 6
  Leroy Eason 7 Lucy 4 Marie 10
  Marvin Roosevelt 7 9-10 Mary 4
  Mary Frances 9 Mary Jane 6 Minnie 5
  Minnie Elizabeth 7 Minnie Lee 6
  Nancy 6 Newton 4 Norma Jean 10
  Ollie V 7 Patricia Diane 11 Paul
  Anthony 10 Pickens 5 Ray M 125
  Robert Hosmer 7 Robert Howell 10
  Robert Timothy 10 Robert Yancy 5-6
  Ronald Eugene 9 Roxie Elizabeth 6
  Ruth Elizabeth 6 Sally 5 Samuel J 3
  Sarah 3 Sarah (Sally) 5 Sarah
  Elizabeth 28 Shelby Jean 10 Susannah
  3-4 Sylvester 6 Viney 4

ATCHISON (cont.)
  Wheeler Eugene 8 William
  Yancy 5 Willie Gertrude 7
  Winnie Lee 8 Yancy Dwyer 3-4
ATKINSON, Agrippa 50
AUGUANA, Doris Faye 8 Roy 8
AUSTIN, Amanda 133 D
  Washington 133
AUTREY, Sarah 94
BAGLEY, Jacob 51-52 Prisoner 51
BAILEY, Betty 152 Catherine 6
  Henry 36 Henry Jr 36 176
  Henry Sr 176 Mary 36 176
  Rosie 75 Walter 6
BAIRD, Oregon 95
BAISDEN, Beverly Jean 138
  Beverly M 138 Norma Jean 138
BAKER, Jenny 24 Lou 25 Martha
  Viola 25 Viola 149
BALCH, Anne Marie 152 Barbara
  Lynne 152 Dawn Elizabeth 152
  Evie Lorene 152 Hilda Carol
  152 Samuel Allen 152
BALDWIN, 93
BALL, Frances 19
BALLARD, Isaac 22 Phoebe 22
BALTIMORE, Lord 118
BARNETT, Matilda 174
BARRETT, Susan 97
BARRON, Barnabas 34 Polly 34
BARTHENA, Lindsey 31
BASKERVILLE, Bettie 171
BASS, Aaron 171 Edward (Edin)
  171 Hartwell 171 Martha Hill
  (Patsy) 35 170-171
BATES, Lucinda 50 52 Sidney 50
  52
BAXLEY, Martha Jane 213
BAXTER, Capt 211
BEALL, Elvira 84 Washington 84
BEASLEY, Anne Alexander 161
  Very 137
BEAUVILLE, 12
BECK, Aerie 34 172-174 Brenda
  151 Charles 151 Ezekiel 174
  Jeffrey 174 Kevin Dewayne 151

BECK (cont.)
  Martha 174 Sabra 174 Susannah 174
  Weatherford 174
BEEMAN, Nathan S 181
BELL, Amanda S 184 John D 184
BENSON, Elizabeth 111 Sarah 111
  William 111
BENTLEY, Joel 14 Mary (Polly) 14 Sarah
  14
BENTON, 76 Ethel Margaret 7 Martha 42
  Mary 43
BERRY, 106
BEVILL (see also BEVILLE), Adolphus
  15 Amy 12-13 Ann 13 Ann P 15
  Chevis 15 Edward 13 Elizabeth 13-14
  Essex 12-13 Essex Jr 13 Family 82
  Frances 13 Francis K 15 James 13
  John 12-13 John Jr 13 Joseph 13-14
  Lord Bruton 12 Lucy (Susan) 14
  Martha 12-13 Martha Jane 15 Mary
  13-14 Mary (Polly) 14 Mary Ann 15
  Mary Ellen 14 Miriam 15 Napoleon D
  14 Paralee 15 Parker 13 R D 14
  Rardon 14-16 Rardon (Riordan) 12
  Rardon G 14 Riley 14 Robert 13-14
  Robert Jr 13 Ruthia 15-16 Sarah 13-14
  Sarah Ann 14 Simpson D 15 Tom 15
  William 13 William A N 14 William
  D 14 Zippar 15
BEVILL-BURTON, 16
BEVILLE (see also BEVILL), 16 Family
  98 Mary 99 Rardon 99 Sara Ann 89
  99 104-105 Susan 90
BIBB, Elizabeth 33
BILLINGSLEY, Ann 189 J B 118
BINGHAM, Jane 95 L A 95
BISHOP, Jake 94 Mamie 94
BLACK, Mary Ellen 14
BLANKENSHIP, Elizabeth 43 John 213
  Mary 213
BLOW, Willie 75
BOONE, (Family) 41
BOOTH, Lela 44
BORAM, Nancy P 46
BOSTON, Hannah 181
BOTT, Amy 12 Ann 13 Thomas 12

BOWYER, Peter 118
BOYD, Clarence 44 Daisy 44
BOYVILL, 12
BRADFORD, A P 86 Dedima 86
BRAGG, Gen 59
BRANDON, Col 83
BRANTLEY, Brenda Darlene 10
　Donald Joe 10
BRENT, Frances A 168 John 168
　Julia Ann 168 Mary 19
BREWER, Ada 44 Phillip 44
BRICE, J 60
BRISTOW, Ann 107 Anne 107
　Elizabeth 107 James 107
　Jedediah 107 Johannah 107 John
　107 Mary 107 Michal 107
　Nicholas 107 Sarah 107 Thomas
　107 William 107
BROADHEAD, Minnie Elizabeth 7
　Tom 7
BROCK, Cynthia 49 John 49
　William 49
BROOK, Cynthia 41
BROOKSHIRE, Mary 46 William
　46
BROWN, 38 Janna 120 Lila 190
　215 Mary Elizabeth 108 Ruby
　76 William 108
BRYANT, Stephen Franklin 184
BUCKELEW, Melisha 44 Zebedee
　44
BUCKNER, Daniel 111 Elizabeth
　111 Mary Elizabeth 108 Mr 108
BUFFINGTON, Ezekiel 174 Mary
　174
BUFORD, Temperance 117
BUNN, Amanda 73 Ellen 44
BURDGE, Michael 180
BURKE, Margaret 41 48
BURNETT, Alice Faye 10 Donald
　Brooks 10 Elizabeth 105
BURNETTE, Elizabeth 29 J R 29
BURT, Haywood 9 Mary Frances 9
BURWELL, Lucy A 171
BURY, 106
BUSBY, Family 119 123

BUSBY (cont.)
　Leroy 53 Meredith (Maraday) 123
　Meridith 118
BUTLER, Amy 12
BYLAND, Mahala W 189
BYRANT, Susan A 184
BYRD, Elizabeth Downing 181
BYRUM, Miriam 31
CADDELL, Martha 155
CAFFE, Orell 2
CALDWELL, Melissa 207
CALIHAN, Joyce 188
CALL, Bessie 117
CALVERT, 117 Lord 118
CAMP, Ann Eliza 202 Eliza 202 John 202
CANNON, Eliza 1
CARLSON, R 13
CARMICHAEL, David 204 Elizabeth 204
CARROLL, Esther 137 Letha 47
CARTER, (Mama) Maybelle 21 Abraham
　22-23 Alvin Pleasant 21 Amye 18
　Ancell 18 Ann 19 Anne 18 Ansyle 18
　Arabella 19 21 Araminta 24 Belma
　Elizabeth 150 Bobby Kay 25 Bobby
　Lee 25 Catherine 19-22 Caty 22
　Charles 20-21 25 Christie 24 Cynthia
　21 Dale 20-21 Daniel 20 Edward 19-
　20 Elisha 22 Elizabeth 18-19 21-22 24
　Elizabeth Lou 149 Elvi 25 Emma 44
　Estelle 25 Ezekiel 22-23 Florence 25
　Frances 19 Frank 42 Franklin 25
　George 18 20-21 Henry 20 Henry
　Skipworth 19 Isaac 20 Jack 24 Jacob
　20 James 17 19-20 22-24 James Jr 23
　25 James Robert 24 Jane 18 Jean 21-
　22 Jenny 24 Jimmy E 25 Job 20 John
　18-19 21-23 John Jr 22 Joseph 19-22
　Joseph D 24 Joseph Jr 21 Judith 20
　Katelyn 25 Katharine 19 Katherine
　18-19 Laurana 24 Lee 44 Lelia
　Ernestine Goodwin 56 Lou 24-25
　Lucy 20 Margaret 19 22-23 Margaret
　Ann 150 Martha 22-24 Martha Viola
　25 Mary 17 19 21 23 107 Mary Ann
　23 Mashac 22 Mattie 24-25 104
　Megan 25 Millicent 17 Molly 24

SOME ALABAMA PIONEERS 219

CARTER (cont.)
Nancy 22 Nell 24 Norris 20-21
Paradise 17 Peter 19-21 Peter Jr
20 Phoebe 22 Polly 23 President
19 Rachel 21 Rebecca 22-23
Reuben Green 149 Reuben Lee
(R L) 25 Rhoda 23 Robert 18
21-22 Robert E 24-25 104
Rueben Green 25 Ruth 24 Sara
Elizabeth 21 Sarah 21-23 42
Solomon 20 Susan 23 Susannah
20 Temperance 18 Terry 24
Thomas 18-21 23 Thomas Jr 19
21 Ursula 18 Velma Elizabeth
26 149 Viola 149 Walter Dean
25 149 William 17-18 24
William C 23 Winifred 17-18
CARY, J W 39 Mary Ann 23
CASSELS, Elias 129 133 Elizabeth
129 133 Henry 129 Margaret
129 133
CATES, Pearl 46
CHANDLER, James 97 Sarah 97
CHAPMAN, Clement 82
CHARLES I, 118 King 106
CHEDZ, Martha 170
CHERRY, Lela 6
CLARK, Alexander 27 Ann 27
Cinthia M 27 David 27 Dollie
Adelia 27 Elizabeth 44 Flora 27
Gilbert 27 Hugh 27 James
Crawford 27 Jane Caroline 178
Lannern 44 Ruth Mae 27 Victor
E 27 Victor Earl 27 Walter 63
CLARKE, Berry 1 John F 1 Nancy
1 Sarah 1
CLENDENNING, Jael 107
CLETION, Joseph 40
COBB, Alexander 52 Bethany 52
Bethney 50 C B 53 James 58
COBURN, Ambrose 28 Amelia 28
Charles J 28 David F 28 Ecsastis
28 George W 5 28 George W Jr
28 Isaac M 28 James M 28
Jessie R 28 John L 28 Sarah
(Sally) 5 Sarah Elizabeth 28

COBURN (cont.)
William N 28
COCHRAN, Melinda 178 Patricia Diane
11 William Richard 11
COHEN, Greg 139 Tracy Elaine 139
COKER, Nancy Jane 132 Noah L 132
Patience 55 Phillip 50 55
COLE, Bertha 146
COLLIER, Harriet B 53 Vic 53
COLLINS, Mary Etta 185 Mr 185
COLSON, Abraham 14 Martha 12-13
Sarah 13-14
COMER, Antoinette Susannah 92 93
Jason 93 Nancy 89
CONNELL, Ora 193
COOLEY, Martha 35
COOPER, Amci 192 Carrie 192 216 Holly
89 John 192 216 Mary Emma 192
COPELAND, Eli 1 Ellen 1 Sidney Emma
1
CORLEY, Columbus 132 Eva Clara 192
216 Manerva 132 Mary 192 William
192
CORLOSS, Rachel 118 Robertson 118
CORPEW, C E 178 Mary 178
COST, Adam 30 Allen 31 Amos 30
Andrew 31 Bailey 29 Barthena 31
Caroline 30 Cathy 31 Clarence 30
Clint 30 Daisy 30 Eli 31 Elijah 15 30
104 148 Elizabeth 29 31 Emily D J 31
Enoch 30 Ephrian 30 F M 31 Fred 30
James C 31 John 29 31 Jolly 30
Joseph 30 Joshua 31 Kinney 31 Lizzie
30 Margaret 30 Maria 30 Martha 31
Mary 31 42 Mary A 42 Matt 29
Miriam 31 Nancy 29 31 Norman 30
Peter 31 Polly 29 Rebecca 31 Robert
29-30 Ruthia 15 Samantha 29 Sarah
29-31 Sarah Evaline 31 Sinda 31
Susie 29 Thomas 30-31 Thomas Jr 29-
31 Thomas Sr 29 Walter 30 William
29 Yearby 30
COSTON, Lucy 4 Mr 4
COUCH, Edward 34
COWAN, Elizabeth 84 Gabriel 84
COX, 167 Anne 158-159 Nancy A 167

COZART, Ann Page King (Hannah) 120 Wiley 120
CRANFIELD, Elizabeth 17 Katharin 17 William 17
CRASFORD, Ora 193
CRAWFORD, Dedima 86 Edward 193 Elizabeth 111 Evelyn Doris 193 George 86
CREEL, 141 Ida 141 Joshua 61 Mary Frances 61 Mary Ozanna 61
CREW, Benjamin F 190 215 Lillie Belle 190 Lucinda S 190 Marcus Eugene 190 Morton Harrison 191 Robert 190 Sarah Matilda (Mattie) 215 Sarah Matilda (Sallie) 190
CRIDER, Viola 65 195
CRISLER, Blanton 85 Catherine 86 George 86 James 85 Joseph 86 Juliann 85 Julius W 85 Lucinda 86 William 85
CROCKETT, Davy 21 Jean 21-22
CROFFORD, Elizabeth 84 Lucy 4 Mr 4 William 84
CROSSLAND, Alicia 117 Ann 117 Edward 117-118 123 Temperance 117 William 123
CROWSON, W B 60
CRUSE, Nettie 75
CRUZ, Ramon II 9 Rosemary 9
CUMMINGS, Edward 137 Linda Ann 137 Thelma Doris 137
CURRAN, Bob 38-39
CURTIS, Crystal 149 Dawn Marguerite 149 Kasi 149 Troy 149
DAILEY, Bazie 207
DALE, Diane 19 Edward 19 Katherine 19 William 63
DANELLY, Amelia 5 28
DANIEL, Sturdivant 170
DAUGHERTY, Dale 140 David 139 Michael 139 Mildred Yvonne 139 Sara Elizabeth 21 Scott 140
DAVIDSON, W L 63
DAVIS, 137 Allen 137 Anne Alexander 161 Hilliard 161 Linda 168 Linda Ann 137 Robert Scott 32 173 Rosanna 200
DAVIS/HONEYCUTT, 59
DAY, John 159
DEALE, Enoch 108
DEASON, David 139 Denise 139 Dewey 139 Douglas 139 Marion Faye 139
DEAVERS, Charlene Cecilia 10
DEERMAN, Lillie 137
DELAGRANDE, Ralph 82 William 82
DENNY, Anthony 17
DENSMORE, Mr 4 Viney 4
DENTON, Elizabeth 179
DICKENSON, Martha 131 Robert J 131
DOOLEY, 11 33 Abraham 33 Ann 33 Bennett 34 Daniel 33-34 Elizabeth 5 33-35 41 48 101 172-173 196 Family 173 Henry 33 James 33-35 37 172-173 James F 37 James Sr 32 Jesse 37 John 159 Lucy 33 Margaret 33 Martha R 37 Mary 32 35 37 172 Mitchell 159 Nancy 34 Patrick 33-34 Permelia 37 Polly 34 R J 37 Sarah Ann 37 Thomas 33 37 Thomas Jr 33 William 33-35 172-173 William Harrison 37
DOOLY, 33
DORSE, George Washington 130 Jane Jameston 112 130 155
DORSEY, Lorena 191
DOSS, George Washington 131 John W 213 Sarah Jane 213
DOULLY, 32
DOWLEY, 33
DOWNEY, Anne Alexander 161 Elizabeth 160-161 James 160-161 Polly 161 Samuel Smith 161 Sarah Pomfret 161
DOWNING, Elizabeth 33-34 John 34 172 174
DRAGGING CANOE, 34 173
DRURY, Family 205
DUFFEY, Iris 62
DULA, 33
DULEY, 33

DUNKIN, Derrick Wayne 150
    Devin 150 Margaret Ann 150
    Randall Lee 150 Suzanne 150
    Wayne 150
DUNN, 159 Lucy 159
DYCUS, Birdie Mae 136-137
    Harriet Rodesta (Hattie) 136
    James 136
DYSON, Jean 138
EADES, Mr 24 Patricia Ruth 24
    Stephen 24
EATON, Lethy 161
EDDINGS, Mary E 124
EDDINGTON, Callie 48
EDDINS, Martha 145
EDMONDS, Rebecca 23
EDMONDSON, Mary 160
EDWARDS, Rebecca 22
ELIZABETH I, Queen 12
ELKINS, Ader 127 Ader (Ada) 112
    Johnston 112 127-128
ELLIOTT, Charles W 97 Lena Kate
    6 Rebecca 97
EMORY, Mary 174
ESSMAN, Charles 25 Sintha Kate
    25 Susan 25
ESTES, Sarah 41 48
EWITT, Dollie Adelia 27
FANCHER, Bobby Kay 25 Bryan
    25 Horace B (Nicky) 25
    Madison 25 Melissa 25
FANT, Sara Araminta 96
FARNHAM, Suzy 144
FAUST, John 123
FERGUSON, Elizabeth 192
FERUE, Emma Lou 144 George
    144
FIELDER, John 177 Sallie (Casey)
    177 Vicey 177
FIKES, Vesta 16
FISH, Bertie 48
FLETCHER, Charles 8 Doris Faye 8
FLOWERS, Jame T 116 Laura Scott
    116
FORBES, Elizabeth 85 Elizabeth
    Louise Helen 85 Molline 191

FORBES (cont.)
    Molline (Lilla) 215 William 85
FORD, Ann 184 Martha Frances 183-184
    189 Nathaniel 184
FORTNER, Arthur 84 Martha 84 Sarah 84
    Susan E 84
FOSHEE, Frances 158 Noah 158
FOSTER, Matilda 179
FOWLER, Wiley W 155
FREDERICK, 143 Estelle (Dodge) 143
FREEMAN, Garrett 3 Judia 3 Julia 204
FRITZ, Ruth Elizabeth 6
FULLILOVE, John 84 Pernesia 84
FURCRON, Minnie Lee 1
FYSSHER, Catherine 18 Richard 18
GADDY, Beverly Jean 138 Roger 138
GALLMAN, Mary Susan 90-91
GANN, Bradley 146 Freda 146 Thomas
    146
GARNER, Betty 9 Carolyn Sue 9-10
    Clyde 9 Clyde Earl 8 Doris Faye 8
    Evelyn Lucille 8 Gladys Theo 151
    Hershel Wayne 9 Jimmie Ruth 8-9
    John Robert 9 Laymon Wallace 9
    Maudie Lee 8 Millard 7-8 Millard
    Eugene Jr 8 Myrtle Jo 9 Pauline
    Virginia 8 Phyllis Jean 9 Rosemary 9
    Ruby Jean 8 Willie Gertrude 7-8
GASKEY, Elizabeth Ann 132 Harriet
    Elizabeth Ann 131
GAYLAND, Thomas 155
GENTRY, Charlotte 4 Flemming 140
    Mary 140 Mr 4
GEORGE, Elizabeth 19 May 44 William
    19
GIBSON, Austin 38-39 Sarah 38-39
    Susannah 3-4
GIDEON, Daniel Murphy 95 Frances 95
    George Joseph 95 Laura Ann 95
GILBERT, A B 122
GILCREASE, Nancy 204
GILLIAM, Frances (Frankey/Fanny) 93
    Julia A 95 Julian F 95 Winnie 67
GLASCOCK, Laurana 24
GLASSCOCK, Benjamin 53 61 John
    David 62

GLOVER, Birdie Mae 136-137 Dr
136 Carolyn? 136 Katharin 17
William 17
GOLDEN, Old Man 78-79
GOLHARD, G W 53
GOODGAME, Elverena 184 John
Chapman 184 Lucinda Eliz 216
GOODWIN, Belle 75 Frances 161
GOOLSBY, Betsy 211
GORDON, Eli M 90-91 Rhoda
Palmer 90 Rhoda Palmer Porter
91
GRAHAM, Anna Maria 121 I G 51
James 121
GRAMMAR, Betty Jean 145 Jimmy
Dale 145 Tim 145
GRANT, Gen 59 Ludovic 174
GRAY, Colie 196.
GREAVES, Joseph 210
GREEN, Frances 168 Sarah
Elizabeth 116
GREGG, Alexander 214
GREGORY, 93 Ferdinand 92
Frances 92
GUNN, Emma 178
GUNTER, Minnie 75
GUTHREY, Anna 163
GUTTERY, Florence 188 198 John
188 198
GUY, Carrie 191 Ernest 191
GWYNETH, Owen-Prince Of
Wales 77
GWYNN, J W 131 Susan 131
HADRIAN, Emperor 63
HALL, Andrew 200 Margaret 200
HALLOM, Sarah 169
HAMAKER, Samuel 49
HAMILTON, Rebecca 165
HAMMOND, Charles 47 Lillian 47
HANCOCK, 83 Isaac Sterling 95
Laura Ann 95
HAND, Belton 4 Crockett 4 Mary 4
Mr 4
HARGROVE, Susan 170 William
170
HARKINS, Vicky Kathryn 144

HARKNESS, Rosa M 42
HARMON, (Squire) 46-47 Ada 44 Agnes
45 Alice 45 48 Allen 40-42 44 Allie
42 Alva 45 Ann 41 Annie 45-47
Audrey 44 Bertie 48 Betty 45 Callie
45 48 Catherine 40 Charles 45 Chris
44 Clarence 44 Cynthia 41 43 47 49
Cynthia J 46-47 Daisy 44 David 43 45
49 David H 44 49 Dora 43 Earl 46
Edna 45 Elbert 45 Elijah 43 46
Elizabeth 41 43-44 46 Elizabeth
(Dutch) 47 Ellen 44 Elser 45 Emma
44 Ethel 45 Eula 44 Frank 46 48
Georgia Ann 48 Gilbert M 48 Hannah
40 Hattie 46 Henry S 47 Ida 45 48
Iona 43 Ira 44 J M 46 J William
Lafayette 44 Jack 45 James 41 47 49
James F 46 James Frank 46 James L
42 44 John 35 40-41 43 47-49 John H
42 John Jacop (Jacob) 40 John L 43
46 John Leonhard 40 John M 47 John
M William 49 John S 48 John Thomas
Andrew 47 Johnnie 45 Joseph 42
Joseph A 48 Joseph E 43 Joyce 44
Kate 45 Laura 46 Lela 44-45 Letha 47
Lila 45 Lillian 47 Little Steve 43-44
Louie 45 Luna (Lou) 47 Lydia 42-43
48 M A 48 M D 48 Malinda 48
Margaret 41 48 Margaret E 48 Marie
46 Martha 42-45 Martin 41-49 Marty
46 Mary 40-41 43 46 48 Mary A 42
May 44 Melisha 44 Morgan 48 Mynia
47 Nancy 43 45 Nancy P 46 Nannie
47 Ollie 46-47 Oscar 47-48 Othie 45
Parthenia 42 Pearl 46 Peter 43 47-48
Rebecca 40-42 48 Robert 45 Rosa M
42 Rosie 47 Rufus N 42 Ruth 45 S W
48 Sara 43 Sara Estes 35 Sarah 40-41
43-44 48-49 Sarah E 48 Sarah Estes
35 175 Sarah L 49 Stella 46 Stephen
41 43-44 48 Stephen G 48 Steve
Luther 44 Tempie 43 47-48 Thomas
48 Tilda 43 Tillman 44 Val 49 Val D
45 Virgil 45 49 Walter 47 Warren 46
Wheeler D 47 Wiley 47 Wiley D 47
William 45 William A 42 49

HARMON (cont.)
  William J 43 William James 46
  William R 48 Willie 47
HARRIS, Pattie 68 West 68
HARRISON, Elizabeth 160-161
  Henry 109 Jane 161 Maria
  Swann 201 Marie Swann 205
  Richard 201 205 Sally 180
HART, Winifred 17
HARVIN, John William 116
  Leonora Virginia 116
HASTINGS, Nancy E 184
HATHCOCK, Elizabeth Lavell 144
HAYES, 147 Betty Joyce 137 Billy
  Claude 137 Emma Victoria 7
  Esther 137 James Claude 137
  James Newton Erasmus 137 139
  Jerry 129 John Martin 137 Kay
  137 Kenneth 137 Lillie 137
  Marguerite Elizabeth 139
  Maude Elizabeth 137 139 Peggy
  137 Rasie Mae 137-139 Thelma
  Doris 137 Vera 137
HEATH, Maureen 139 Wiley 51
HEFLIN, Rachel 73 103 213
  William C 73
HENDERSON, Caroline 76 Daisy
  76 Elaine Stewart 168 Elizabeth
  73 Florence 76 Henry 76 Holly
  41 Horace 76 Martha 76 Mary
  Pleasant Evaline 73 Michael 36
  173 Miss 3 Nancy Jane 166
  Nora 76 Pleasant 73 Roxie Mae
  2 Sarah 41 William 166 Williard
  76
HENLEY, Elisha 50 55 Martha 50
  55
HENLY, Henry 50 Sally 50
HERMANN, Melchior 40
HERRING, Flora 75
HERRINGTON, John 98
HETH, M H 46 Nancy 46
HICKS, Hilda Carol 10
HIGGINBOTHAM, 72 Eula 44 Joe
  44 Lottie 75
HILL, Adam J 215 Amanda F 215

HILL (cont.)
  James 216 Margaret F 190 Sarah Ann
  216 Tom 143 147-148
HINES, 120 Ann 120 Eliza 120 M 120
  William 56
HINTON, J 29 Mary 36 175 Susie 29
  Thomas 36 175 Wesley 36 175
HOBBS, Caroline Martha 178
HODGE, Nora 75
HOLCOMB, Hosea 99 Jesse 99 Maj 46
  Mary 46 Nancy 99
HOLCOMBE, Martha 35
HOLLAND, Charity 165 Mr 147
HOLLEY, John 146 Mattie 146
HOLLINGSWORTH, Arlevia 74 Leon 98
  Maggie 74 Neata Della 74
HOLLIS, Harriett Rembert 181
HOLSENBECK, Ida 45
HONEYCUTT, A H (Zachariah?) 53
  Alexander 56-57 Alpha Ann 57
  Amanda 53 Amy Denise 62 Anderson
  55 57-58 Angeline 53 Arena 55 Arvel
  Jefferson 62 Ballina 54 Ballina
  (Barthena) 55 Bartheny 54 Bathsheba
  53 Besteny (Barthena) 54 Bethany 52
  Bethney 50 Catherine 56 Charles W
  58 Daniel 59 Daniel Crawford 60
  Doctor 52 57 Doctor Blewford 58 Ed
  50 56 Eddard 58 Edward 51 53 58-62
  Edward Henry 52 Edward W 62
  Edward Walter 60-61 Elisha 56 Eliza
  56 Elizabeth 52 Elmira Bagley 52
  Elmira D 56 Emily 59-60 Emily
  (Emma) Elizabeth 61 Emily A 58 Eva
  Dora 61 Eyvonne 62 Fanny 56 Francis
  Asbery 58 G W 53 George M 53
  George Newton 57 George W F 52
  Glen Edward 62 H 54 H B 53 Harriet
  B 53 Hazel Cecil 62 Herschel 61-62
  Iris 62 Isadora 56 J J (Jefferson
  Jasper) 55 James 50 52-54 61 James J
  52 James M 53 James Matthew 57
  Jane P 57 Jane Sabrine 55 Jasper
  Marion 53 Jefferson Jasper 57-60
  Jesse Garfield 60-61 John 56
  Josephine 50-51 56 Leah Malinda 55

HONEYCUTT (cont.)
  Leah Paralee 59-60 Levi
  Anderson 53 Lewis 56 Louisa
  52 57 Lucinda 50 52-53 58
  Martha 50 55-56 Martha
  Elizabeth (Patsy) 51 Martha
  Jane 52 Mary 50 52 55-56 59
  Mary Missouri 60-61 Mary
  Ozanna 61 Nancy 56 Pall O 52
  Parthenia 42 Patience 50 55
  Richard 42 Riley M (Monroe)
  53-54 Sally 50 52 Sarah 58
  Sarah B 52 Susan 56
  Temperance 55 Tennessee 53 61
  Thomas 50-51 56 58 Thomas
  Anderson 57 Thomas R 51-52
  Vera Agrath 62 Vivian Nellie 62
  Ward 59-60 William 51-52 57
  William (Billy) 59 William L
  (Billy) 60 William T 52
  Zachariah 52
HOOD, Clarissa 203 Maudie Lee 8
  Ruby Jean 8
HOOKER, Gen 59
HOPKINS, Capt 34
HORTON, Arthur 7 Brandy
  Michelle 146 Hugh 63 Isaac 64
  Jacqueline 146 James 63 193
  James M 64 James W 66 John
  63-64 194 John W 64 66
  Margaret 194 Margaret Emeline
  64 75 193 Martha 64 66 Mary
  63 Mary Frances 61 Melvin 146
  Minnie Elizabeth 7 Nimrod 63
  Nimrod Wells 63 Perry 63 66
  Prince 64 Saphronia 85
  Susannah 63 Violetta 64 66 193
  William 63
HOSEY, Ann 4
HOUSE, Minnie Lee 6 Thomas
  Pickens 6
HOUSTON, Martha 43-44
HOWARD, Audrey 44 Martha 41
  Melisha 44 Newie 44 Pete 76
  102 Ruby 65 76 102 197 Sally
  76 102 Sinda 31 William 31
HOWTON, Ollie 46-47
HUDGINS, Betty Jean 145 Charles 145
  Charles Richard 145
HUDNALL, John 83 Mary 83
HUDSON, Elizabeth 170 Hall 170
  Permelia 37
HUGER, Elliott 116
HUNNICUTT, Thomas 50
HUNT, 144
HUNTER, Robert 210
INGE, Richard 171
IRWIN, Col 210
IVEY, Charlotte 183 Dicey 183 Jane
  Jensy 183 Peebles 183
JACKSON, Alsey 69 Andrew 35 38 162
  205-206 Betty Delois 10 Elizabeth
  146 Howard O 146 Jacqueline 146
  Ralph 67
JAMES, Ann 110-111 Francis 111 John
  111
JAMESTON, Isaac 112 130 155 Jane 130
JARVIS, Ann 108
JOHNSON, Elizabeth 24 James M 31
  Martha 31 Mary J 124 Rachel 73
  Rebecca 31 Sarah Elizabeth 85
  William 124
JOLLY, Annice 96 Family 82 Jane 96
  John 96 Letitia 89 Lucinda Lucy 96
  Mahala 96 Mary 96 S J 94 Theda 94
JONEBY, Quitlawe Of 18
JONES, Amos 133 Betty Jean 145 Elisha
  165 Francis 71 Georgia Ann 48 Lenna
  145 Luther 94 Mary (Polly) 133
  Nannie 94 Polly 71 Reynolds 145
  Ridley 71 Rita 151
JORDAN, Ben 41 Charlie 41 George 41
  Georgean 42 Jim 41 Lessie 103 197
  Ludie 42 Manerva 41 Martha 41 76
  Rose 41 Rose Peel 75 Samuel 41
  Sarah 42 Uriah 41
JORDON, Lessie 65
JOURDAN, Uriah 41
KELLY, James 47 Mary A 212 Nannie 47
KEMBALL, 67
KEMBOLDE, 67
KENDRICK, Palmore 155

KENNEDY, Lillian 47 Tom 47
KENT, Agnes 180 Amy 12 Henry 12 William 180
KEUHL, Nancy 156
KIMBALL, Alsey 69 Alsey Jackson 70 Bartholomew 67 Benjamin 70 Buckner 68 70 Charles 68-69 72 Harris 68 Joseph 67-68 Lewis 69-70 Pattie 68 Peter 68 70 Sarah 68 William 67 69 Winnie 67
KIMBELL, Armistead 71 Benjamin 69-71 Charles 71 Christopher 70 David 70 Francis 71 Gideon 70 James 70-71 John 70 Leonard 71 Lucy 69 Ransom 70-71 Rebekah 71 Robert 70 Thomas 70 William 71
KIMBLE, 67
KIMBREL, 67 Amanda 73 Arlevia 74 Belle 73 Berryman 67 72-73 Caroline 76 Charles 72-73 Clayton 74 Feriby 72-73 G C 74 Genie 75 George 74 Gracie 73 Helen 74 Jacob (Jack) 74 James B 73 Jesse 75 Joe 75 John 73 Lucinda 74 Martha J 73 Mary 74 Mary Pleasant Evaline 73 Melvin 74 Missouri Alice 75 103-104 Nancy 73 Neata Della 74 Nellie 74 Nelson 74 Permelia 73 Pleasant 73 Rachel 73-74 103 213 Ransom 67 72-74 103 213 Rose Peel 75 Sadie 75 Sally 76 Susan Lee Ann 213 Susan Lee Anne 75 Thomas 74 William 73-74
KIMBRELL, 67 Benjamin 72 Berryman 72 Betsy 72 Catherine 72 Charles 71-72 Charles M 72 Crowder 72 Elvy 72 Jacob 72 Jenny 72 Jesse 72 John 72 Nancy 72 Peterson 71-72 Rachel 72 Sally 71 Thomas 72
KIMBULL, 67
KIND, Florence 2

KING, Andrew 110 Elizabeth Downing 181 Frederick 84 George Clark 181 Martha Louise 84 Sophia Clark 181
KIRBY, Sandra 140
LACEY, George 146 George Wesley 146 Jacqueline 146 Julie Lynn 146 Michael Howard 146
LAGRANT, Betty 9
LAMBERT, Junior 104 Minnie 104
LANIER, Barbara Diane 138 Frederick 33 Stewart 138
LANKFORD, Mary 40 William 40
LAUDERDALE, Luanne 216
LAWES, Elizabeth Adeline 121 Salem 121
LAWHR, James 51
LAWLEY, Minnie 167
LAWRENCE, Theresa 166 William 166
LAWSON, John 19 Katharine 19 Mr 4 Viney 4
LEDBETTER, 76
LEE, Emily D J 31 Thomas Helm 182
LEITH, George 129
LENOIR, Elizabeth 116 Napoleon P 116
LETSON, Emma Rosella 4
LEWIS, Comfort 25 212 Emaline 97 Florence 16 Jane 201-202 Mary 211-212 Robert 201 Seaborn 97
LICHLITER, Asselia 16
LINDSEY, Joseph 41 Rebecca 40-41 Sarah 41
LITTLE, Donna Adelia Jane 186
LOCKHART, 46
LONG, Mary 14 99 157
LOVE, Mynia 47
LOVELADY, Julia Mary Ann 7
LOVELESS, Elvy 72
LOWE, Elizabeth 120 Family 205 Fernando 120
LOWERY, Nettie 1
LUTTON, Holly Frances 150 Laurence 150
LUTTRELL, Catherine 72
LYMAN, Bruce 116 Elizabeth 116
LYNCH, Mary 23
MADOC, Prince Of Wales 77 79 81

MAHAN, Desdemona 123 James 123 Susannah 123
MANN, ---- 36 Beulah 36 176 Mary 36 176
MANNING, Family 205 James 72
MARCUS, Emily A 58
MARDIS, 93
MARION, Francis 117 210 Gen 211
MARKHAM, Elizabeth 106
MARSHALL, M A 48
MARTIN, Alexander 63 Amanda 54 Amanda Honeycutt 54 Carol Virginia 9 Clarance 54 George 54 Glois 60 Isaac B 54 Isaac Bird 54 J 54 J B 54 Mandy 54 Maria 30 Mary 54 Virgil 60 William 54
MARY QUEEN OF SCOTS, 12
MASON, Gilbert 153 Susan J 153
MASSENGALE, Amelia 184 John Cobb 184 Mary Jane 183 Stokely D 183
MASSEY, Ruth Mae 27
MASTIN, Miss 120
MATCHAN, Billy Dwain 10 Shelby Jean 10
MAXWELL, Nancy Elizabeth 184
MCBRIDE, Evie 143 Herbert Luville (Hub) 136 Marie Imogene 136 Maylene 136 Nancy Matilda 136 Patrick 136 Robert 136 U L 136 William 136
MCCAIN, Richard 192
MCCALL, Charles S 162
MCCART, Jack 139 Jacqueline Ann 139 Mark Edward 139 Shirley Ann 139 Terry Russell 139 Tracy Elaine 139
MCCLANAHAN, Mary 86-87
MCCLENDON, F M 31 J 189 James Darcy (Dart) 2 Julia Ann Billingsly 189 Lillian 2 Luther 2 Mary 75 Nancy Ida 2 Ollie (Pete) 2 Thomas Luther (Dick) 2
MCCLURE, Fanny 104

MCCLURE (cont.) Mayhew 104
MCCOLLUM, Sarah 140
MCCOOL, Lydia 144
MCCRARY, Elizabeth 3 Sinclair 3
MCCRAW, Malinda 48
MCCULLOUGH, Francis 94 Mary Ann 94
MCCULLY, Amanda (Polly) 167 Lafayette 167
MCDONALD, Madge 103
MCDOUGAL, Margaret E 48
MCELROY, 143 Mary 165 William R 165
MCFERRIN, Missouri 66 Mr 66
MCGOWAN, 158
MCINTOSH, Celia 215
MCINTYRE, Ann 119 Ann Page King (Hannah) 120 Annie Lou 120 Archibald Charles Crossland 120 Edward Legare 119 Hamilton 120 Janna 120 Peter 119 Peter Mastin 120
MCKINNEY, Harris 183 Jane Jensy 183 Lou 24 Verlinda 183
MCKISSICK, Margaret 90
MCLAUGHLIN, Elizabeth 174
MCLEAN, Flora 27
MCNEAL, J A 60 Mary Ann 60
MEADOWS, Nancy 165 167
MEDLEY, Ann 159 Eleanor 159 James 159 James Sr 159 Susannah 159
MEEKS, Norma Jean 10
MERIWEATHER, Lucy 159
MERONEY, J 29 Samantha 29
MILLER, 166 George W 164
MILLS, Ann P 15 James 168
MILSTEAD, Amanda 24 Jade 24 James Donald 24 Jarrod 24 Kyle 24 Larry Ray 24 Patricia Ruth 24 Penn 24 Ruth 24 Timothy 24 William Ronald 24
MIMS, Alto Sue 10
MODOC, 78-80
MONK, Mary 192
MONTOE, Christie 24
MOODY, George 123 Susan M 123
MOONEY, Elizabeth 127

MOORE, Anna Rivers 117 Elliott Huger 116 Gladys 104 James 129 133 Leonard 104 Margaret 129 133 Marion Percival 116 Morgan 48 Richard Manning 117 Roxie Elizabeth 6
MOORER, Robert J 121
MORGAN, Mary J 190
MORRIS, Elizabeth S 16 Laura 4 Tom 4
MORRISON, Alexander 109
MORROW, Deborah Paige 138 Earl 138 Joyce Elaine 138 Patricia Lynn 138
MOSELY, William 205
MULL, Goldie Earnestine 8
MUNSEY, Rhoda 23
MURCHISON, Donna Adelia Jane 186 Evie Lee 185-187 Rora McKeever 186
MURPHY, Alexander 161 Jane 161
MUSE, Drury 155 Lydia 108 Sophie Pope 108
MYERS, Mary Alice 116
MYLES, Jane 18 John 18
NEAL, Benjamin 34 Nancy 34
NEELY, John 124 Mary 124
NEGRO, Amanda 70 Andrew 70 Betty 70 Esther 71 Fanny 70 Hannah 70-71 Hilah 70 Indah 71 Jack 87 Lilah 71 Lucy 71 Marc 71 Mell 68 Mengo 71 Ned 71 Peg 71 Peter 71 Riddle 71 Rose 71 Susanna 71
NEWTON, Francis 169
NICHOLAS, John 42 Lydia 42
NICHOLLS, Mary 17
NICHOLS, Michal 107
NICHOLSON, Ada 191 215 Mollie 191 215
NICKSON, Mary 206
NOBLES, Pinney H 105
NOLAN, Ida 48
NORRIS, Judith 20
NORWOOD, 46 164 Ann 181 Cynthia 43 47 Cynthia J 46-47

NORWOOD (cont.) Hannah 181 James 181 Joseph 164 Richard 164 Tempie 43 47
O'DONLEY, Eyvonne 62
OGLESBY, Ira 44 Jona 44
OGLETREE, Mary Emeline F 215-216 Thomas R 215-216
OWEN, Elizabeth 84 Gadi 84 Mary Elizabeth Newsome 85 Thomas McAdory 182
PACE, John 189 Matilda 189 215
PALMER, Ellis 88 Joshua 88 Rhoda 88 91-92 95 Winneyfred 83
PARKER, Elizabeth 163
PARR, Mathias 71-72 Sally 71
PARRISH, Joel 206
PARROTT, Mary 154-155 (Polly) 153
PARSONS, Nancy 45
PATILLO, Henry 201
PATTERSON, Adam 64 Betty 45 Luna (Lou) 47 Mary (Polly) 162 Melvin 47 Violetta 64 66 193
PATTON, Richard 168
PAYNE, Mary 205 Robert 205
PEARCE, Arthur 118 Arthur Jr 118 Temperance 118 Temperance Crossland 117
PEEL, Rose 41
PEGRAM, John 170 Martha 170
PELL, Puseyline 213
PENDERGRIST, Florah 94 James 94
PERKERSON, Cinthia M 27
PERRY, Clyde 1 Ivy 1 Wallace 1
PETTIT, Holly Frances 150 Madge 66 163 William Francis 150
PHILLIPS, Alline 104 Bennett 206 Melissa 206 Minerva 206 Reuben 193
PIERCE, Annie 46-47
PINES, Ann 19
PITTS, Joyce 44
POCAHONTAS, 63
POELNITZ, Baron De 118 Rachel De 118
POGUE, Seth 34
POND, Ebenezer 64 66 Violetta 64
POPE, James Michael 139 James Michael Jr 139 Jerry Michael 139

POPE (cont.)
Lisa Louise 139 Maureen 139
Nancy Louise 139 Stephen
Sumner 139
PORTER, 15 Addison Thomas 85
Adeline 95 Alline 104 Andrew
Jackson 93-94 104 Andrew
Jackson G 94 Andrew Jackson
Jr 93 Ann 82 90 Antoinette
Susannah 92-93 Avis 88 Benj
Franklin 85 Beulah 5 Calvin 83
98 Camillus 92 Charles 75 104
Chloe 88 Christopher Columbus
(Lum) 95 Cier 89 Clovis A 89
Cluff 94 Comer 88 Cora 85
Cynthy 87 David 91 99 Dedima
86 Dorothy 91 Draper Roman
85 Edward 82 86-87 89 Edward
Sanders 83 88 91 96 98-99
Elisha 89 Elisha P 90 Elizabeth
82 84 88 90 96 Elizabeth Louise
Helen 85 Elvira 84 Emaline 97
Emeline 92 Epaphroditus 83 96
Epaphroditus III 98
Epaphroditus Jr 97 Epaphroditus
Sr 97 Family 209 Fannie 75
Fanny 104 Flora 104 Florah 94
Frances 92 95 Frances
(Frankey/Fanny) 93 Francis 82
Francis A E 93 G C 94 G N E
90 Geo Washington 85 Gideon
99 Gillis 95 Gladys 75 104
Grace 95 Grayce 94 Hancock
82-83 86 89 96 Hancock Jr 86
Henry 89 Hezekiah 99-100
Hezekiah Sylvanus 90-91 Holly
89 95 Homer 93 Hosea
Holcomb 92 Ibzan 5 100-101
176 Idella 85 Isom 97 J S 99
Jack 75 Jackson 94 Jacob 82
James H 94 James N 93 James
Palmer 84 James Robt 94 James
T 90 James Walden 85 Jane 86-
88 95 Jeditha 89 Jedithan 87-88
91-92 95 97-98 Jedithan Jr 96
Jedithan P 90 Jefferson Davis 85

PORTER (cont.)
Jemima 88 Jennett 87 Jeremiah (Jerry)
84 Jesse 75 104 John 82-83 88-89
John Abraham (Ibzan) 5 36 100 105
176 196 John B 105 John Backster 90
John H 84 John M 93 John Monroe 65
75-76 102-103 197 John N 93 John
Palmer 88 91 96 John Palmer Jr 92 96
John Wesley 85 John William 36 65
75-76 101 103-104 147 176 196-197
208-209 Jonathan 98-99 Joseph 83 91
Joseph Anthony 93 Joseph N 91
Josephus 89 Joshua P 96 Julia A 95
Juliann Retty 85 Kiah 89 Kier 89
Landlot 83-84 87 93 98 Landlot
(Lotty) 92 Laura Ann 95 Lemuel Lott
93 Lemuel Teague 92 Lessie 65 103
197 Letitia 89 Lizzie 85 Lucian 104
Lucinda 83 98 Lucion 75 Lucy
(Susan) 14 M J 93 Mamie 94 Margaret
90-91 Margaret Fatima 65 75-76 196-
197 Margaret Fatima Thomas 66 102
Margie 103 Margie Eugenia 26 65-66
75 102 104 147 150-152 197 Marion
Sanford 96 Martha 84 98 Martha Ann
84 Martha Louise 84 Marthe 92
Martin 84 98 Mary 36 82 86-87 96
101 105 176 196 Mary Ann 93-94
Mary C 89 Mary Elizabeth Newsome
85 Mary Sturdivant 5 Mary Susan 90-
91 Massina 92 Matthew 99 Mattie 24-
25 75 104 Melvina 91 Mildred 88
Milly S 93 Minnie 75 104 Missouri
Alice 75 103-104 Monroe 103-104
Nancy 86 89 99 Nancy A 89 Nannie
94 Nathaniel 99 Newbert 95 Odellus
95 Omia 95 Ophelia 92 Oregon 95
Oscar 94 Palmore 86 Paralee 90 Paul
95 Pernesia 84 Peter 82 Phoebe 87-88
Pinkney Prentiss 85 Pleasant 88
Prentiss 84 Rardon 100 Rebecca 97
Rhoda 86 88 91 95 Rhoda Palmer 90
92 Robert 82 105 Robert Chandler 85
Roy 94 Ruby 65 76 197 Rufus 75 104
Russell 84 Russell V 96 S Lott 94
Sallie 91 Samuel 83 103

PORTER (cont.)
Samuel David 65 75 103 197
Saphronia 85 Saphronia Paulina
84 Sara Ann 89 99 104-105 Sara
Ann Beville 100 Sara Araminta
96 Sara J 89 Sarah 82-83 94 97-
98 Sarah Ann 14 Sarah
Elizabeth 85 Shadrach 83
Shadrack 86 Simpson 96 Stark
14 82 89 96 99-101 104-105
Stark Jr 104 Stark W 91 Susan
84 90 97 Susan Elizabeth 84
Synthy 87 Theda 94 Thomas 82
Tillman 97 Tresuvar 97 Uriah
87-88 98 Virginia Elizabeth 95
Waitus 95 William 83 86-88 98
102 197 William E 14 William
Edward 82 90 William Forbes
85 William Jr 84 William Sr 87
Winney 87 Winneyfred 83
Zachary Taylor 89
PORTY, Ruby 102
POTTS, Eritta Jane 3-4
POWELL, A P 17 Phillip 159
Powell 212 Wethleyan 17
PRESCOAT, Jane 202 Martha 202
Mary 202 204 Thomas 202
PRESTRIDGE, G W 53
PRICE, John 9 Mrytle Jo 9
PRIDE, Parker 13
PRUITT, Arvel 8 Pauline Virginia 8
PUGH, Lethy 161 Maj 161
PULLEY, Beverly Jean 138 Bryan
138 Mike 138
RAGSDALE, Frances 13 John 13
RAINS, John 33 Margaret 33
RAMSEY, Rhoda 204
RANDALL, G W 53
RANDALL-RICHARDSON, 154
RAWLS, Emma 178 Ida Elizabeth
178 Jabez P 178
RAY, Caroline 30 Christopher 138
Cynthia 176 Deborah Paige 138
Gareth 138 Isaac 176 Jennifer
138 John 32 173 Lucy 4 Mary
35 37 172 Mr 4 William 32

RAY?, Mary 32
REACH, Amanda (Polly) 167 James 167
Kissiah 166 Sara 165
REDD, Al 166 Azalie 167 Bud 166
George 167 Joe 167 John 166-167
Mary Jane 166 Minnie 167 William
166
REDDING, Ann Mariah 52 Ann Mariah
Honeycutt 50
REID, Elizabeth 190 215
RETTY, 83
RICE, Charles 137 James Anderson 137
Peggy 137
ROBBINS, Ada 192 Ada B 215 Paul 164
Sarah 189
ROBERTSON, Miss 4 T G 53
ROBINS, Elizabeth (Dutch) 47 Philip 47
ROBINSON, Christopher 169 Pink 29
Polly 29
ROCKETT, H H 122
ROGERS, Catherine 19 Lucinda 98
ROPER, Lucy 4 Mr 4
ROSE, Susan E 84 Susanna 163 William
H 84
ROSS, Idella 85
ROY, Andy 103 Madge 103
ROYALL, Joseph 13 Mary 13
ROYLAND, Elizabeth 159
SAILE, 159 Ruth 159
SANDERS, 38 Edward 83 Elizabeth 83
Mary 83 Sarah 82
SANDY, Ann 87 Mary 87 Uriah 87
SAUCER, Allie M 126
SCOTT, Phillip B 85 Sarah Elizabeth 85
SEAL, Joyce Jones 156 Lucille 4 Wright
156
SEALE, 147 Ader 127 129 153 Ader
(Ada) 112 Alexander N 122 Alice 132
Allen 132 Allie M 126 Alma E 156
Amanda 133 Andrew 132 Ann 107-
108 111 114 119 121 Anna Eliza 127
Anna Maria 121 Anna Rivers 117
Anne W 155 Annie 125 Anthony 106
108 111 Anthony II 107 Barnabas
131-132 134-135 Barnabas (Uncle
Barney) 140-141 146

SEALE (cont.)
Barnabas Bass 140 147 153
Barnabas Bass Jr 147 Barnabas
Bass Jr (Bassy) 141 Barnabas
Bass Sr 141 Barnabas Jr 132
140 Benjamin 111 126 Bertha
124 Bessie 117 Brooks C 126
Caroline 123 Caroline J 120
Charles 107-108 112 123 126-
128 131-132 156 Charles H 126
Clyde 115 Cora 132 D A 126
Daniel Thomas 123-125 130
David 107-108 112 118 121-123
127-129 134 153-155 David Jr
154 David Thomas 130
Desdemona 123-124 Dorothy
109 Drusillah 156 Edward 126
Edward Crossland 123-124 130
Edward F 124 Eli D 114 Elijah
108 128 Eliza 120 Elizabeth
106-111 114 116 118 120 123
127 129 132-133 135 141 154
Elizabeth A 123 Elizabeth
Adeline 121 Elizabeth Ann 132
Elliott Huger 116 Elmos P 114
Elvie H 122 Emeline 124-125
Emma J 155 Ermon O 126
Estelle 114 Family 156 168
Felix 123 Finias 114 Flaurence
114 Floy 113 Frances Jane 133
Frances Leonora 116 Geneva
156 George 113-114 132
George W 123 H H 156 H M
115 156 Harriet 114 Harriet
Elizabeth Ann 131 Harriet
Rodesta (Hattie) 136 Helen 156
Henrietta 131 Henry 114 Henry
C 125 Henry Thomas 125
Hester 114 Hopkins 115-116
127 Hopkins Jr 116-117 Icey
115 Ida 141 Isaac Hopkins 126
130 153 155-156 Jael 107 James
108 112 114 116 James A 124
154 James Pinkney 127 James
Thomas 133 Jane 114 Jane
Jameston 112 130 155

SEALE (cont.)
Jesse 121-122 Jesse D 126 Jessie 132
Joan 115 John 108 113-115 117 126-
131 136 153 John A 133 John
Anderson 135 141 John Anderson Jr
137 John Arthur 117 John B 130 133-
135 140-141 153 John C 114 John
Comer 126 John J 113 John Milton
113 Joshua 108 112 Kathleen 137
Laminta 115 Laura Scott 116
Laurence E 114 Leonora Virginia 116
Lizzie 114 Lorene 137 Lucinda 125
Lucinda C 155 Lydia 108 M D 126
Madena 114 Mahala 153 Mahalia 127
Manerva 132 Marietta 126 Martha 111
114 127 131-132 141 155 Martha A
113 Martha Jane 125-126 Martin 113
Marvin 126 Mary 113-116 124 132
140-141 153-155 Mary (Polly) 133
153 Mary Alice 116 Mary Ann 131-
132 Mary E 124 Mary Elizabeth 108-
109 111 Mary J 124 Mary L 156
Matilda 134-136 140-141 153 Matilda
J 113 Matthew 153 Mattie 113 Maude
Elizabeth 137 139 Minnie 125 132
Mortimore 153 155 Nancy 113 133
140-141 Nancy Jane 132 156 Nancy
Matilda 136 Naomi 126 Oliver 124
Phillip 130 Phillip P 126 Phillip Seale
130 Rachel 118 124 Rebecca 115 122
132 Rebecca Watson 117 Rev David
W 121 Rev David William 117 120
Rev William 117 120 123-125 129
156 Robert A 114 Robert W 113 Sara
131 Sara F 155 Sara Jane 122 Sarah
107-108 111 116 140 Sarah A 113
Sarah Elizabeth 116 Sidney Miron 126
Sophia 110 Sophie Pope 108 Susan
131 Susan J 153 Susan M 123
Susannah 123 Temperance Crossland
117 Temperance Crossland Pearce
118-119 124 Terissa 114 Thelma 115
Thomas 106 108-112 132 Thomas III
132 Thomas Jefferson 156 Thomas Jr
106 108-109 112 118 123 125-133
153 155

SEALE (cont.)
Thomas Sr 111 115 117 126-128
Tishy 113 William 106 108 118-119 126-127 130 132 William A 113 124 William D 114 William H 114 116 132 William Henry 116 William Jr 106 William Morgan 131 141 William Riley 133 William T 115-116 William Thomas 116 134 Willie 113 Wilson 133 Winifred 108
SEALES, Anna Lu 144 Becky 151 Bertha 146 Betty 141 143-144 146-147 152 Billie Jean 151 Billy 142-144 146-147 Bobby Joe 25 Brenda Gale 151 Charity Lynne 151 Charles 130 Christy 151 Dorothy Nell 150 Elizabeth 165 167-168 Elizabeth Lavell 144 Elizabeth Tabitha 141 143 152 Eugene Thomas 151 Evie 143 Evie Lorene 152 Family 209 Frances 38 Gladys Theo 151 Glen Ralph 143 Harold 146 Hazel Jane 150 Herman 143 Horace Dale 151 Hubert 143 James Riley 143-144 152 Jason Dale 151 Jennifer Michelle 151 Jessie Mae 152 John Anderson 165 167-168 John B 168 John Robert 146 John Scott 152 Joseph H 197 Joseph Horace 26 65 104 147 150-152 Jos Horace Jr 150 Julie Christine 152 Margie Eugenia 26 65 104 150-152 197 Margie Eugenia Porter 147 Martin 147 Mary Madge 150 Matilda 168 Mattie 146 Michael Glen 151 Ralph Frederick (Freddy) 144 Richard Clinton (Clint) 144 Richard Glen 144 Rita 151 Robert Glen (Bobby) 144 Rufus B 143 Sarah 38 Suzy 144 Thomas Jeffrey 151 Velma Elizabeth 26 149-150 Vicky Kathryn 144

SEALES (cont.)
William Joseph (Little Bill) 151
William Keith 152 William Martin 146 William Sturdivant 151 William Thomas 143 152-153 165 167 William Thomas (Billy) 141
SEALES?, Brandon Michael 152 Christopher 152
SEALS, Frances 38 Sarah 38
SEAMONS, Elizabeth 73
SEGAL, Eloise 145
SEILE, Henry 106 Thomas 106 William 106
SHACKELFORD, Elizabeth 212
SHANKS, Phyllis Jean 9
SHARP, Elizabeth 14 Napoleon D 14
SHARPE, Nancy 6
SHAW, Bradley Paul 140 Jennifer 140 Marguerite Elizabeth 139 Marion Faye 139 Marion Michael 139 Michael 140 Mildred Yvonne 139 Ronald Wayne 140 Sandra 140 Tessie 140
SHEARIN, Joseph 69 Lucy 69
SHELBY, Pauline Virginia 8-9 Polly 11 28 Reif O 9
SHERMAN, Gen 59
SIDES, Billie Jean 151
SIMMONS, Effie Dee 7
SIMPSON, Mrs Walter 105 Walter 89 100 105
SIMS, Adam 67 Elihu 131 Mary Ann 131
SIRMON, 126 Martha Jane 125-126
SKIPWORTH, Diane 19
SLOVENSKY, Alice 48
SMART, Mary Ann 132
SMITH, (Hell Nation) 157 (Hellstone) 157 Alexander 158-159 161-162 164 Amanda (Polly) 167 Amy 161 Ann 159 Anna 163 Anne 158-161 Anne Alexander 161 Archibald 165 Betty 144 Bob 1 Carlton G 171-172 Catherine 40 Clyde 1 Elisha 165 Elizabeth 135 160-161 163 165 167-168 Elizabeth Mary 171 Elizabeth Tabitha 141 143 152

SMITH (cont.)
Emeline 142 167-168 Emily 211
Frances 158 161 Frances A 168
Francis 159 163 Greenberry 168
Henry Clayton 1 Hiram J 172
James 158 James Riley 141
James Webb 161 Jane 161 208-209 Jasper 168 Job R 168 John 29 157-158 162-164 185 John Granville 161 John R 166
Jonathan Newton 129 Joseph 158 Joshua 165 Julia Ann 168 Kissiah 166 Leeberry 168 Lethy 161 Lucy 159 Mariah C 168 Martha Elizabeth (Patsy) 51 Martha Ella 185 Martha J 166 Martha Logan 185 Martha W 172 Mary 141 157-158 160 162 164-165 168 190 Mary (Polly) 162 168 Mary Jane 166 168 Maurice 161 Meriweather 159 Minnie Lou 1 Nancy 135 165 167 Nancy A 167 Nancy Ann 168 Newton 168 Nicholas 159 162 Odell 1 Peter 157 162-165 167 Rebecca 165 Richard Norwood 164 Riley 165 167 Rufus 141-142 147 167-168 Ruiah 135 Ruth 159 Samuel 159-161 165 Samuel II 160 Samuel III 160 Sara 165 Sarah 29 Sarah Pomfret 161 Senah 165 Susanna 163 Susannah 159 Sylvania 167 Tammy Gail 150 Theresa M 166 Thina Ann 168 Thomas 40 161Uriah 29 157-158 162-168 Uriah III 165 Uriah Jr 164 Uriah P 168 Wilbur 1 Wiley 158 165 William 158-159 161-162 164 William R 166 Zachariah 162 164
SMITHSON, Ann 41 Anson 41
SNEAD, Ann 117 Samuel 117
  Temperance 117
STANDLEY, 198 Family 188
STANLEY, Martha 22
STANTON, Suzanne 150
STARNES, Mary 41 48
STARR, Emmett 34 172
STEELE, Catherine 200
STEPHENS, Catherine 20-22 Dorothy Nell 150 Henrietta 131 James 21
STEVESON, Gen 58
STEWART, Levin 166 168 Mary Jane 166 Nancy Jane 166
STOKES, Caroline J 120 J T 120
STOUGH, Frances Lucille 7 9
STOVALL, Joseiah 84 Sarah 84
STRIBLING, Dorothy 109 Family 107 Francis 109
STRINGFELLOW, Sarah 107
STUART, Royal Family 106
STUBBS, Claudine 138
STURDIVANT, 11 Aaron 171 Aerie 34 172-174 Agnes 180 Allen 170 Allen Cannon 177 179 Allen Dudley 178 Ann 169 181 Ann M 172 174 Armistead 171 Arnold Cannon 178 Benjamin B 174 Bettie 171 Caroline Martha 178 Charles 171 175 Charles J 178 Chichester 169 Commodore 178 Cynthia 36 176 Cynthia Ray 7-8 148 177 Daniel 169 Dempsey 179 Dempsey Jr 179 Edmond Troup 182 Elizabeth 35 41 48 101 170 172-175 179 196 Elizabeth (Sis) 36 177 Elizabeth Dooley 8 32 Elizabeth Mary 171 Family 169 182 Frances 170 Fred F 179 George 41 48 George W 35 175 Hallom 169 Harriett Rembert 181 Helen 179 Henry 169 178 Herbert 179 Hollum 178 180 Ida Elizabeth 178 Isabel A 174 James 170 James Norwood 181 Jane Boston 181 Jane Caroline 178 Joel 170 173 178 John 35 169-171 180 John Calhoun 174 John Marion 181 John S 178 John T 174 Joseph 34-35 171-175 Joseph A 178 Joseph Allen 171 Joseph H 174 Lewis Lafayette 182 Lillie M 174 Lucy A 171 Martha 170-171 174 Martha Elizabeth 181

STURDIVANT (cont.)
  Martha (Patsy) Hill 35 170-171
  Martha J 178 Martha W 172
  Martin Butler 174 Mary 5 35
  101 170-171 175 178-179 196
  Matilda 174 179 Matthew 169
  178 Matthew Jr 178 180
  Matthew Parham 179 Matthew
  Sr 178 180 Melinda 178 Paul H
  174 Randolph 176 180
  Raymond 179 Rebecca A 36
  177 Richard 171 Robert 170-
  174 178 180-181 Robert Daniel
  181-182 Roxanna Hollingsberry
  182 Russian Edward 178 Sabra
  174 Sallie 36 177 Sally 180
  Sarah 41 48 170 Sarah Estes 35
  175 Sherrod 5 32 34-36 41 48
  101 173 175 196 Sherrod Aaron
  169 171-172 177 Sophia Clark
  181 Susan 170 Susan Turner
  182 Thomas 179 Thomas S 178
  Vicey 177 William 5 170 179
  William H 175-176 William
  Harrison 5 7-8 32 36 101 104
  148 173 175-177
STURDIVANT-HENDERSON, 173
SUGG, Lizzie 85
SULLIVAN, Maude 75 Whitmill
  207
SUMNER, Barbara Diane 138 Carol
  Ann 138 Carol Max 138
  Claudine 138 James 138-139
  James Arthur 138 James Arthur
  Jr 138 James William 138 Jean
  138 Joyce Elaine 138 Nancy
  Louise 139 Norma Jean 138
  Rasie Mae 138-139 Shirley Ann
  139 Wayne Hayes 139
SWANN, Elizabeth 202 205 Mary
  Ann 200 205 Thomas 202 205
  Thomas Jr 201 205 Thompson
  201 205
TABB, Katharine 19 Mr 19
TATE, Donna Hope 10 Stephen
  Wayne 10

TATUM, Mary 74 Sadie 75
TAYLOR, Annie Lou 120 Elizabeth 120
  Mr 120 William Dana 120 William
  Dana Jr 120
TEAGUE, Dorothy 91
TEDD, Margaret 19
TEMPLETON, Polly 23
THAMES, James 60 Mary Missouri 60-61
THOMAS, Aaron Bartley 186 Ada 191-
  192 215 Ada B 215 Albe Virgil 186
  Albert 189 Albert McKinney 184
  Albert Reed 192 215 Allan J 189
  Amanda S 184 Ann 189 Annette 185
  Arthur Lee 186 Arthur Patrick 185-
  187 Benjamin 188 190 Carey T 192
  Carl 191 Caroline 190 Carrie 191-192
  216 Carrie Mae 192 Charlotte 183
  Clara 186 Clara Ann 190 215 Claud
  216 Claude Lewis 193 Claude Lewis
  Jr 193 Coleman 66 195 Colie 196 Coy
  191 Cullen 192 Dicey 183 Edgar 190
  215 Elizabeth 192 Elizabeth (Betty)
  190 215 Elverena 184 Emeline 195
  Emma 66 Emmie 192 Ethel 65 194
  Ethel Inez 192 Ethelred 188 Ethelred
  Watson 183 Ethelred Watson Jr 184
  Eva Clara 192-193 216 Evelyn 198
  216 Evelyn Doris 193 Evie Lee 185-
  187 Ezekiel 188 Family 103 Florence
  192 Frances Amelia 184 Fred 193
  Fred Duncan 193 Gen 59 George 65
  188 195 George Braxton 193 George
  Duncan 192-193 216 George M 190
  Gertrude 186 Henry C 190 Herbert
  192 Houston 184 Ina Lois 191 James
  H (Jim) 191 215 James Rufus 191-192
  Jeremiah 188 John 65 188-189 193-
  194 197 215 John M 64 75 102 190
  193 John Sebron (Seaborn?) 186 John
  Seldon 191 215 Joseph 188-189 198
  Joseph Carey 192 Josephine 66 196
  Joshua 188 Joyce 188 Julia Ann
  Billingsly 189 Julius 184 Lennie 65
  195 Lila 190 215 Lillie Belle 190
  Lorena 191 Lucille 191 Mahala W
  189 Mahalia 127 Margaret 194

THOMAS (cont.)
  Margaret Emeline 64-65 75
  Margaret Emiline Horton 102
  Margaret F 190 Margaret Fatima
  65 75-76 102 147 194 196-197
  Mariah 195 Marjorie Hazel 186
  Martha 65 195 Martha Ella 185
  Martha Ester 186 Martha
  Frances 183-184 189 Mary 183
  190 Mary Eleanor 193 Mary
  Emeline 190 Mary Emeline F
  215-216 Mary Etta 185 Mary F
  190 Mary J 190 Mary Jane 65
  183 194 Mary Susan 189
  Matilda 185 189 193 215
  Michael 183 Michael L 183
  Missouri 65 Missouri E 195
  Mollie 191 215 Molline 191
  Molline (Lilla) 215 Moriah 65
  Nancy E 184 Nancy Elizabeth
  184 Nancy Scott 185 Patience
  183 Patrick 183 Ralph Waldo
  186 Randy 187 Raymond 192
  Rhoda 204 Robert 65 194 Ruby
  65 191 195 Ruth 192 Sarah 189
  Sarah Matilda (Mattie) 215
  Sarah Matilda (Sallie) 190
  Seaborn Jones 183-184 Seaborn
  V 190 Selden Burtram 189-190
  193 198 Seldon Bertrand 191
  215-216 Seldon Robbins 192
  Sudie 191 Susan A 184 Vera
  Mae 191 Verlinda 183 Verna
  Blanche 192 Viola 65 195 W Ed
  191 William 65 189 195-196
  William Aubrey 193 William B
  191 William Callihan 188
  William H Jr 185 William
  Horton 183-184 William
  Houston 185 189 William P 183
  Willie C 191 215 Yvonne Marie
  193
THOMAS/HORTON, Family 66
THOMPSON, Ann 169 201-202
  Ann Eliza 202 Asa 202 Bazie
  207 Callie 45 Caroline 203-204

THOMPSON (cont.)
  Catherine 200 Clarissa 203 Clifton
  202 Col 87 David 202 205 Dock 199
  Eliza 203 Elizabeth 199-206 Emily
  207 Emily W 199 Eunice 202 Family
  209 Fleming 203 Frances Leonora 116
  Hannah 204 Hattie 46 J W 199 James
  200 203 James William 199 Jane 201-
  202 Jesse W 207 Jessie 199 John 101-
  104 176 196 200-209 John Daniel 201
  Joseph 199-203 205-207 Josiah 200-
  201 203-205 Julia 203-204 Katherine
  203-204 Lydia 202 Margaret 200 207
  Margie 202-203 Maria Swann 201
  Marie Swann 205 Martha 201 203
  Mary 169 200 202 204-206 208-209
  Mary Ann 200-201 205 Mary E 204
  Melissa 207 Nancy 199 203-204 207
  Oliver 203 Ophelia 204 Rev William
  205 Rhoda 203 Rhodes 201 Rosanne
  200 Salina 203 Samuel 200-202 204-
  205 Samuel Jr 203-204 Sarah 202
  Susan 203 Thomas 200 202-204 W P
  129 Waddy 201 203-205 Waddy III
  201 Waddy Jr 201 Waddy Sr 202
  Wallace 207 Whitmill 199 207
  William 157 199-202 206-207
  William Jr 204-205 William Morris
  200 William Sr 204-205
THORNELL, Florence 192
THORNLEY, Capt 210
THORNTON, Elizabeth 19
THRASHER, Anna 145-146 Anna
  Frances 145 Anna Lu 144 Annette 144
  Bart 166 Bobby 144 Charles Thomas
  144 Elizabeth 146 Eloise 145 Emma
  Lou 144 Freda Jones (Johnnie) 145
  Henley 145 Henry Wayne 145
  Herschel 145 Hersery (Buster) 145
  Hobert 144 Isaac 144-146 Lenna 145
  Lydia 144 Martha 145 Mary Sue 145
  Preston 145 Rosella 145 Wesley 145
TIBBS, Laura 46
TILERY, Wanda 137
TILLERY, Betty Joyce 137 Billy 137 Joan
  137 Mary 165 Wiley 165

TOLLEY, Rev N 121
TUCK, Mary Susan 189
TURNER, Elizabeth 170 Hannah 40 James 111 Martha 111
TYLER, Alabama 213 Alexander G 212 Allie 42 Amelia 6 Ann 213 Asa 212 Belle 75 Benjamin 210-211 Benjamin Jr 210 Betsy 211 Bob 76 Britton C 211 Comfort 25 212-213 Daniel 213 David T B 213 Elizabeth 212 Elizabeth Ann 213 Emily 211 Enoch 25 210-213 Fannie 76 Flora 75 George 76 210 Grover 76 H Alonzo 213 Henry N 212 Henry Newton 212-213 Homer (Tiny) 76 Homer T 213 Isabel 213 James 214 James L 6 Jane 210 Jeannette 76 John 76 210 213 Lewis 211 Lottie 75 Lucy 213 Lucy Ann Valinda 212 Mae 76 Martha 213 Martha Jane 213 Mary 75 211 213 Mary A 212 Maude 75 Minnie 75 Mourning 211 Nettie 75 Nora 75 Oscar 76 Owen 212 Parthenia 213 Pauline 213 Puseline 213 Richard 212-213 Rosie 75 Ruby 76 Samuel 211 Samuel S 212 Sarah Jane 213 Susan 214 Susan Lee Ann 213 Susan Lee Anne 75 Thomas 210 212 214 Wiley 212 William 210-213 William Andrew Jackson 75 213 Willie 75
VARDMAN, Mary 4
VEDLE, Jane 130 John C 130 155
VINING, Emeline 195 Emma 66 Feriby 67 72 John 67 72 Joshua 65 Mary Jane 65 Roman 66 195 Tilda 43
WADDY, Anthony 200 Family 205 Mary 200
WAITES, Adie 186
WALDROP, Carrie Mae 192 Theo 192
WALLACE, Charlotte 10

WARD, David 130 Sara 43 Sarah 44
WARREN, Brenda 151 Ivey 151
WASHINGTON, Geroge 200
WATKINS, Martha R 37
WATSON, Rebecca 115 Sarah 115 William 115
WEALE, Mattie L 155
WEAVER, Christine 4-5 Sally 5
WEBB, Amy 161 Elizabeth Ann 132 Francis 160 James 160 Jesse 132 Lucy 33 Mary 160 Polly 161
WEBBER, Nell McBurnett 24
WEEKS, Alex 150 Clarence 149 David Shane 149 Dawn Marguerite 149 Elizabeth Lou 149 Joseph E 149 Michael Kavell 150 Shane 149 Tamara 149 Tammy Gail 150 Tammy Jean 149 Virginia Hereford 149
WELDON, Sarah 97
WELLS, Susannah 63
WEST, Cecil 145 Connie 145 Eugene 146 Freda Jones 145 Kimsey 74 Maggie 74 Massina 92 Richard 69
WHALEY, Clarence 65 195 Irene 66 195 Leona 66 195 Missouri 65-66 103 Missouri E 195 Otto 66 195 Paul 65 195 Starling 65-66 195
WHATLEY, Betty 4 Fanny 56 Lucille Seal 4 Tyre 4
WHEATLEY, Catherine 18 Elizabeth 18 Robert 18
WHEELER, Carol Ann 138 Emeline 142 167-168 Joe 142 167 Phil 138 Tyson 138
WHETSEL, Carl 9 Rosemary 9
WHITE, M D 48 Tom 48
WHITMER, Howard Edward 9 Myrtle Jo 9
WIDE, Allen 49
WILEY, Mary Ann 93
WILKERSON, Amanda F 215 Benjamin 216 Celia 215 Clara Ann 190 215 Elizabeth 190 215 James R 216 Joseph B 216 Luanne 216 Lucinda Elizabeth 216 Mary Emeline 190 Mary Emeline F 215-216

236   *SOME ALABAMA PIONEERS*

WILKERSON (cont.)
  Robert Thomas 215 Sarah Ann 216 Sidney 190 215 Thomas 216
WILLIAM THE CONQUEROR, 12 32 82
WILLIAMS, Arabella 19 21 Betsy 72 Curtis 183 Edward 17 Lightfoot 183 Mary 183 Miles 68 Ollie V 7 Paradise 17 Patience 183 Permelia 73 Winnie Lee 8
WILLIAMSON, Mary 160 William 160
WILSON, Becky 151 Jenny 72 John T 129 Mariah 195 Moriah 65 Samuel Glen 129 Sarah Ann 37 William 72
WILSON'S RAIDERS, 74
WINGARD, Tammy Jean 149
WOOD, Elizabeth 82 John 106
WOODS, Penuel 68 Sarah 68
WOOLEY, Elizabeth 123
WRIGHT, Colie 66 Family 196 Josephine 66 196
YATES, Frances Jane 133 Mary 115-116 Robert E 115-116
YORK, Danny 11 Patricia Diane 11
YOUNG, Elizabeth 160 William 160